# HOW TO WRITE A HORROR MOVIE

*How to Write a Horror Movie* is a close look at an always-popular (but often disrespected) genre. It focuses on the screenplay and acts as a guide to bringing scary ideas to cinematic life using examples from great (and some not-so-great) horror movies.

Author Neal Bell examines how the basic tools of the scriptwriter's trade – including structure, dialogue, humor, mood, characters and pace – can work together to embody personal fears that will resonate strongly on screen. Screenplay examples include classic works such as 1943's *I Walked with a Zombie* and recent terrifying films that have given the genre renewed attention like writer/director Jordan Peele's critically acclaimed and financially successful *Get Out*. Since fear is universal, the book considers films from around the world including the 'found-footage' *[REC]* from Spain (2007), the Swedish vampire movie, *Let the Right One In* (2008) and the Persian-language film *Under the Shadow* (2016).

The book provides insights into the economics of horror-movie making, and the possible future of this versatile genre. It is the ideal text for screenwriting students exploring genre and horror, and aspiring scriptwriters who have an interest in horror screenplays.

**Neal Bell** is a writer and professor of play and screenwriting at Duke University and has received grants from the Rockefeller and Guggenheim Foundations, and the National Endowment for the Arts. Winner of an Obie Award for sustained excellence in playwriting, he's been a script consultant for HBO, and also received an Edgar Award for Best Mystery Play for *Spatter Pattern*.

# HOW TO WRITE A HORROR MOVIE

*Neal Bell*

Routledge
Taylor & Francis Group
LONDON AND NEW YORK

First published 2020
by Routledge
2 Park Square, Milton Park, Abingdon, Oxon OX14 4RN

and by Routledge
52 Vanderbilt Avenue, New York, NY 10017

*Routledge is an imprint of the Taylor & Francis Group, an informa business*

© 2020 Neal Bell

The right of Neal Bell to be identified as author of this work has been asserted by him in accordance with sections 77 and 78 of the Copyright, Designs and Patents Act 1988.

All rights reserved. No part of this book may be reprinted or reproduced or utilised in any form or by any electronic, mechanical, or other means, now known or hereafter invented, including photocopying and recording, or in any information storage or retrieval system, without permission in writing from the publishers.

*Trademark notice*: Product or corporate names may be trademarks or registered trademarks, and are used only for identification and explanation without intent to infringe.

*British Library Cataloguing-in-Publication Data*
A catalogue record for this book is available from the British Library

*Library of Congress Cataloging-in-Publication Data*
Names: Bell, Neal, author.
Title: How to write a horror movie / Neal Bell.
Description: London ; New York : Routledge, 2020. | Includes index.
Identifiers: LCCN 2019055915 (print) | LCCN 2019055916 (ebook) | ISBN 9780367151645 (hardback) | ISBN 9780367151652 (paperback) | ISBN 9780429055416 (ebook)
Subjects: LCSH: Horror films--Authorship. | Motion picture plays--Technique. | Motion picture authorship.
Classification: LCC PN1995.9.H6 B45 2020 (print) | LCC PN1995.9.H6 (ebook) | DDC 808.2/3--dc23
LC record available at https://lccn.loc.gov/2019055915
LC ebook record available at https://lccn.loc.gov/2019055916

ISBN: 978-0-367-15164-5 (hbk)
ISBN: 978-0-367-15165-2 (pbk)
ISBN: 978-0-429-05541-6 (ebk)

Typeset in Bembo
by Taylor & Francis Books

For my brother Richard – who's helped me with a lot more than Winged Monkeys, over the years.

# CONTENTS

*Acknowledgments*    *viii*
*A note on transcription of dialogue and screenplay format*    *ix*

1. "Who goes there?": A brief introduction to horror    1
2. What scares you?    13
3. Basic horror movie structure    27
4. Building Act One    37
5. The changed world of Act Two    46
6. Ending and beginning    56
7. Dialogue    64
8. Fearful landscapes    78
9. Humor in horror    89
10. "Beyond this point are monsters" – digging up inspiration    101
11. Politics and global horror    113
12. "Our name is legion" – varieties of horror    132
13. "Dead man's chest" – the economics of horror    142
14. The future of horror    151

*Index*    *166*

# ACKNOWLEDGMENTS

There are so many people I need to thank, for their help and encouragement – including my colleagues in Theater Studies at Duke University, Duke's tireless librarians, and my students in a course I teach – "The Dramatic Monster" – who've given me the gift of watching movies I've seen many times before, with fresh eyes.

I'd also like to thank *Duke Magazine*, which solicited a short piece from me for "The Fear Issue", in the fall of 2018. That piece, expanded, ended up as a section of Chapter 1 of this book.

# A NOTE ON TRANSCRIPTION OF DIALOGUE AND SCREENPLAY FORMAT

Most of the screenplays I write about haven't been published; so for the script excerpts in this book, I've relied on my own transcriptions. I've attempted to be as accurate as possible; any mistakes in transcribing are my own.

For languages other than English, I've relied on the films' subtitles.

To save space on the page, the script excerpts in the text are not in industry-standard screenplay format. There are many good books on this standard format, including *The Hollywood Standard* by Christopher Riley. And there are also many sites online that give the same basic information.

## And a word of warning

To be thorough in discussing the films in this book, I've had to give away plot twists and endings. So this is a Spoiler Alert that applies to *everything* that follows.

# 1

# "WHO GOES THERE?"

## A brief introduction to horror

The first horror movie to scare the daylights out of me was *The Wizard of Oz*. It was also the very first movie I saw without the protection of Grown-ups; my older brother (nine, at the time) was given the solemn duty of getting me safe to Oz and back again (within the confines of an old and – my parents thought – ringworm-infested revival house.)

The tornado that opens the movie I managed uneasily, but ok, so far; ditto the threatening trees ("I'd turn back if I were you!") and the Wicked Witch of the West herself, keeping track of our heroes' progress in her ominous crystal ball.

But then – when I least expected horror, and all of a sudden, there it was: winged monkeys. I peeped again, through my fingers. Yup, a lot of monkeys. With wings. And, weirder, all of them dressed like bell-hops, plummeting down on our hapless heroes, in flapping simian squadrons. Why were the monkeys dressed like bell-hops? *More important – because more horrific – why did they have wings?*

How my big brother handled a panicking six-year-old, I no longer recall. I probably spent the rest of the movie under my seat – though I must've popped up long enough to see the Wicked Witch melting, at this fiendish movie's climax. That inexplicable death unnerved me even more than the monkeys. Water can melt you? Bottom line: this movie was full of things (angry trees, flying monkeys, old ladies dissolving) that were plainly and simply wrong (see Figure 1.1).

Which was one of the defining characteristics – I later learned – of horror movies: category confusion, the blurring of boundaries, binaries breaking down. Living/dead, human/non-human, sane/insane – horror movies challenge fundamental distinctions we cling to, trying to make any sense at all of a baffling world. And these provoking confusions were there, from the earliest days of cinema: is Dr. Caligari a medical miracle man, or a raving loon? (*The Cabinet of Dr. Caligari*, 1920). Is that giant monster made of clay a savior of the ghetto, or its worst nightmare? (*The Golem: How He Came Into The World*, 1920.) Does the 1930s Dracula want to make love to us? Or suck our blood? Or both?

**2** "Who goes there?"

**FIGURE 1.1** A Winged Monkey gets his orders from the Wicked Witch (Margaret Hamilton) in *The Wizard of Oz*.

In many of the great horror movies, this fundamental uncertainly is expressed as a simple but chilling 'what if':

1. What if witches are real, and my fears for my unborn child aren't paranoia? *(Rosemary's Baby*, 1968)
2. What if aliens are replacing the people we love with soul-less look-alikes? (*Invasion of the Body Snatchers*, four versions so far – beginning in 1956.)
3. What if being stalked and killed by a stranger is some kind of curse that can be passed on, like a supernatural STD? (*It Follows*, 2014).
4. What if I have the god-like power to bring inanimate matter to life – then learn that I can't control it? [*The Golem* (1920), *Frankenstein* (1931), the computer HAL in *2001* (1968), *Ex Machina* (2014)].

In a sense, these 'what ifs' are all variants of our earliest fears from childhood. What if there is a monster under the bed? Or in the closet? Our parents check out all the hiding places – "nope, no monsters there." And we're reassured – momentarily. But the ritual has to be repeated, night after night after night, because – ok, there wasn't a monster last time… but how do I know it didn't sneak into the closet, while we were at dinner? [1]

A classic that takes this suspicion and makes it skin-crawlingly real is *Poltergeist* (1982), a movie that had a great tag-line: "It knows what scares you … " And 'it' is happy to show you that you weren't just imagining Things in the Dark. There is a monster under the bed (a clown-doll, natch), and earlier in the movie, one in the shape of an eerily twisted dead tree (shades of *Wizard of Oz*) right outside your window…And you can count the seconds, between flash of lightning and rumble of thunder – as the little boy does, in *Poltergeist*, to try to distract himself from his fear; but while you do, that haunted tree is about to send a branch crashing through your bedroom window, to grab you…

Or – to take a step back to the days of written horror, before the cinema: your sister, who you thought was dead (or you wouldn't have locked her away in the family tomb, in the mansion's basement) would seem to be breaking out of her coffin … something's making that terrible crashing sound! … "Have I not heard her footstep on the stair? Do I not distinguish that heavy and horrible beating of her heart?…I tell you that she now stands without the door!" (Poe, "The Fall of the House of Usher", 1839).

And indeed, as the heavy doors swing open, Madeleine Usher – once buried alive – is standing there in the doorway:

> There was blood upon her white robes … For a moment she remained trembling and reeling to and fro upon the threshold – then, with a low moaning cry, fell heavily inward upon the person of her brother, and in her violent and now final death-agonies, bore him to the floor a corpse, and a victim to the terrors he had anticipated.

"The terrors he had anticipated" – Poe's a master of the worst-case "what if". So – given the predilection of cinema's pioneers for horror[2] – it makes sense that Poe was one of the first great American writers whose works were made into movies. Before the silent era was over, "The Fall of the House of Usher" had already been filmed twice – both in French and American versions (1928).

In his gruesome poem "The Conqueror Worm", Poe describes life itself as a kind of lurid, nightmarish performance:

> With a phantom chased forever more
> By a crowd that seize it not,
> Through a circle that ever returneth in
> To the self-same spot,
> And much of Madness, and more of Sin,
> And Horror the soul of the plot.

That feeling – of being pursued by some terrible thing, and not ever escaping – is central to many horror films. It's a visceral (and visual) metaphor for the unwelcome truth: that behind the masquerade of 'normal life', Revelation is waiting to pounce. Morality is a sham, madness lurks in us all, and death (often protracted and painful) cancels out whatever meaning our lives may have had. In the middle of the grotesque performance Poe imagines our lives to be,

# 4 "Who goes there?"

> ... A crawling shape intrude[s].
> A blood-red thing that writhes from out
> The scenic solitude!
> It writhes! – it writhes! with mortal pangs
> The mimes become its food,
> And seraphs sob at vermin fangs,
> In human gore imbued.

Horror movies challenge us to examine how we live our lives. The "conqueror Worm" will devour us all – and how to exist, with that knowledge? Live in denial, like Norman Bates, who has to keep forgetting what he knows about his crazed mother? (*Psycho*, 1960). Face the pain of traumatic loss (2005's *The Descent*) by setting oneself a daunting physical challenge? (Hint: if the 'challenge' is an unexplored cave system, this will not be a good plan.) Assure your baby-sitting charges there's no such thing as the boogeyman – though he's out there, at that very moment, stalking and killing your friends? (*Halloween*, 1978.)

In the most extreme horror movies, people come face-to-face with annihilation that seems to wipe out everything. They're defeated, sometimes long before the movie ends – and in the final 'act', we're forced to watch as the characters suffer and die. For example, in the brutal French movie *Martyrs* (2008), a young woman who was abused as a child seeks out and murders – in very cold blood - the family who had tormented her, before killing herself in despair. Then the childhood friend she'd called to help her discovers that the murdered family was just a part of a larger group of sadists with mystical leanings – who imprison the friend and torture her for the almost-unwatchable final third of the story. There's no denying the skill with which this movie was made; the tension, in the first half, is almost unbearable. And it has its defenders, who find – in the last victim's 'martyrdom' – some kind of awful transcendence. But, because the woman is utterly helpless, the viewers end up feeling helpless, too.

This is probably why a much more entertaining movie – John Carpenter's *The Thing* (1982) – failed to find an audience, on its initial release. The movie – set in a desolate research facility in Antarctica – is about a shape-shifting alien that takes on the form of each creature it kills. As the movie goes on and the body-count mounts, the survivors become wholly justified in their paranoid fear and suspicion of who is human and who may not be. (The 1930s sci-fi story on which the movie is based has the very apt title, "Who Goes There?".) By the movie's haunting end-game, only two humans are left – or is that one? Our hero MacReady runs out of options; all he can do is blow up the base, knowing he'll freeze to death along with the other survivor, his colleague Childs – who may or may not be The Thing-in-hiding. So – BLAM! There's some desolate satisfaction in the explosions that end the movie ... but it's bleak as hell, to have our protagonist saving the world by killing himself. Another sci-fi movie, *E.T.*, which also opened in 1982, grossed $359 million; The Thing took in $19.6 million. Admittedly, apples and oranges; though the differences are suggestive, perhaps, since both are about "close encounters" with an alien intelligence. *E.T.* was a heart-warming fable about embracing the Unknown; in *The Thing*, the Unknown kills you.

*The Thing* is classic horror, with the sturdiest of templates: man meets Monster. Chaos ensues. Order is restored, or it's not. The threat we clueless humans meet keeps shifting, over time and space – though often enough the threat is a then-current version of the Other: from East Europeans immigrants (in the late-Victorian *Dracula*), to the maybe-too-friendly white liberals in the recent hit movie *Get Out*.

And in some of the greatest horror flicks, this confrontation – man vs. monster – builds to a moment of nerve-shredding recognition: that the Other we're so terrified of meeting isn't so 'other' … In fact, in the brilliant 1950s film, *Invasion of the Body Snatchers*, (#2, on our earlier list of horrific 'what ifs), the monsters look exactly like your mother, or your Uncle Ira … except they aren't Uncle Ira or Mom, in some uncanny way you can't quite explain … you just know. But who the hell are they?

Human beings are being replaced with identical-looking aliens (who we see, in one nightmarish sequence, being 'born' – life-sized - from giant pea-like pods in a greenhouse). And this transformation is so suggestive, of so many dreadfully plausible scenarios (are the pod-people brain-washed Communists? or conforming bourgeois Americans?) that the film's producers – worried about how truly disturbing the movie was – insisted on a new, more hopeful ending. (Not to mention a new voice-over narration that climaxed with the movie's most risible line [and spoiler alert, by the way]: "I never knew the true meaning of fear … until I kissed Becky … ")

Becky fell asleep – and that's when she changed: she's become a pod-person. In the film's original ending, the protagonist flees the horror of kissing pod-Becky, ending up on a busy freeway, trying to stop the unheeding cars racing by in the night: "You're next! You're NEXT!"

But are we? Do we have to be? Before the horror-writer puts a single word down on paper, there's a basic decision to make, regarding the world of the story she's building: is this a place where the characters can encounter the monstrous, and live? Or is it a world where the story's logic closes down on hope like a trap?[3]

Either way, we need to care about the characters in jeopardy. This is all too often the problem with the 'body-count' slasher movie. The victims are barely characterized – the Jock, the Nerd, the Bimbo – and the only thing generating suspense is the manner in which the victims will die. Carried to an absurd extreme, the cruelly ingenious murder becomes the entire point of the popular *Final Destination* films. So intricate are the ways of death in these movies – like lethal Rube-Goldberg machines – that the ultimate effect is much more comic than horrific.

There is a place for laughter, in horror; often a comic moment gives the audience needed breathing room, a momentary easing of tension before the build-up begins again. (We'll look more closely at comic aspects of horror – including comedy/horror hybrids like the great *Shaun of the Dead* - in Chapter 9.) The danger of such a strategy comes when comedy's at the expense of character; when we're invited to laugh at, and not with, the characters, we lose that connection that makes us care that the characters' lives are in danger.

When we talk about creating characters audiences can care about, we're talking about something more than a simple 'we like them!' kind of sympathy. In great horror flicks, the protagonists are often far from perfect. They steal (like Marion Crane, setting the *Psycho* plot in motion), they fantasize about revenging themselves on their enemies (like the bullied Oskar in *Let the Right One In*), they rage at their needy, precocious, maddening children (like the harried, haunted mother in *The Babadook*). But because of their imperfections, these characters are very human. And it's with their basic humanity that we empathize - even when we want to shout at them not to do what they're doing: "Don't steal that money! Don't fall asleep! And – no, for the love of God! - don't go in the basement!"

What complicates matters more – for both the characters, and the audience – is the recognition (mentioned before) that the Other we're all afraid of may turn out to be some version of Us. For example, in James Whale's *Frankenstein*, the Creature's child-like qualities are both touching and appalling. But either way, we connect with him, in a way that we don't with the arrogant, manic Doctor who proclaims, "Now I know what it feels like to be God!" – and then proceeds, cold-heartedly, to abandon his creation. That doctor is the ostensible protagonist of the movie. But to the public, "Frankenstein" became the name of the monster ... the one with whom we feel at least some sense of identification.

Fast-forward from Frankenstein's creature to a modern monster who also evokes a conflicted response from the audience. Hannibal Lecter's a savage killer who eats his victims (or parts of them); but in his 'star' appearance, in *The Silence of the Lambs*,[4] the imprisoned Lecter's also a patient (albeit cunning) guru. Sensing how damaged the FBI agent is, who's become his 'protégé', he lures her into confronting her own inner demons, as he helps her track down another killer and save a young woman's life. And he's mesmerizingly clever (and equally dangerous), as he does all this. So we fear him and we cheer for him. We may even be relieved, at movie's end, when he escapes.

Because – we need our monsters. They teach us about the dangers of the world; and they teach us about ourselves. They begin to answer the questions raised by the haunting and haunted tales of Poe: what are we most afraid of? And how do we live with that fear?

*How to Write a Horror Movie* will look at 'fear itself' as the place to start, when writing a horror movie. Specific fears generate the plot (often a version of 'what if?'), as well as the monster/menace/threat that embodies the fear, and even the 'right' protagonists – whose particular strengths and weaknesses will make them the most intriguing people to follow into the nightmare.

The trick is to find a new way to embody fears that are universal. The South Korean blockbuster, *Train to Busan* (2016) is a good example. On the surface, it's just another (incredibly well-made) zombie flick, with the twist that most of the action's confined to a claustrophobic speeding train. The fear of infection (and losing one's humanity) is familiar; but the writers – Joo-Suk Park and Sang-ho Yeon – have burrowed deeper. What else might be at stake, for someone trapped in this situation?

What about your child's belief in you, as a decent human being? At the center of *Train to Busan* is a divorced and overworked businessman, escorting his little girl on an hour-long train-trip to visit her mom. The little girl knows her dad is selfish; and she's even more heart-broken when he acts without generosity, as a zombie infection spreads through the train. Again and again she offers a better example of how he ought to behave; and the movie generates real suspense out of whether or not the father will learn – in time - from his brave but frightened child.

That fear – of failing to live up to your child's best expectations – gives a satisfying, unexpected shape to the plot of *Train to Busan*. It also suggests a relationship – between a too-busy father and his neglected little girl – that determines who the main characters need to be (see Figure 1.2). Similarly, the harried, neglectful dad suggests an opposing human (non-zombie) nemesis, in the person of another businessman so far gone into selfishness that he'd throw a helpless grandmother to the zombies (and does.)

In the course of *How to Write a Horror Movie*, we'll look, in turn, at each of those aspects of horror-moving writing – from plot, to protagonists, to Menaces – as they relate to an organizing fear. And we'll also look at how that fear suggests specific locations – particularly the "Bad Place" where a horror movie often ends up (e.g., the basement of the Victorian house that looms above the forlorn motel in *Psycho*, the mysterious blocked-up closet in the apartment of *Rosemary's Baby*, the train itself in *Busan*, which goes – in a matter of minutes – from sunlit and civilized modern mode of transit to a thundering chain of linked-up carloads-of-horror).

Other chapters will take up the use of humor in horror tales, the craft of scene-building and dialogue, and sources of inspiration – all the elements you can use, to embody the fear you're writing about. And how to choose that particular fear, to

**FIGURE 1.2** Preoccupied father Seok-woo (Gong Yoo) tries to comfort his daughter Su-an (Kim Su-an), on the *Train to Busan* full of zombies.

begin with? To echo that tag-line from Poltergeist: "You know what scares you". (We'll examine several sources of inspiration in Chapter 10.)

For Dorothy in *The Wizard of Oz*, the Fear is about being lost, in a very strange place, unable to find a way home again. It's a stretch, of course, to call this a 'horror' film; it's also (and maybe more accurately) a "Wisdom Quest', with our hero learning she has the strength to survive in the 'home' she misses so much – the bleak and often lonely world of Depression-era Kansas. What's odd about the movie – and what links it to the subversive message of Horror – is how totally disappointing it is, when Dorothy succeeds in her quest, and finds herself returned to home, in a black-and-white world where any chance of adventuring is gone for good. In the dangerous world of Oz – despite her fear – she was learning and growing. Now that she's back in Kansas, her education comes to a crashing halt.

Horror movies are often about gaining knowledge – frightening though it may be. But unlike *The Wizard of Oz*, where Dorothy's life returns to 'normal', there is no normal left, at the end of the great horror films; the world has changed. And this is the secret exhilaration of horror, no matter how bleak it is. The characters have moved beyond the confines of convention, the limits of everyday life – into a place where, if they survive, they'll have to re-invent themselves.

We see a darker version of this moment in the cave-explorer flick *The Descent*, where one of the women spelunkers has to hide from the creature hunting her by submerging herself in what looks – in the lurid light of flares – like a pool of blood. When it's safe – or she thinks it is – she emerges slowly from the red water (much like Martin Sheen rising out of the river, on his way to kill Colonel Kurtz in *Apocalypse Now*).

She's a different woman now, from the damaged innocent at the top of the film; she knows what lurks in the darkness (both in the cave itself, and in the hearts of her fellow spelunkers). She began the story as victim of a sudden and terrible tragedy (when – in the film's shocking prologue – her husband and child were killed in a freak car accident); now she's a hardened survivor. When she finally finds a narrow opening out of the cave, her emergence into the light of day is like a re-birth (and is filmed that way). We're left with the question of what she's had to lose, to survive – a question that haunts the ending of many horror films. "After such knowledge, what forgiveness?"[5]

It's a common complaint of horror fans – that a film they like falls apart in the end. So we need to think about our endings carefully, before we begin. The chapters on structure (3–6) will conclude by examining 'where we end up', with the story we're telling – and how that ending has to inform our story, from the beginning. Maybe the monster does get away, vanishing like the murderous Michael Myers in *Halloween*. But even that 'open' ending has to be earned, by what leads up to it.

A few final thoughts on the genre, before we launch into the specifics of craft.

Horror movies take as many shapes and forms as the monsters who shamble through them – from slashers to psychological thrillers, creature features to tales of the supernatural. And each of these genres divides, like a virus gone wild, into many subgenres. The haunted-house story, for instance, covers a lot of sinister real-estate – eerie apartment buildings (*Candyman*, the Philippine chiller *Sigaw*, Japan's *Dark Waters*), elaborate mansions (*The Changeling*, South Korea's *A Tale of Two Sisters*), summer places (*Burnt Offerings*, Iceland's *Rift*), and even the good ol' suburban home (*Poltergeist, Sinister, The Conjuring*).

Also monster-like are the ways horror movies often tend to be hybrids – like *Alien* (a sci-fi thriller crossed with a haunted-house movie), or *Train to Busan* (a zombie flick aboard an action-adventure story.) As I mentioned earlier (quoting "Monster Culture [Seven Theses])", the monster always eludes us, always escapes – in part because the meaning of 'the monster' is always shifting, from one historical era to the next, from culture to culture. And similarly, the movies that try to contain these monsters also shift, escaping our attempts to come up with a single, all-encompassing definition.

Consider the simple assertion: horror movies want to scare us. Even that seemingly straightforward statement needs further clarification. Because, as Stephen King points out, fear itself exists on a spectrum, from exalted 'terror' to 'gross-out'.[6]

An example of the former comes in the indie thriller *Monsters*. A space-probe has fallen back to earth – and brought with it some kind of teratogenic contamination, turning northern Mexico into a quarantined 'infected zone', crawling with the ungodly spawn of earth-meets-alien DNA. Our protagonists, a journalist and the daughter of the journalist's boss, miss the last boat out and have to find a way through the infected zone, with a motley crew of mercenaries, none of whom survives the trek. After terrifying encounters with some of the crypto-creatures that haunt the 'zone', they reach the U.S. border – just as two unearthly (and very large) creatures appear above them, floating high up in the night-time sky. Like Portuguese men-of-war the size of zeppelins, these jellyfish-like monstrosities engage in what seems a kind of dance – maybe even a mating dance? – mid-air, pulsating like summer heat-lightning. It's a stunningly beautiful moment – what the English Romantics would have called a sublime and 'awful' (awe-filled) one.[7] And it's terrifying, too – because the creatures are so unknowable. Do they have a purpose, beyond surviving – which seems to involve exterminating the pesky humans they run across? The movie ends before we find out, though our prospects don't look good at all. What we do know, as the credits roll, is that life itself is more various – and more threatening – than we'd dreamed of.

To stay for the moment with King's taxonomy, we have a sublime kind of terror, at one end of the horror spectrum; and revulsion and disgust oozing unpleasantly at the other. As King is frank to admit, of his aims in writing his fiction: "I will try to terrorize the reader. But if I find I cannot terrify him/her, I will try to horrify; and if I find I cannot horrify, I'll go for the gross-out. I'm not proud." [8]

Horror-movie writers, as we will see, mostly follow King's example. In this book, our emphasis will be on terror and horror. But let's look at one example of the 'gross-out', before we move on. In *Saw III*, a man is chained by the neck to the floor of a pit, above which an endless conveyor belt is feeding rotting hog corpses into a row of circular saws. (Where one finds an infinite supply of rotting hog corpses is a question the movie doesn't address.) The putrid and pulverized pigs rain down on the victim, slowly filling up the pit and threatening to drown the man. He's a character we've barely met; so we don't have more than a cursory sort of sympathy, for his horrible plight. What we do feel is a sense of disgust, for this terrible way of dying. And whatever suspense the scene generates has less to do with 'will-he-survive?' – and a whole lot more with 'can I/should I keep watching?' Sequences like this are a dare to the audience: "how much can you take?" These scenes, and the movies containing them, are playing with a basic contradiction in human nature – that what repels us also exerts a terrible fascination. We close our eyes – but then we always start to peek through our fingers …

In movies with more on their minds than making us gag, this kind of tension – 'I don't want to watch – but what's happening?' – can be extremely effective. A notorious example is the 'chest-buster' scene in *Alien*. A crew-member of a deep-space ship is attacked by an alien life-form, a bile-colored octopus-wannabe, which attaches itself to his head and face. An X-ray shows that the creature's extended a tube down the crew-member's throat, apparently breathing for him; and the sickening thing can't be removed by force (its blood turns out to be highly corrosive acid). But eventually it drops away, apparently dead. And the crew member thinks he's recovered … till the moment when he's having a 'welcome back' dinner with his colleagues. Unexpectedly, he starts to choke – then convulse – and then, as the frightened crew tries to hold him down, on the tabletop – there's a sudden explosion of blood and gore, that splatters the horrified onlookers … And an alien creature – looking a lot like a glistening phallus with razor-teeth – pokes out of the dead crew member's chest, surveys the 'alien' humans, and shoots for an exit out of the room, before anyone can move to stop it.

It's a moment with the power to shock, no matter how often you've seen it. Like the equally infamous shower-sequence in *Psycho*, the chest-buster sequence is more than just a 'boo!', intended to startle or gross us out. Instead it's a rupture, a violent break in the way we've been understanding the world of the story. We assumed this world – however exotic – resembled our own in basic ways, e.g., life-cycle stages. But we learn – with the crew of the ill-fated ship – that we were completely and totally wrong. From this point on, we can't afford to take anything for granted. Which means we're now watching the movie in a state of hyper-vigilance. The alien could be anywhere in the ship, and – worse, it could be any form; we don't even know what the monster will look like, when we next encounter it.

We're suspended in uncertainty, which the script-writers Dan O'Bannon and Ronald Shusett play with beautifully – for example, in the sequence leading up to the death of the likeable slacker Brett (Harry Dean Stanton). Brett's gone in search of the crew-members' mascot Jonesy, a cat with more than nine lives in this film. Jonesy needs to be caged, so he won't throw off the motion-detector the crew are using, to try to locate the alien (see Figure 1.3).

For almost four minutes, the movie slows down to one simple, quiet activity: Brett moving through a vast and uninhabited part of the spaceship, calling out,

FIGURE 1.3 Doomed crewman Brett (Harry Dean Stanton) searches for a lost cat, in *Alien*.

"Here kitty ... Jones? Jonesy?" No music on the soundtrack – just the echoing steps of a frightened man, as he tries to do his duty ... condensation falling like rain, in one of the cavernous ship's industrial spaces... the eerie clinking of chains that dangle down from the far-away ceiling ... And because of the hyper-vigilant state we've been in, ever since the chest-buster scene, the tension keeps building and building. We know that something terrible is just about to happen – but we don't know when, or how, or where.

Brett stands, for a moment, taking off his baseball cap, so the condensation-rain can hit his face – and we sense, as he instinctively pauses for one brief moment of pleasure, how far from Earth this man has been (for months, or even years), how alone he and his colleagues are, in the endless dark of the universe. It's very close to one of those moments of wonder we mentioned earlier – when we sense our insignificance, in a vast and indifferent cosmos. How very fragile we are – and yet, how amazing that we can contain, in our dreaming minds, the entire universe. Brett stands in the dripping condensation, maybe remembering rain on a distant earth – and his simple humanity makes his onrushing death even more upsetting. He does find Jonesy, but it's too late – because Jonesy sees Something rearing up, very high above Brett's shoulder ...

In the following chapter, we'll look at how, to write an effective horror movie, you need to start with those Things rising up from your own imagination. When you hear a sound in the dark, late at night – what do you think might be waiting for you, too patiently, in the shadows? You closed your bedroom door – so why is it open now, at 3 a.m.? What's out there is exactly what you're going to want to write about.

## Notes

1 In his influential essay "Monster Culture (Seven Theses)", Jeffrey Jerome Cohen asserts that "the monster always escapes" (emphasis added). "Regardless of how many times Sigourney Weaver's beleaguered Ripley utterly destroys the ambiguous Alien that stalks

her, its monstrous progeny return, ready to stalk again in another bigger-than-ever sequel. The anxiety that condenses like green vapor into the form of the vampire can be dispersed temporarily, but the revenant by definition returns. And so the monster's body is both corporal and incorporeal; its threat is its propensity to shift." Jeffrey Jerome Cohen, *Monster Theory: Reading Culture*, (Minneapolis: University of Minnesota Press, 1996), pp. 4–5
2 In 1910, inventor Thomas Edison's company, Edison Studios, made a short film of the novel *Frankenstein* – considered by some to be the first horror movie. Another candidate is George Melies' *The House of the Devil* (1896)
3 Andrew Tudor makes a basic distinction between 'closed' narratives – in which the monstrous is contained at the end, and 'open' narratives, which suggest that the monster – in whatever form – remains at loose in the world. Andrew Tudor, *Monsters and Mad Scientists: A Cultural History of the Horror Movie*), (Cambridge: Wiley-Blackwell, 1991), pp. 81–105.
4 Hannibal Lecter – a character created by Thomas Harris in a series of books that begins with *Red Dragon* – made his first, less spectacular screen appearance in 1986, in the film *Manhunter* (an adaptation of *Dragon*), with British actor Brian Cox playing Lecter (or, as the credits had it, 'Lecktor').
5 T.S. Eliot, "Gerontion".
6 Stephen King, *Danse Macabre* (New York: Gallery, 2010), p..37.
7 The most often-quoted definition (in English) of 'the sublime' appears in Edmund Burke's treatise on aesthetics, *A Philosophical Enquiry into the Origin of Our Ideas of the Sublime and Beautiful*, (1757)
8 King, op. cit

# 2
# WHAT SCARES YOU?

"The oldest and strongest emotion of mankind is fear," wrote H.P. Lovecraft, creator of a pulp-fiction world of dreadful gods and monsters. "And the oldest and strongest kind of fear is fear of the unknown."[1] We'll keep coming back to this subject of fear – but for now, I want to look at the screenwriter's very specific and fearful unknown: that blinking cursor, on the blank screen, the blank page. What do I write about?

The best answer is also the obvious one – write about what scares you. Spiders? Arachnaphobia. Snakes? *Anaconda* or *Snakes on a Plane*. Open water? *Open Water*. Strangers? *It Follows*, or *Ils* (or its American rip-off, *The Strangers*). Loneliness? Many examples – it's one of the central subjects of horror, including the very great *Psycho* (which we'll look at in more detail, in Chapter 7).

Whatever the fear, most horror movies work on more than one level. There's the obvious menace – spiders, aliens, strangers, children, zombies, clowns; then beyond the things-that-go-bump-in-the-night, is the Night Itself: disorder, chaos, rupture, violent separation from the comforting-if-numbing everyday of most of our lives.

For instance, *Rosemary's Baby* is – on the surface – a film about ancient witchcraft in modern Manhattan (circa 1968). Some critics have even panned it for its ostensible subject matter, claiming the film's director/screenwriter, Roman Polanski, was a religious skeptic, and didn't himself buy into the horror with which he was trying to frighten us.[2]

This criticism misses the point – because the film's deepest fears aren't the lurid ones of its surface story. These bedrock fears revolve, instead, around the common condition of pregnancy (with all the anxieties that accompany it), and betrayal by people you love the most. Fears anyone can relate to, no matter what their religious beliefs. In this context, witchcraft is not so much the film's subject as its metaphor. And it generates some serious jolts, in particular, a ghoulish nightmare (or is it?) where Rosemary, semi-conscious, is impregnated by the Devil (or her husband, who at that moment is possessed by the Devil incarnate). "This is no dream," she moans, looking up at the jaundice-yellow eyes of a demon, "this is really happening!"

Despite being drugged and traumatized, Rosemary is seeing clearly – and what she sees is a horrifying betrayal of her, by the man she loves. So painful is this knowledge that, the next morning, Rosemary has to shrug it off, as a dream – a denial that starts a kind of 'ticking clock' for the audience – as we wait, with mounting anxiety, for Rosemary to figure out that the things she fears aren't delusions at all. She *is* being threatened – both from without (by her husband's betrayal), and from within (by the baby itself she's carrying, through a nightmarishly painful pregnancy).

Amniocentesis, as a routine procedure, was still in its infancy, when the novel *Rosemary's Baby* was written (1967). And the tragic consequences of thalidomide – prescribed as a tranquilizer for pregnant women, but found (in the early 1960's) to cause horrific birth defects – were still very much in the public's consciousness. Rosemary's concerns, at first, are those of any pregnant woman unnerved by the graphic photos, in papers and magazines of the time, of babies born with deformed hearts, missing limbs, blind or deaf.

Below that conscious fear is another, regarding the fetus itself (whether the pregnancy is 'normal' or not). Women often report that the fetus can feel like a kind of invasive parasite – taking sustenance and strength from the mother, and giving nothing back in return. This definitely seems to be the case, during Rosemary's first trimester – when she's losing weight, instead of gaining, and feeling a constant pain – 'like a wire getting tighter and tighter' – that her new doctor (who's in on the fiendish plot) dismisses as 'perfectly normal'. Rosemary's friends are shocked by her appearance – and she's ready to throw in the towel, and go to a different doctor ... when the searing pain she's been living with suddenly stops. Rosemary laughs and cries in relief, thinking her very worst fears – that she'll lose the baby, or it will be grossly deformed – are finally unfounded. In a moment that should be joyous, she feels the baby moving – and invites her husband Guy to touch his child. He demurs – and when she takes his hand and places it on her belly, he jerks his hand away. What exactly does he know, about this baby, that she doesn't?

In his fascinating book, *Religion and Its Monsters*, Timothy Beal suggests that horror arises out of threat, at several different levels: the personal (threats to our bodies and/or sense of self, our identity), the societal or cultural (one's specific circumstances), and the global or cosmic (one's understanding of, and place in, the larger world). Horror conjures the seismic shift, when we lose our sense of being 'at home', in our bodies, in our societies and in our world.[3] As we've seen in *Rosemary's Baby*, Rosemary starts to lose the sense of self she'd always taken for granted, as her pregnancy begins to take over her life, both physically (as she loses weight and suffers from constant pain), and mentally (fearing, as she does, that something must be wrong with the child she's carrying). Then her fears begin to radiate outward, as she starts to suspect that her neighbors, her doctor, and even her ambitious husband are all conspiring against her. When her best friend Hutch – who's harbored suspicions about Rosemary's 'friends' – is suddenly struck down by an illness, lapses into a coma and dies – Rosemary's left completely alone, without anyone she can trust, as her delivery date approaches. Her sense of self is shattered; next, the community in which she lives. Even a kindly doctor she turns to, at the last desperate moment, thinks she's suffered a psychotic break and delivers her to her enemies. And finally, when the baby is born – and Rosemary sees its little hooves, and its cat-like eyes ("He has his Father's eyes," says elderly head witch Roman Castavet, intending a compliment), Rosemary's understanding of how the world works – specifically the place within that world, of good and evil – is demolished. Evil isn't a concept; it's a little baby fussing in its pitch-black bassinette.

For her final confrontation with the Satanists-next-door, Rosemary arrives with a very big, very sharp kitchen knife – to kill her tormentors, or maybe herself, or possibly even the baby … But now, in the movie's last chilling moment, coven leader Roman suggests that she comfort the crying child. "Rock him," he says. Rosemary hesitates: "You're trying to get me to be his mother … "

"Aren't you his mother?", Roman replies, with the straightforward logic of nightmare.

And those are the final words of the script. Rosemary stares down at her baby (who, by this point, we're pretty certain is Satan's spawn) – and the camera closes in on Rosemary's face, as a look of helpless maternal love possesses her. She's trapped – more completely than by any spell the devil-worshippers could've cast. More disturbingly, the final image – Rosemary looking with love at her child – implies that she accepts her trap, and maybe even embraces it. She and her baby have both survived; it's a kind of happy ending, of a devastating sort.

To recap: to frighten your audience, you should write about what frightens you. And your fear should be something that poses a threat: to your characters' sense of self, to their community, or to their basic beliefs about the world and how it works.

As we've seen, *Rosemary's Baby* activates threats at every level – as the movie builds relentlessly, from the personal to the cosmic. What is it about Rosemary that makes her such an effective character, to entangle in a demonic plot?

For starters, she's a lapsed Catholic – and though her guilt about that is a little clearer in the novel, it's definitely a part of what defines her in the movie. The movie is set in 1965 – the year the Pope first visited America, appearing to an overflow crowd at Yankee Stadium. Paradoxically, it's also within a year of the moment when *Time* magazine – for the first time ever – ran a cover without a photo, just red letters against a black background: "IS GOD DEAD?"[4] Organized religion – like many other forms of authority – was being questioned, during the turbulent decade of the 1960s. And in fact it comes up, the very first time Rosemary and her husband Guy have dinner with their new neighbors, Roman and Minnie Castavet (an eccentric but seemingly harmless older couple, who turn out to be the leaders of the coven).

**16** What scares you?

> ROMAN
> No pope ever visits a city where the newspapers are on strike.
> MINNIE
> I heard he's going to postpone and wait till it's over.
> GUY
> Well, that's show biz.
>
> *[Mr. and Mrs. Castavet laugh, Guy along with them. Rosemary smiles and cuts her steak. It is difficult to cut, and flanked by peas and mashed potatoes. From her expression we can gather that it doesn't taste good either.]*
>
> ROMAN
> *[still laughing]* That's exactly what it is! All the costumes, the rituals – all religions ...
> MINNIE
> Uh-oh – I think we're offending Rosemary.
> ROSEMARY
> *[uncomfortable]* No, no ...
> ROMAN
> You're not religious, dear, are you?
> ROSEMARY
> I was brought up a Catholic. Now I don't know.
> MINNIE
> You looked uncomfortable.
> ROSEMARY
> Well – he is the Pope ...
> ROMAN
> Well, you don't need to have respect for him just because he pretends that he's holy.
> GUY
> That's a good point.
> MINNIE
> When I think what they spend on robes and jewels ...

Because she was raised a Catholic, Rosemary isn't at ease with the cynical dinner-table banter. But, as she says, she doesn't know what she believes, any more. So she's vulnerable. She still feels the guilt instilled in her, by her early religious training – but she no longer has the comfort and strength of a firm belief, to defend herself. If God is dead, then wouldn't it follow that Satan is moribund, also? Or to put it in the oft-quoted words of Baudelaire, "The Devil's greatest trick is to make us believe he doesn't exist."[5]

The night of the satanic rape, Minnie treats the young couple to little pots of her special chocolate mousse (or 'mouse', as Minnie mangles the word). It's drugged –

and if Rosemary ate it all, she would have been knocked out cold. But she notices a 'chalky undertaste'; she only eats a few spoonfuls, dumping the rest but pretending to finish it off ... So she's woozy but dimly – horrifically – aware, when the nightmare rape begins. At the very end, still naked and tied down on a bed, she hallucinates that she's seeing the Pope, who bustles over to comfort her:

>                         POPE
> They tell me you have been bitten by a mouse.
>                       ROSEMARY
> Yes. That's why I couldn't come to see you.
>                         POPE
> Oh, that's all right. We wouldn't want you to jeo-
> pardize your health.
>                       ROSEMARY
> Am I forgiven, Father?
>                         POPE
> Oh – absolutely!

And the dream – that's only partly a dream – fades out, as the Pope holds out his ring, for Rosemary's penitent kiss.

Rosemary's learned submission – but has lost the belief underlying it. This moral fog also shadows her relationship with her husband, Guy. She's aware of his self-absorption, but also makes excuses for it. And she's touchingly grateful when he decides it's time they had a baby.

The morning after the rape, when she wakes up, as if from a blackout, she finds scratches on her body – and realizes, dumbfounded, that Guy had sex with her, even though she was 'out'. He pre-empts her protest, telling her he 'didn't want to miss baby night.'

>                          GUY
> ... and a couple of my nails were ragged –
>                       ROSEMARY
> [dazed] While I was out?
> [Guy attempts a kind of lecherous grin.]
>                          GUY
> ... and it was kind of fun, in a necrophile sort of way ...
> Rosemary sits on the edge of the bed, struggling to
> remember.
>                       ROSEMARY
> I dreamed someone was ... raping me ... someone inhuman ...
>                          GUY
> Thanks a lot! [She turns her back on him.] What's the
> matter?

```
                        ROSEMARY
    Nothing.
                          GUY
    I didn't want to miss the night.
                        ROSEMARY
    [plaintive] We could've done it this evening, or
    tonight - last night wasn't the only split second …
                          GUY
    Well, I was a little bit loaded myself, you know …
```

Rosemary doesn't reply, and the awkward moment comes to an end. Shortly afterward, she learns from a doctor that she's pregnant. Guy's delighted by the news – and rushes off to tell Minnie and Roman. By now, Rosemary's managed to completely repress the 'baby night', and also the morning after. She's forgotten the horrible "dream" – and even Guy's grotesque 'apology', when she woke to find her body scratched: "it was kind of fun, in a necrophile sort of way!" As Mathias Clasen writes, in *Why Horror Seduces*,

> Rosemary's willingness to overlook Guy's moral flaws, as well as her naivete, makes her vulnerable to his monstrous betrayal … Guy's selfish ambition is so strong that he is willing to sacrifice his own wife and use her deepest desire [for a child] against her, in exchange for professional success.[6]

Rosemary Woodhouse has specific strengths and weaknesses that make her the perfect character to embody a specific fear – of a truly monstrous betrayal by a loved one (see Figure 2.1).

**FIGURE 2.1** Rosemary (Mia Farrow) wakes from a terrible dream (or was it?) in *Rosemary's Baby*.

The Swedish film *Let the Right One In* (2008) – with a screenplay by John Ajvide Lindqvist, adapting his own novel – is another haunting match-up of Fear and Character. Young Oskar is a bullied kid, whose separated parents are too distracted to see his distress. Friendless and most often alone, Oskar daydreams of retaliating against the kids who torment him. In fact, the first words we hear – against a dark screen lit only by falling snow – are 'Squeal like a pig … So, squeal." We cut to an apartment, where we meet Oskar – a pale blond pre-teen – only as a reflection in the window, looking out at the night. Bare-chested, wearing only briefs, he looks completely defenseless – but then, jarringly, we see that he has a knife in his hand; and what he's play-acting, alone in his room, is turning the tables on the bullies. He pretends he's forcing his nemeses to do what he's been made to do: debase himself and "squeal like a pig."

But Oskar can never translate his violent daydreams into reality. Though he doesn't realize it, what he's looking for is a catalyst. And one appears – in the form of a young girl, Eli, who moves in next door. Eli's definitely an outsider, like Oskar, with an odd smell at times, and impervious to the freezing weather. When she first meets Oskar, he's playing again through his fantasy, this time stabbing a tree outside his apartment building. Feeling a presence behind him, he turns – and Eli's appeared, atop the snowed-up jungle gym.

```
                    ELI
What are you doing?
                    OSKAR
Nothing. What are you doing?
                    ELI
Nothing.
                    OSKAR
Do you live here?
                    ELI
Yeah … I live right here, in the jungle gym.
                    OSKAR
Seriously, where do you live?
[She points.]
                    ELI
Next door to you.
                    OSKAR
How do you know where I live?
[She jumps down, crunching through the snow to approach
him.]
                    ELI
Just so you know, I can't be your friend.
                    OSKAR
What do you mean?
                    ELI
Does there have to be a reason? That's just the way it is.
```

>
> *[She turns and moves off-screen. Oskar calls after her:]*
>                          OSKAR
> Are you sure that I want to be your friend?
> *[In response, he hears the door to the building open and close, as Eli slips away.]*

Oskar takes her rebuff without flinching; he's used to being rejected. But Eli's reasons for keeping her distance are more than simple pre-teen angst – because, in fact, she's a vampire. She's been an outsider much longer than Oskar, and recognizes in him a kindred spirit. Slowly the human boy and the vampire girl become unlikely friends – while a series of killings rocks the small community where Oskar lives (Eli has to feed); and Oskar's tormentors at school continue to bully him, relentlessly. Eli teaches Oskar that he has to fight back; and he finally does, hurting one kid so badly that the kid's older brother plots revenge. Meanwhile, Oskar has figured out – at last – that Eli's not human. When he knocks on her door, she sees that he knows; and she's hesitant to let him in.

>                          OSKAR
> Are you a vampire?
>                          ELI
> I live off blood. Yes.
>                          OSKAR
> Are you dead?
>                          ELI
> No. Can't you tell?
>                          OSKAR
> But ... are you old?
>                          ELI
> I'm twelve. But I've been twelve a long time.
> *[Oskar's overwhelmed, and starts to leave.]*
>                          OSKAR
> I'm going home. I have flyers to distribute tomorrow.
>                          ELI
> To make money? I can give you money. *[handing him some paper]* Here. Take it if you like.
>                          OSKAR
> You stole this ... *[He puts the money down]* ... from the people you killed, right?
>                          ELI
> It was given to me.
>                          OSKAR
> By who?
>                          ELI
> By different people.

OSKAR

I want to go home now. *[She doesn't move.]* If you'll let me. *[She steps aside, he exits.]*

Oskar's finally brave enough, to ask his friend who she truly is – but not quite strong enough to accept her, as she's accepted him. So, in a following scene, she comes to his door – where his fear and uncertainty make him act like the bullies he loathes.

ELI

Hey …

OSKAR

Hi.

ELI

You have to invite me in.

OSKAR

What happens if I don't? What happens if you walk in anyway? Is there something in the way?
*[He mocks her, by miming a barrier between them in the doorway. Then he steps aside, challenging her to enter. Reluctantly, but determined, she does so. And as she stares at him, he sees her beginning to bleed – everywhere: through her blouse, from her scalp, her eyes and ears. Horrified, he shouts the necessary words.]*

OSKAR (cont'd)

No! You can come in!
*[Moved in a way he can barely understand, he embraces her bleeding body.]*

OSKAR

Who are you?

ELI

I'm like you.

OSKAR

What do you mean?
*[Not cruelly, but forcefully, she quotes his earlier words:]*

ELI

"What are you staring at? Well? Are you looking at me? So scream! Squeal!"
*[Pause.]*

ELI

Those were the first words I heard you say.
*[He takes this in.]*

                              OSKAR
```
I don't kill people.
```
                              ELI
```
But you'd like to ... if you could. To get revenge. Right?
```
                              OSKAR
```
Yes.
```
                              ELI
```
I do it because I have to.
[She draws close to him, blood streaking her face.]
```
                              ELI
```
Be me, for a little while.
[He closes his eyes - and, just for a moment, we see his
vision of her as a much older
woman, still pleading.]
```
                         ELI (cont'd)
```
Please. Be me, for a little while.
```

In that moment, we come face to face with the Fear at the heart of this 'vampire' movie: of never being 'seen' or understood, of always having to be a monstrous 'other' (see Figure 2.2). And Oskar begins the painful and beautiful task of seeing another (perhaps not as clearly as she sees him, but then, she's had more experience with all the mortals she's had to live among). Unfortunately, the moment can't last. Eli is being hunted down, and has to leave town abruptly. And Oskar, alone once more, becomes a target for the worst of the bullies – a sadist who isolates Oskar, in the school swimming pool, and gives him a choice: stay underwater three minutes (held in place by the thug, who's grabbed his hair) ... or be stabbed in the eye with a switch-blade.

In a terrifying sequence – much of it shot below the water's surface – Oskar struggles, starting to drown ... and then – something Horrible/Wonderful

**FIGURE 2.2** Oskar (Kåre Hedebrant) learns why a vampire (Lina Leandersson) has to be invited to enter, in *Let the Right One In*.

happens: as the camera stays on Oskar's face, we hear shouting, see the feet of someone being dragged along the pool's surface … then suddenly, a decapitated head plunges into the pool behind Oskar, who doesn't realize yet he's been saved … till at last the arm holding him down also drifts to the bottom, detached from its shoulder. A different hand reaches down to help Oskar up to the surface – to light and life; Oskar finally opens his eyes and sees Eli, who's come just in time to save him. For a moment, he just stares at her – and then he breaks into a radiant smile. We see only Eli's eyes, looking back – and are left to wonder if she's smiling, too – after having killed (in fact, ripped to pieces) three of Oskar's tormentors.

The next cut is to the aftermath: three bloody bodies, at the pool's edge, and the most conscious-stricken bully – the one Eli spared  horrified by what's happened, alone in the bleachers, quietly crying. Then a cut to a shot that repeats the movie's opening – snow falling against a black sky. And then – a scene in daylight, a coda: Oskar, running away from home, on a speeding train, at his feet a large trunk. He hears tapping from the trunk, and taps back – the Morse code he and Eli had learned, to 'talk' through their apartment walls. Oskar's escaped his loneliness – though we're left to wonder what will happen, as he gets older and Eli stays twelve, forever.

Sometimes the attempt to match character with fear can seem either comic, or too obvious. For example, in the classic *Jaws* (1975), Roy Scheider plays the sheriff of a tiny island community – who happens to be afraid of being out on open water. For a man in charge of defending an island, this fear is a real liability; you wonder why he didn't look for a job somewhere in Nebraska. The screenwriters can play this problem for laughs – because they have a much darker fear they're building to, as the danger grows from the giant shark that's besieged the town. By then, the sheriff's joined forces with a goofy marine biologist and the captain of a fishing boat who has his own personal reasons for wanting to hunt down any and every shark. In a wonderful moment of seeming calm, before the film's furious climax, the captain delivers a truly hair-raising monologue, that connects the film's local problems to an even more terrible tragedy in the Pacific, in World War II. (We'll look at this brilliant speech in Chapter 7, on dialogue.) As the captain, Quint, tells his story, we hear a man who's completely obsessed – putting the sheriff and the biologist in even more danger than they'd imagined; Quint isn't going to stop until either the shark is dead, or he is (making the ever-more possible deaths of his companions 'collateral damage').

As a final example – one where the linking of character/fear is problematic – I want to look at the indie hit *Lights Out* (2016), which began as a two-and-a-half-minute short that went viral, a "miniature master-class in terror", as one critic put it.[7] In the short, a woman comes out of her bathroom, getting ready for bed – and then notices something ominous: when she turns off the light in her hallway, she can see a figure in silhouette at the hallway's end, standing in shadow. Turn the light back on? The figure is gone. The puzzled woman tries this several times, with the same result: something is lurking there in the dark, and vanishes in the light. Completely unnerved, the woman tapes the hall light-switch in place, leaves her bedside light on, and cowers under her blankets. But protections like that are not going to work. The woman hears floorboards creaking, in the hallway; then the lights – despite the switch taped 'on' – go out. And so on, till a final shock-cut, as the woman thinks the Creature has gone. She turns, and it's right by her bedside, sharp teeth glistening in a savage grin. Lights out.

And that's all there is to it. Swedish director David Sandberg had made the short (starring his wife Lotta Losten) as an entry in a contest. But when it went viral, Hollywood came calling. Producer Lawrence Grey spoke to what grabbed him about the short:

> It's this big genius universal idea. We all know it. We're all afraid of the dark. We all know the feeling of, "I saw this thing out of the corner of my eye. Is that a tree? Is that my laundry? Or is it something more sinister than that?" There was real craft in how [Sandberg] did it. [8]

Grey spoke to writer/director/producer James Wan (*Saw*, *The Conjuring*), who was also intrigued, but (in Sandberg's words), "didn't know if there was enough there for a movie, so I wrote a treatment of what I wanted the story and characters to be … [Wan] really felt there could be a movie."[9]

What Sandberg came up with – and screenwriter Eric Heisserer expanded into a full-length script – was a story of a family besieged by the light-fearing shadow-creature from the original short. In terms of matching up Fear with Characters, the challenge for Sandberg was this: to what characters would it make most sense, for this kind of demonic figure to appear? And what strengths and weaknesses would they bring to the fight, when they had to deal with this creature?

"I figured I wanted to do something about depression," Sandberg said in an interview,

> because I've suffered from depression over a decade now. And I had a friend who committed suicide. To me, it's the most terrifying thing there is. So I wrote [the] treatment for something that was a bit more arthouse, where it was very much an allegory for depression.[10]

In Sandberg's story, the troubled character is Sophie, a woman with a tragic past: she spent time, as a child, in a mental institution. And her best friend there was a girl, Diana, who suffered from a deadly sensitivity to light. As *Lights Out* starts, the ghost of Diana's begun to haunt Sophie, threatening her children – who spend the movie fighting to protect themselves from their mother's 'friend' – the ghostly figure Sandberg chose to represent Sophie's depression (see Figure 2.3).

Sophie's childhood – told via flashback – is awkwardly shoe-horned into the movie. And the reason for ghostly Diana's phobic reaction to light - she was killed by doctors attempting an experimental cure using light - is so literal, that (like the sheriff's fear of water, in *Jaws*) it becomes laughable.

FIGURE 2.3 Businessman Paul (Billy Burke) confronts a creature who only appears in the dark, in *Lights Out*.

Even more problematic is the movie's abrupt conclusion: deciding that ghost-Diana only exists because of the link to her, depressed mother Sophie 'saves' her children by shooting herself in the head. As the reviewer for online magazine *Slant* describes it, "The film resolves its running interest in mental illness with an act of emotional terrorism that's at once offensively lazy and massively counterproductive."[11]

Director Sandberg was taken aback by reviews that pointed out the implicit message of the film – that people with mental illness were "gigantic burdens on their families", burdens they could only lift by offing themselves, as *A.V. Club* reviewer A.A. Dowd suggests.[12] In an interview for *Indiewire*, Sandberg addressed concerns about the ending, explaining –among other things – why the running time of the film is so short (it's less than eighty minutes).

> The movie actually went on for almost 10 more minutes where we find out that this [the mother's suicide] didn't get rid of Diana, you know, and now depression has consumed [her son] Martin instead, because his mom's suicide affected him that much. She came back one more time and they dealt with her once and for all.

But Sandberg says test audiences hated this ending.

> They felt that Sophie was sort of sacrificing herself for her children and to save their lives, and if Diana just came back right after, then, you know, she'd done that for nothing. But now [with those final 10 minutes lopped off] it was this feeling of "Oh, shit." Even though people loved it, it could kind of be interpreted as … that suicide helped them, that it was the solution.[13]

In other words, neither ending was completely satisfying – and I think the problem has to do with the less-than-organic connection between the Fear which sparked the original short (fear of the dark, and the creatures that might be hiding in it), and the fear that's really haunting Sophie's daughter Rebecca – that of her mother's mental illness. This wouldn't be so troublesome, if the film depicted the horrors of depression *from the mother's point of view*. (In fact, the Australian film *The Babadook* sets out to do exactly that, and does it more successfully.)

But *Lights Out* spends very little time, exploring the troubled mother's life. Most of the story is told from the point of view of her suffering children; and to them, the threat in the film is the mother's absorption in her own illness. As reviewer A. A. Dowd describes it, the film's subtext "is so close to the surface that it's basically text with a few handfuls of graveyard dirt thrown on top. The film is blatantly, unmistakably about mental illness, and that makes it hard to ignore or forgive what it ends up saying (hopefully by accident) on the subject."[14] In *Lights Out*, mental illness is a destructive raging demon – and although it provides some effective jump-scares, that central metaphor doesn't offer us any deeper insights into the characters. In effect, the metaphor swallows up the story, which ends incoherently. To quote director Sandberg, "Some people have sort of said, 'Oh, it's a happy ending; she shoots herself and everyone's happy.' But I think it's going to ruin them … "[15] That discrepancy – between the director's intentions and the audiences' response – is some indication of just how muddled a movie can get, when its Characters and its Fear(s) aren't organically connected.

## Notes

1 H. P. Lovecraft, *Supernatural Horror in Literature* (Dover Publications, 1973), p. 12.
2 E.g., Harrison Engle, 'Film Comment 5', Fall 1968, p. 5.
3 Timothy Beal, *Religion and its Monsters* (New York: Routledge, 2002), p. 5.
4 *Time*, April 8, 1966.
5 Charles Baudelaire, *Paris Spleen* (Middletown, CT: Wesleyan University Press, 2009), p. 60.
6 Mathias Clasen, *Why Horror Seduces* (New York: Oxford University Press, 2017), p. 89.
7 A.A. Dowd, "The Scariest Thing about Lights Out is What It Says about Depression," avclub.com, 7/21/16, https://film.avclub.com/the-scariest-thing-about-lights-out-is-what-it-says-abo-1798188358 (accessed 10/7/19).
8 Rebecca Murray, "'Lights Out': Lawrence Gray Interview on Horror Films, Revealing the Monster and the Cast," showbizjunkie.com, 4/8/16, https://www.showbizjunkies.com/movies/lights-out-lawrence-grey-interview (accessed 10/7/19).
9 Heather Wixson, "Lights Out Interview: Director David F. Sandberg and Lotta Losten on Journeying from Sweden to Hollywood & The Advantages of Technology for Emerging Filmmakers", dailydead.com, 7/22/16, https://dailydead.com/lights-out-interview-director-david-f-sandberg-and-lotta-losten-on-their-journey-from-sweden-to-hollywood-and-the-advantages-of-technology-for-emerging-filmmakers, (accessed 107/19).
10 Liz Calvario, " 'Lights Out': Director David Sandberg Explains the Film's Shocking Ending", indiewire.com, July 31, 20, https://www.indiewire.com/2016/07/lights-out-director-david-sandberg-explains-film-ending-1201711861/16 (accessed 10/7/19).
11 Christopher Gray, "Review: Lights Out", slantmagazine.com, 7/21/16, https://www.slantmagazine.com/film/lights-out, (accessed 10/7/19).
12 Dowd, op. cit.
13 Calvario, op. cit.
14 Dowd, op. cit.
15 Calvario, op. cit.

# 3

# BASIC HORROR MOVIE STRUCTURE

You've chosen a fear you'd like to explore (or it's chosen you); and you've had some thoughts about characters who can activate your nightmare. The next important question to answer is: *What do your characters want?*

To say the characters want to survive may seem like the obvious answer. And in many films – from *The Texas Chainsaw Massacre* to the great home-invasion movie *Ils* – the story's focus rapidly narrows, until survival's the only goal. The protagonists either escape, or they die.

But 'survival' doesn't answer a deeper question: why survive? What attaches us to the world? Why is it such an incredible gift, just to be alive? What hopes and dreams are we willing to fight to the death for, when we're threatened?

Paradoxically, it's often loss that first defines a character. He or she has been living happily, till a tragedy – like a death in the family – shatters the character's world. That seismic moment can be in the past – or a film can begin with that breaking point.

*The Descent*, for example, opens with a group of women happily completing a white-water rafting trip. As protagonist Sarah drives away from the river, with her family, she's in a horrific car-crash; she survives, but her husband and daughter are killed. In the equally shocking opening of *Wake Wood*, a couple's young daughter is badly mauled by a dog, and dies of her wounds.

In each of those films, the protagonists have an initial stark decision to make: whether or not to go on with their lives, after suffering catastrophic loss. In *The Descent*, directed and written by Neil Marshall, we jump forward a year. Sarah's friends – wanting to help her re-engage with life – come up a new adventure for the group: cave-exploring. In the course of the film, as things go wrong – and then rapidly very, *very* wrong – Sarah's instinct to survive does kick in. And the change begins, dramatically, after an unexpected cave-in – as Sarah struggles to crawl through a narrow passage, and finds herself firmly stuck. She starts to panic, until her friend Beth crawls back to her, to help her through:

**28** Basic horror movie structure

> BETH
> Okay, breathe. Breathe, okay? Hey, listen to me. What are you so afraid of?
>
> SARAH
> I can't fucking move!
>
> BETH
> You can move! Sarah, look at me. Look at me! The worst thing that could've happened to you has already happened. Okay? And you're still here. This is just a poxy cave. And there's nothing left to be afraid of. I promise. Okay?
> *[Beth's efforts work; Sarah starts to calm down, and Beth even gets her to laugh:]*
>
> BETH (cont'd)
> Hey? Hey, listen. Listen. Listen to me. You'll love this one. How do you give a lemon an orgasm? Goddamn it, let me hear you say it. How do you give a lemon an orgasm? What do you do? You tickle its citrus. *[Sarah laughs.]* Okay, that's better. Come on. Okay. We're gonna move now.

Sarah squeezes through the passage – and the friends move deeper into the cave. Sarah's begun her re-entry into life – but she isn't the person she used to be, before she lost her family. Some part of her knows that Beth's comforting words aren't true: "The worst thing that could've happened to you has already happened … This is just a poxy cave. And there's nothing left to be afraid of." In fact, the women discover that there are plenty of things to fear, in the dark. And the worst aren't monsters, or cave-ins; they're inner demons, like selfishness.

In *Wake Wood*, after the loss of their child, the parents – a vet and his pharmacist wife – move away from the place where their daughter died, and try to start their lives over again. Patrick finds a new job in a rural clinic, and throws himself into exhausting work. And Louise gets another pharmacist's job – but she seems to have too much time to brood. She's stuck in her loss (like Sarah stuck in the cavern); and Patrick can't help her.

He comes home one night to find Louise curled up on the floor, surrounded by their daughter's clothes and toys – painful reminders. In his desperation to help her, Patrick starts to gather up all the mementoes, thinking that holding onto them is keeping Louise from moving on. But she protests, in anguish:

> LOUISE
> What are you doing?
> *[Patrick keeps shoving things into a garbage bag.]*
>
> PATRICK
> You know what I'm doing. These *[the child's posses-sions]* are like a black hole in here.

```
                        LOUISE
[horrified] You're not just throwing Alice's stuff away.
                        PATRICK
No, we can't keep them.
                        LOUISE
D'you not understand? I'm not ... I'm not ready. [Silent a
moment, they watch each other.] You'd forget her if you
could.
[Stung, Patrick stares at his wife, in love and
frustration.]
                        PATRICK
What can I do?
                        LOUISE
You can let me go. [He shakes his head, heart-broken but
determined.] It's not you, Patrick. It's not because of
you.
                        PATRICK
You know what? All I want is for you to be okay.
                        LOUISE
Drive me to the station.
```

In this beautifully written short scene,[1] Patrick fights for what he wants – he wants his wife back from the grief that's consuming her. Louise is fighting, too – to hold on to the memory of her beloved child; and the struggle is making her cruel, in the low blow that she lands: "You'd forget her if you could." Patrick knows that any answer to that accusation is useless. Instead, he asks Louise, simply, "What can I do?" – in other words, 'What do you want?'

She replies, "You can let me go … " She wants release – the very last thing he's willing to give her. He spells out what he hopes for: "All I want is for you to be okay."

And the knock-out punch is her reply: "Drive me to the station." He's lost this fight – and we cut to them silently driving off into the night.

But then fate intervenes: their car breaks down, and they approach the home of a neighbor (Patrick's boss Arthur), to call for help. Though it's late, Patrick knocks on Arthur's door. Louise tries going around to the back – and then stumbles upon a nightmare scene: a crowd of villagers, lit by torches, conducting what seems like a strange sort of rite. From out of a human-sized chrysalis, something's struggling to emerge – is it human? Terrified, Louise runs back to Patrick and – without telling him what she's seen – says they have to get out of there. Now. So they flee the scene – only to find that their neighbor has brazenly entered their home, where he's been waiting to make them an offer. It seems the good folks of Wake Wood have perfected a very disturbing kind of magic. If a loved one has been dead and buried – for less than a year – the Wake Wood magic can bring that person back to life … but just for three days. Patrick's dumbfounded, thinking at first that his boss is making a horrible joke. When he realizes Arthur is serious, he angrily orders him out of the house. But then, with a jolt, he sees that Louise knows more than she's told him, about what she saw behind Arthur's house.

And the conflict between the grieving husband and wife flares again, as he demands that she tell him what she knows.

>                         LOUISE
> I told you already.
>                         PATRICK
> You didn't tell me anything. Please, stop this.
>                         LOUISE
> Stop this, stop what? What is it you think I'm doing?
>                         PATRICK
> Oh come on, babe. Please, come on, be straight with me. What did you see? *[She moves away from him.]* What did you see?
>                         LOUISE
> I saw something like …
>                         PATRICK
> What?
>                         LOUISE
> … a birth?
>                         PATRICK
> And?
>                         LOUISE
> I believe. Patrick, I believe what Arthur said.
>                         PATRICK
> If we do this, will you stay? *[She faces him.]* Louise?
>                         LOUISE
> I just want her back.

This scene contains, compactly, all the basic elements of dramatic action:

- the characters *want* something;
- what they want puts them *in conflict*;
- and they *negotiate*, attempting to resolve the conflict to get what they want.

In the previous scene – when Patrick determined to throw away the possessions of their daughter, and Louise stopped him – Patrick tried negotiating, to get what he wanted, and failed. That sets up the necessity for another attempt; in that second scene, Patrick gets another chance to hold onto Louise: "If we do this, will you stay?" Her ambiguous 'yes' – "I just want her back" – is an indication that even now, they have different goals: he needs his wife, she needs their daughter … But for the moment, at least, they agree on a course of action.

The barbaric rite is performed, and their child is 'born' again, as old as she was when she died and with some recall of her life before, but no memories of her terrible death.

And then the darker side of the transformation starts to play itself out. For one glorious day, Louise and Patrick have their daughter back, playing games in the yard with her, watching her sleep – all the simple but soul-satisfying routines of 'normal' family life they had lost when she was killed. But of course, this life isn't 'normal', because of the one condition that darkens it all: daughter Alice can only be with her parents three days – and then she has to 'return to the woods.' Louise and Patrick try not to think of the ticking clock; and when the townsfolk tell them Alice needs to go back even earlier because something is 'wrong' with the child – they hold on even more fiercely (see Figure 3.1).

But the villagers are correct – there is something very wrong with Alice. Because Patrick and Louise have lied about a key requirement of the rite – Alice had been dead and buried more than a year. So the magic that brought her back has been corrupted – like the child herself. Unwilling to admit that their beautiful daughter's becoming a stranger, the parents try to flee the town – another thing they were warned against – and find, to their horror, that there's a magical barrier around the town. When they pass beyond it, Alice collapses, bleeding – so they have to return.

Finally Alice murders some of the locals who wanted to send her back. And her parents have to make the most painful decision of all – to give their daughter back to the magical woods. To lose her forever. Alice hides from them, but they lure her out, and trick her into crossing the boundary line a final time. The little girl passes out, and her parents carry her lifeless body into the woods, to bury her. In a moment recalling the shocker ending of Brian De Palma's *Carrie*, the monster-Alice reaches up from the grave to grab her mother, dragging her into the ground that swallows them up.

**FIGURE 3.1** Something's not right with the girl (Ella Connolly) who's come back from the dead, in *Wake Wood*.

A coda suggests we may be doomed to keep repeating the same mistakes. Patrick has joined the villagers, as they prepare for another 'birth'. This time it's Louise who's born from the dreadful cocoon, falling into her husband's arms. Will three days be enough, this time? We're left without an answer.

I chose to look at *Wake Wood*, instead of its better-known predecessor, Stephen King's *Pet Sematary* (both novel and film) because it's less familiar (and, to my mind, it's even more powerful). But both stories are modern variants of the Edwardian tale of terror, "The Monkey's Paw" (1902) – itself a horrific version of the "three wishes" fairy tale (the pattern of which is a frivolous wish, a second wish in reaction to the first which makes things worse, and a final wish that's wasted, in reversing the consequences of wishes one and two). King even acknowledges his debt to "The Monkey's Paw", quoting from it, at the top of Part 3 of his novel, which was made into a financially successful film (1989) and a less successful sequel; a remake is opened in April 2019.

Why has W.W. Jacobs' story been so effective a template, not just for the movies discussed above, but for numerous adaptations of the story itself? I think it's because it's is a textbook example of *"three-act structure"* – the one most commonly used in traditional narrative movies. In fact, the story breaks into three parts, which are numbered as such by the author. In Part One, an older couple – Mr. and Mrs. White – and their son Herbert are visited, one cold wet night, by Mr. White's former colleague, a Sergeant Major Morris, who's been serving in India twenty-one years, and has just returned to England. Among his souvenirs is a very strange curio – a monkey's paw, "an ordinary little paw, dried to a mummy." The paw, according to legend, can grant three wishes – but it's trouble; and the sergeant major ends his story by throwing the paw on the fire. Mr. White, intrigued by the magical object, snatches it out before it burns; the sergeant major, resigned, can only warn his friend to be careful: "If you must wish, wish for something sensible."

When their visitor has left, the family chats about what they could ask for. Son Herbert suggests his father wish for £200 – enough to pay off the mortgage on the house. And so the father does – crying out, because he seemed to feel the paw move in his hand.

In Part Two, the following morning, the family laugh at their gullibility, wondering how they could have believed in the power of the monkey's paw. "The idea of our listening to such nonsense!", says Mrs. White. "How could wishes be granted these days?"

"Well, don't break into the money before I come back," Herbert jokes to his father as he's heading off to work. "I'm afraid it'll turn you into a mean, avaricious man, and we shall have to disown you."

As the day wears on, the couple receive another surprising visitor – a well-dressed man they don't recognize, who announces he comes from 'Maw and Meggins' – the factory where the couple's son Herbert works. And he has terrible news – Herbert was been in a gruesome accident: "He was caught in the machinery." Maw and Meggins "admit no liability at all… but they wish to present you with a certain sum as compensation." The sum is £200. The old man faints.

Part Three picks up a week after the funeral.

> It was all over so quickly that at first they could hardly realize it, and remained in a state of expectation as though of something else to happen – something else which was to lighten the load, too heavy for old hearts to bear. But the days passed, and expectation gave way to resignation – the hopeless resignation of the old, sometimes miscalled apathy.

And then, one night, Mrs. White is seized by a terrible hope. "The monkey's paw!", Mr. White tries to argue her out of her plan; but she insists – so the old man makes his second wish: "I wish my son alive again."

At first nothing happens – and with a sense of uneasy relief, the husband joins his wife in bed. But the dark is oppressive, and neither can sleep. Mr. White goes downstairs for a candle, and then – as he starts to light a match, "a knock, so quiet and stealthy as to be scarcely audible" sounds on the front door. He's terrified, and retreats upstairs, but his wife has heard the knocking, which is continuing, getting louder. "It's my boy; it's Herbert!", she cries. "For God's sake, don't let him in," replies the old man, trying to hold his wife back. "You're afraid of your own son," she cries, "Let me go. I'm coming, Herbert; I'm coming."

Breaking away from her husband, she runs downstairs and struggles with chains and bolts, to unlock the front door – as Mr. White, terrified of the mangled 'thing' outside, makes his third and final wish. "A long loud wail of disappointment and misery from his wife gave him courage to run down to her side, and then to the gate beyond. The street lamp flickering opposite shone on a quiet and deserted street."

Robin Wood, in a famous essay on the American horror film, offered this simple underlying formula: "Normality is threatened by the monster".[2] In the case of "The Monkey's Paw", the 'monster' isn't a drooling creature or a psychopathic killer; it's just a slightly sinister curiosity, a small severed limb. But it holds the power to turn the life of its possessor upside down. It's what the monstrous always does – it forces people into new realms of experience never dreamt of. As Dante says, right before his long descent into the Inferno: "In the middle of the journey of my life, I came to myself in a dark wood." *In horror movies, the monstrous is the thing that wakes you up.*

So *Act One* is the place where your characters 'come to themselves' and see that their world has changed. The 'normal' has broken down, and some kind of chaos is starting to take its place. Whatever it was that the characters began the story wanting - fame, fortune, someone's love - is now being put in jeopardy by the intrusion of the 'not normal'.

This pattern of events can be seen in the earliest horror movies. In *The Cabinet of Dr. Caligari* (1921), for example, the story begins with two friends Francis and Alan deciding to visit a traveling carnival. Though they're rivals for the love of Jane, they enjoy each other's company – and they think a carnival visit is just what they need, to escape their humdrum lives. At the fairgrounds, they're intrigued by one attraction in particular – a mysterious "Dr. Caligari", whose 'exhibit', Cesare, is a

## 34  Basic horror movie structure

man who's been in a trance-like sleep all his life. Dr. Caligari wakens Cesare, who's advertised as a fortune-teller. When Alan – as a joke – calls out from the audience, "How long will I live?", the somnambulist Cesare opens wide his eyes and pronounces his sentence: "Until dawn!" That night, Alan is murdered – and Francis spends the rest of the movie hunting down the killer (see Figure 3.2).

One of the most intriguing things, about this early horror film, is that the meaning of "normal" is already being questioned. As originally conceived by its writers, Hans Janowitz and Carl Mayer, the story builds to a startling climax as Francis discovers that Caligari's been living a double life – carnival showman by night, and by day – the head of a local insane asylum. Francis is able to prove that it's the doctor himself who's crazy; Caligari is locked away in his own asylum, and order's restored. Or at least it is, in the story's original ending. But the studio intervened, not liking the script's implication that figures of authority could be madmen. In the rewritten version – the one that was filmed, despite the writers' protests – a framing story is added, reversing the big reveal at the climax. Now Francis is the lunatic, and the story he's told – the movie we've been watching, up to the big reveal – is Francis's delusional version of events; nothing he's told us is true. Caligari isn't a criminal genius, but instead the benevolent head of the institution where Francis is housed. Having heard how Francis has constructed his twisted version of reality, the doctor thinks he can now begin to treat his patient successfully.

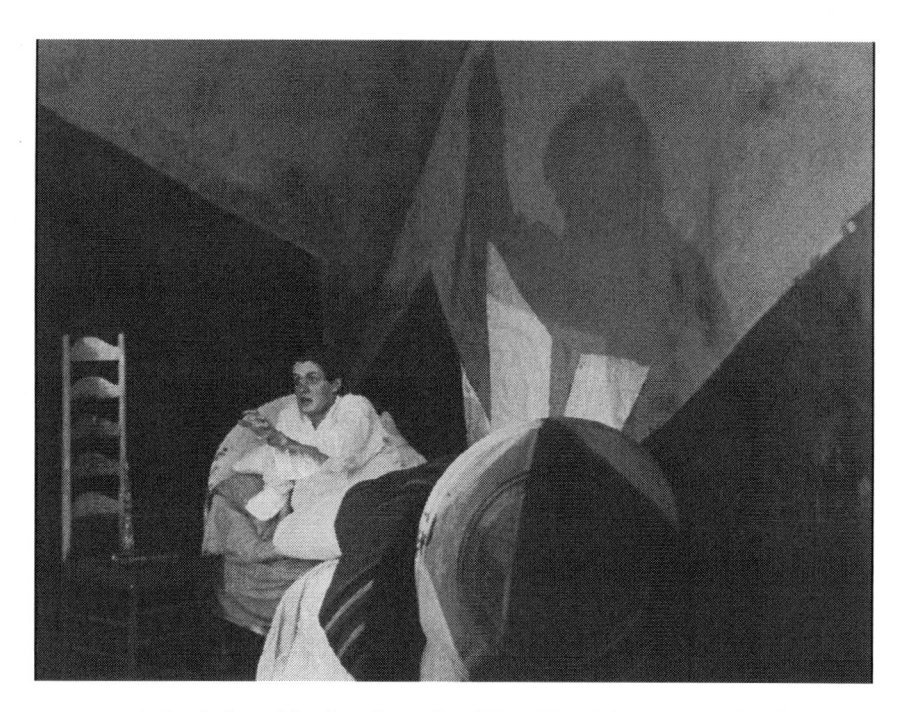

**FIGURE 3.2** A death foretold, of student Alan (Hans Heinrich von Twardowski), in *The Cabinet of Dr. Caligari*.

Basic horror movie structure 35

In other words, from the very beginning 'normality' has been a relative term, in the horror film – determined by the culture in which the story is taking place. With that proviso, let's move on to *Act Two* – what has to happen, after the monster's first appearance.

Sometimes the threat won't seem to be a threat at all, to begin with. In *Poltergeist* (1982), for example, the titular spirits seem benign, at first; and the movie's charming Act One follows a family's laid-back mother, Diane, as she encounters forces in her new home that appear to be playful – moving objects around behind her back, or sliding her little daughter, Carol Ann, across the kitchen floor. Perhaps because she's the youngest, Carol Ann seems to have the most direct connection to the spirits. Her family finds her staring at the TV's snowy static, one night; and in the movie's most famous line, she announces what she alone can see: "They're HERE!"[3]

But having lulled the family into an acceptance of the uncanny, the poltergeists turn savage with a vengeance, in the movie's Act Two. Carol Ann's brother is almost snatched away by that wicked tree branch (c.f. Chapter 1, p. 03); while the family struggles to save him, Carol Ann is sucked into some kind of Other Dimension in her closet. Her family searches for her in vain, finally hearing her voice that's coming – eerily - from the TV set. What the characters *wanted* in Act One (real-estate sales for husband Steven, a happy family life for Diane) has changed; mother, father, older daughter Dana and son are united in their desperate hunt for the missing child. In Act Two, the family turn to outsiders – first a team of parapsychologists from University of California, Irvine; and then a professional medium, who determines that Carol Ann has been taken into another dimension. Act Two builds to Diane's decision to go through the portal herself, into the world of restless spirits where her daughter is being held.

Diane disappears through the portal, while the medium screams instructions to her; and at the Act Two climax, mother and daughter – covered in ectoplasm – tumble through another portal that's opened up in the ceiling. Somewhat smugly the medium announces that her work is done: "This house is *clean*."

But she couldn't be more mistaken. In fact, the spirits infecting the house have saved their nastiest tricks for last. After another deceptive lull, all hell breaks loose (almost literally), with killer clown-dolls attacking, coffins and skeletons bobbing up in the unfinished swimming pool out back (see Figure 3.3), and father Steven finally learning the truth about where he's been living. It turns out that his firm had developed land that had once been an Indian burial ground. Steven thought the firm had moved the remains of the dead, before any houses went up. But instead, the firm had simply removed the headstones; the bodies remained in the ground, beneath this sprawling new subdivision.

In *Act Three*, the action narrows down to a frantic attempt to survive the night. Diane and Steven save their children, managing to drive away as their house – the whole shiny split-level thing – collapses into the Void and disappears.

To recap: In Act One, *the threat appears* – and is either recognized as such, or is misunderstood – e.g., the initial manifestations of the spirits in *Poltergeist* or the 'birth' of the creature in James Whale's *Frankenstein* (1931), a moment that Dr. Frankenstein mistakenly hails as a triumph.

**36** Basic horror movie structure

**FIGURE 3.3** Poltergeist's mom (Jobeth Williams), meeting an unexpected guest.

In Act Two, *the characters learn the meaning of the threat*, to their way of life or their very existence, *and begin to fight back*. For example, in 2018's *Hereditary*, a distraught mother begins to suspect that her family is cursed, in some way: her mother has died, at the top of the film, and her little daughter is killed, early on, in a truly gruesome car accident (losing her head). The mother, Annie, turns to the occult for help – with increasingly unnerving results that start to unravel her family.

In Act Three, the characters face *a final confrontation with the threat* – and either survive – forever changed - or die.

Acts One and Three – the story's set-up and pay-off – tend to be shorter, roughly a quarter each of the screenplay; and Act Two is the longest, the one where the characters – under pressure – discover their strengths and weaknesses, as they try to deal with what's threatening them.

Of course, there are infinite variations on this basic pattern – some of which we'll examine, as we look at each separate act, in turn. But in general, this formula will work for your screenplay's basic architecture:

- Normality is threatened by the monster.
- 'Normality' fights back.
- The monster wins (and disorder reigns, at the end), or the monster loses, and we either return to the 'old' normal (the more conservative horror movies follow this pattern), or we enter a 'new' normal, where the eruption of chaos has changed forever the way we live in – and understand – the world.

## Notes

1 Screenplay by Brendan McCarthy and David Keating.
2 Robin Wood, "An Introduction to the American Horror Film", reprinted in *Robin Wood on the Horror Film: Collected Essays and Reviews* (Detroit: Wayne State University Press, 2018), p. 83.
3 Screenplay by Steven Spielberg, Michael Grais and Mark Victor.

# 4
# BUILDING ACT ONE

In her helpful book on TV writing, Pamela Douglas makes an intriguing point about story-telling: "Every story, whether it's a medical show or a cop show or a soap opera, is a mystery. A secret is going to be revealed. When are other people going to find out?"[1]

This notion of story-as-mystery is especially true of the horror genre – which always involves the intrusion, into daily life, of the unexpected (a break-with-the-normal which, at the start, is often inexplicable). This intrusion comes in myriad forms: sleep-walking assassins (*Caligari*), giant ants (*Them!*), aliens who look exactly like us (*Invasion of the Body Snatchers*) or horrifically different (*Alien* and its sequels), the walking dead (*28 Days Later*), the waking predator (*Jaws*, *Backcountry*'s bear), vampires (*A Girl Walks Home Alone at Night*, *Let the Right One In*), children (*The Omen*, *Who Can Kill a Child?*), psychopaths (*Seven*, *The Silence of the Lambs*), djinns (*Under The Shadow*), relatives (*The Stepfather*, *The Visit*), and so on, from the sublimely terrifying (the angelic demon in *God Told Me To*) to the truly ridiculous (giant rabbits, in *Night of the Lepus*, or pollen(!) in one of the silliest horror movies ever made, *The Happening*).

Whatever the threat turns out to be, it most often begins as a secret, something hidden or in hiding: Dr. Frankenstein's 'experiment', tucked away in a lonely tower … the alien incubating in a clueless human's stomach … the motel-keeper's unstable 'mother', only ever glimpsed as a silhouette at an upstairs window. Act One then involves a movement toward *the discovery of the story's threat*. Within that general pattern, there are several variations:

- *The threat is revealed to the audience, but not to the protagonist.*

This is often the template for the typical 'slasher' movie – where the killer is picking off victims, one by one, but no one is aware of the slaughter until the movie's final act. Viewers get the shock of individual acts of violence; but, because the protagonists aren't aware of the danger they're in, until the axe is descending, it's hard for this kind of body-count movie to generate steadily building suspense. This is why *Halloween*, to my mind, is a whole lot scarier than *Friday the 13th*, though they're often lumped together as slashers. They do share in common protagonists who discover, only very late, that their friends have been murdered and they're in mortal danger. But in *Friday*, the surviving teenager never knows there's a threat, until the bitter, bloody end. In *Halloween*, on the other hand, Laurie Strode is picking up clues, from early on, that something's not right in her town. She keeps seeing an ominous figure – outside her school, in a neighbor's yard, or revealed, for a moment, behind some laundry flapping in the breeze. Laurie tries to dismiss her unease, reassuring her babysitting charges that 'there's no such thing as the boogey-man'. But when she discovers how wrong she is – and the boogeyman has stalked her into the house where her charges are upstairs sleeping, it feels like her earlier glimpses of danger have made her alert and primed for the life-or-death struggle that ends the movie.

- *The protagonists consciously follow clues that lead them into the danger.*

The original *Invasion of the Body Snatchers* (1956) is a model for this strategy. In Daniel Mainwaring's screenplay (from a novel by Jack Finney), the protagonist Dr. Miles Bennell is returning from a conference to his home-town of Santa Mira, where he learns that many patients have been seeking him out, with a strange complaint: they insist that a loved one (father, uncle, etc.) isn't the loved one they've always known, that these people have changed, though they look the same and even have the same memories. With the help of a former love (and recent divorcee), Betty Driscoll, the good doctor tries to figure out what's happening in his sleepy town. "A strange neurosis," dismisses the town's one and only psychiatrist, who's not worried at all, "an epidemic mass hysteria. In two weeks, it's spread all over town."

"What causes it?", Dr. Bennell wants to know.

"Worry about what's going on in the world, probably," the shrink replies – an answer that would've made sense at the time, with the Cold War starting and with it, the fear of nuclear Armageddon.

Dr. Bennell would like to believe the shrink's simple explanation. But then he's summoned frantically by a friend, who's just uncovered another ominous piece of the puzzle. Friend Jack has found a mysterious 'corpse' in his house – a body about his size and shape, without fingerprints, and with the facial features still unformed. "It's like the first impression on a coin ... waiting for the final finished face to be stamped onto it," Jack notes.

"But whose face?" Jack's wife Teddy has leapt ahead of her friends in guessing what's happening. The body – in size and shape – is exactly a double of her husband's.

From this point, Dr. Bennell and his friends pursue the clues that uncover the danger they (and the rest of the world are in), from a silent but deadly invasion replacing humans with soul-less look-alikes (see Figure 4.1).

As I mentioned in the introduction, one of the scariest monsters we can encounter is some version of *us*. And *Invasion of the Body Snatchers* makes this nightmare literal. So disturbing, in fact, was the film's first cut, the producers – in a move recalling the treatment of *Caligari* – insisted on a frame-story that would undercut the bleak ending (where a hysterical Dr. Bennell tried to stop unheeding motorists, as he shouted a warning no one would believe: "You're next! YOU'RE NEXT!"). In the added frame-story, Dr. Bennell's been arrested, and now is telling his story to a sympathetic psychiatrist.[2] The rest of the movie – again like *Caligari* – becomes a flashback, complete with voice-over narration working against the film's more subtle build-up of suspense:

> DR. BENNELL (V.O.):
> For me, it started last Thursday … In response to an urgent message from my nurse, I'd hurried home from a medical convention I'd been attending. At first glance, everything looked the same. It wasn't. *Something evil had taken possession of the town.* [My emphasis]

- *The protagonists and the audience are unaware or uncertain of the danger approaching, until it closes in.*

This narrative approach is often called the 'slow burn'; it favors suspense over shock, building tension slowly and carefully, with the audience feeling an ever-increasing sense of dread – until the threat, whatever it is, is at last revealed.

**FIGURE 4.1** Teddy (Carolyn Jones) sees a corpse-like figure suddenly open its eyes, in *Invasion of the Body Snatchers*.

**40** Building Act One

*The House of the Devil* (2009) – from writer/director Ti West – is a good 'slow burn' example. To escape an obnoxious room-mate, college student Samantha wants to rent an apartment of her own. To do so, she needs money fast, and answers an ad for a babysitter. Her potential employer's unsettling – he fails to show up for one meeting, and though he apologizes later, he has another surprise in store, when Samantha and her best friend (and ride) drive out to the employer's house. The employer, Mr. Ulman, reveals that he and his wife don't have children; the person he wants Samantha to 'sit' is his wife's ailing, bed-ridden mother. Samantha's friend Megan (an early role for Greta Gerwig) thinks the whole set-up is screwy, and urges Samantha to bail on the job. But Mr. Ulman triples the amount of money he's offering; and Samantha, badly needing that money for rent, agrees to stay.

For almost one-third of this ninety-minute movie, there are no obvious scares. Samantha finds an apartment she likes, but worries about how to pay for it; she deals with an inconsiderate room-mate (which only makes her want the new apartment even more); she makes an appointment to meet a potential employer, who doesn't show up; and when she's lost that chance at a job (or thinks she has), she consoles herself with a pizza, with her best friend. And for thirty minutes, that's about it – if one didn't know the ominous title, one wouldn't be sure this was horror at all.

Yet Samantha – in her struggle to better her life – has won us over. We care about what might happen to her, once she's entered the old Victorian home where she plans to 'babysit' for a few hours and make her rental deposit. In the following forty minutes (the entire Act Two), Samantha rattles around, alone, in the big spooky house – never seeing the sleeping old woman she's ostensibly been hired to watch. She investigates odd noises (finding nothing); dances to music on her Walkman (the movie is set in the 1980s) and accidentally breaks a vase; she orders a pizza, and tries – without success – to reach her friend Megan on the phone.

Without success, because – in a truly shocking 'aside' to the audience - the director cuts from the house to Megan, on her way home but having car trouble. When she pulls off the road, a man pops up beside the car, out of nowhere. "Aren't you the babysitter?", he asks. When she answers, "No" – he shoots her in the head. Now we're back to 'strategy one' – where the audience knows a *lot* more than the protagonist. And the movie proceeds at its own stealthy pace – but with our sense of the danger Samantha is in increased exponentially (see Figure 4.2).

This variant of the slow-burn - an *unexpected and sudden jolt, followed by a return to seeming normality, as tension builds* – works incredibly well in the very disturbing film *Audition* (1999, screenplay by Daisuke Tengan). In the quiet and moving opening, businessman Aoyama loses his wife Ryoko to illness. Then we move ahead seven years; Aoyama's son (a child, in the opening) is now a teenager, Aoyama himself a lonely widower who hasn't reconnected to life. A friend of his in the movie business has what he thinks is a great idea: he can announce auditions (for a movie he never intends to make), and Aoyama can meet (and select from) the women who come to these try-outs. One of them – the quiet-spoken Asami – is a standout. Aoyama ends up inviting her to dinner; though he knows very little about her (and she doesn't know about the deception involved in the bogus 'audition'), he's

**FIGURE 4.2** Babysitter Samantha (Jocelin Donahue) wonders what bumped in the night, in *The House of the Devil*.

strongly attracted to her. And she – still thinking she's up for a role in his 'film' – enjoys their meal together. We're uneasy about what will happen, when Asami finds out the 'auditions' were fake. And yet, at the end of their first dinner-date, she seems to have had a wonderful time. On the street, as they're saying their goodbyes, she makes a touching request.

```
                        ASAMI
I hope I'm not asking too much of you ... but if you have some
free time, I'd like to talk to you more. That would be
wonderful. I don't have any adult men to be frank with.
                        AOYAMA
If I'm good enough, I'd love to.
                        ASAMI
Really? I'm very happy about that. I'll try not to
bother you. Anywhere is fine. Even just on the telephone
would be fine.
                        AOYAMA
I wrote down my cell phone number on the business card I
gave you. Please call me anytime.
                        ASAMI
Thank you very much. Thanks for the meal, too.
[She turns to smile and give a small bow, before she
joins the stream of pedestrians hurrying down the
sidewalk; smiling himself, Aoyama waves, as he watches
her moving away.]
```

**42** Building Act One

But Aoyama's friend, Yoshikawa, thinks that things are moving too fast. He's tried to do a background check on Asami, and came up with nothing. Her references don't check out, and her former place of employment's abandoned. He cautions his friend:

```
                    YOSHIKAWA
   Promise me one thing. Don't call her for awhile. I hope
   I'm wrong. It's going to affect your whole life. You had
   better not be hasty. Cool down a bit.
   [Aoyama considers, then nods.]
                    AOYAMA
   All right. I promise you.
```

Now the film begins to cross-cut between Aoyama, wanting to call but holding back, and Asami's apartment, which we're finally seeing for the first time. Patiently and unmoving, Asami sits on the floor in the foreground, a phone on the floor beside her, and beyond, a large and mysterious sack. And the film now builds to its first big shudder. Aoyama has a dream – of his dead wife, silent in a snowy landscape, briefly appearing, then vanishing. Next day, he can't hold back any longer; and as he's starting to call, we cut to a close-up of Asami's mouth, as her phone begins to ring. Her lips begin to curl up in a smile … and then, as the phone continues to ring, the sack behind her suddenly *moves*, convulsing and thrashing across the floor before stopping, just as suddenly (see Figure 4.3). It's one of the great jump-scares in the modern horror film; what the *hell* is in that sack? Whatever it is – or *whoever* it is – we know, now, in a frightening way, that Asami's not who she seems to be, and Aoyama's in danger.

**FIGURE 4.3** The mysterious Asami (Eihi Shiina) waits for the phone to ring, in *Audition*.

The movie returns (for awhile) to its less sensational story-telling – Asami and Aoyama have another dinner together, and finally head to a place by the sea, where they plan to spend the weekend. When they're in their room, alone at last, Aoyama is clearly nervous; he starts suggesting things they can do before dinner … but he's stopped by Asami stepping out of her dress and getting in bed. She covers herself, but then pulls the sheet up her legs, revealing some scars on her thighs:

ASAMI
I burnt myself when I was little. I want you to know all about me.
*[She uncovers herself completely; he stares, transfixed.]*
AOYAMA
You're very beautiful.
ASAMI
Please love me. Only me.
AOYAMA
I will.
ASAMI
Everybody says so. But I hope you're different from other guys. Only me. Okay? Only me. Please love me. Only me.

Aoyama bends down to kiss her – there's a cut to movement under the sheets … and then we learn, surprised, that it's the next day. Aoyama struggles out of the sheets, feeling woozy – and Asami is gone. Without a word; Aoyama is desolated. End of Act One.

Aoyama's still in the dark about who Asami really is; but now – with her sudden disappearance – at least he knows there's a mystery, and he has to solve it, to win her back. Act One has followed a lonely widower's quest to find a partner; in Act Two, what he *wants* – his *action* - gets more complex: now he wants what he almost had, and lost – and to do so, he has to investigate the past of this woman who's captured his heart. (We'll be looking at transitioning into Act Two, in the following chapter.)

One final variant on the warning jolt is *an ominous prologue*.

Jordan Peele's *Get Out*[3] is a recent example of a movie that sets us on edge from the top, with a chilling pre-title sequence. Andre, a young black man, is walking at night down the manicured sidewalk of an affluent-looking neighborhood. He's feeling out of place, as he tells his girlfriend on his cellphone.

ANDRE
… The thing I've been asking myself is, what kind of sick individual names a street Edgewood Way and he put it half a mile away from Edgewood Lane? Huh? … It's crazy. You got me out here in this creepy, confusing ass suburb… *[He chuckles, uneasily.]* I'm serious, though.

I feel like a sore thumb out here ... All right, baby. All right. I'll talk to you soon. See you.
*[His unease grows, as a car passes by – and then turns around, to start following him. Now he talks to himself, to keep his spirits up:]*
                    ANDRE (cont'd)
All right, just keep on walking, bruh. Don't do nothin' stupid. Just keep on.
*[But when the car keeps creeping along beside him, he makes a decision.]*
                    ANDRE (cont'd)
Fuck this. I'mma fucking go the other way I came.
*[Reversing directions, he heads away from the car.]*
                    ANDRE (cont'd)
Not today. Not me. You know how they like to do motherfuckers out here, man. I'm gone.
*[He walks faster, then turns to look back at the car. It's stopped, lights on, with the driver's-side door wide open. This doesn't look good at all.]*
                    ANDRE (cont'd)
Yo ... Come on, brother, this is ...
*[Suddenly a figure – wearing what looks like a medieval helmet – steps from the shadows and grabs him. Andre briefly struggles, but the stranger overcomes him, dragging him back to the car and stuffing him in the trunk. And the credits roll.]*

Now the movie seems to start over again, as photographer Chris Washington, another young black man, gets ready to leave for a nerve-wracking weekend, to meet his white girlfriend's parents. This first act plays out as a kind of tense social comedy of manners; but the nightmare opening lingers in our minds, until Chris's story connects – in Act Two – with the kidnapped Andre's story (which turns out to be a whole lot worse than we could've ever imagined).

In his fascinating book, *Into the Woods: How Stories Work and Why We Tell Them*, John Yorke talks about the elements of an archetypal story:

> You have a central character, you empathize with them, and something then happens to them, and that something is the genesis of the story... The 'something' is almost always a problem, sometimes a problem disguised as an opportunity. It's usually something that throws your protagonist's world out of kilter – an explosion of sorts in the normal steady pace of their lives ... [4]

That's a perfect description of what goes on in Act One of a horror film.

As a final example, let's look at the 'found footage' monster movie *Cloverfield* (2008, screenplay by Drew Goddard). A young man, Rob, is leaving New York, heading off for a brand new job in Japan. His friends have thrown him a farewell party; and Hud, Rob's best friend, is recording the happy/sad event. Rob's thrown when Beth shows up at the party; she's the girl he's loved forever – but knowing he's moving away, he's tried to disconnect, emotionally. Tried but failed, he realizes, seeing that Beth has brought a date along. Jealously, he confronts her, she fights back – he's the one who's made himself unavailable. And Beth and her date depart, leaving Rob to lick his wounds.

This whole sad love story plays itself out, in the opening act of the movie. Then, literally out of nowhere, all hell breaks loose. The building shakes, the whole city goes dark before lights come back on … The party-goers rush up to the roof, to discover that Manhattan's under attack; buildings explode in the distance, and Hud thinks he's captured – on his camera – a brief glimpse of a giant … creature? Now there's a mad dash down to the street – where the giant head of the Statue of Liberty suddenly comes crashing. Police are directing the terrified mob to evacuate Manhattan, via the Brooklyn Bridge. But they're too late: something colossal – a creature's *tail?* – smashes the bridge (killing Rob's brother Jason) and forcing the panicked survivors back to a crumbling Manhattan.

At this moment, Rob gets a frantic call from Beth, who's uptown in her apartment, trapped beneath a wall that's collapsed. And Rob suddenly *knows what he wants*: more than a high-paying job, more than anything in the world. He wants to save the woman he loves. To do so, he'll have to make his way uptown, where the danger seems to be greatest. But what's happened in Act One – from his fight with Beth, to the sudden explosion into the world, of the Unexpected – has clarified what matters to him. And *this change in perspective* sends him uptown – and into Act Two.

## Notes

1 Pamela Douglas, *Writing the TV Drama Series* (Studio City, CA: Michael Wiese Productions, 2005), pp. 128–129.
2 In a 'film note' for *Body Snatchers*, Kevin Hagopian (Senior Lecturer in Media Studies at Penn State University) writes that the film's director, Don Siegel, and screenwriter, Daniel Mainwaring, "objected strongly [to the addition of the frame-story], but cooperated in order to make this flashback structure as integral to the rest of the film as possible, but many (including Siegel) felt that it diminishes the power of the film through phony reassurance." Kevin Hagopian, film notes for the New York State Writers' Institute, http://www.albany.edu/writers-inst/webpages4/filmnotes/fnf03n6.html
3 It's intriguing to note that Jordan Peele, writer/director of *Get Out*, named his production company "Monkeypaw", after the W.W. Jacobs story we looked at in Chapter 3.
4 John Yorke, *Into the Woods: How Stories Work and Why We Tell Them* (Penguin Random House UK, 2013), p, 3.

# 5

# THE CHANGED WORLD OF ACT TWO

By the end of Act One of your horror film, the characters' world has changed (whether the characters know it yet or not); the Monster – in whatever form – is already wreaking havoc (e.g. raping the drugged protagonist, in *Rosemary's Baby*), or nerve-wrackingly biding its time (like the sinister couple who've hired a baby-sitter, in *House of the Devil*). Now, in Act Two, your characters have to confront this new reality – which involves reasserting and/or redefining what they want, in this newly changed world.

In David Cronenberg's disturbing re-make of *The Fly*, for example, reporter Ronnie Quaife wants 'the story of a lifetime'. And she thinks she may have found it, when she meets inventor Seth Brundle, who's very close to perfecting an actual teleportation device. Seth and Ronnie start falling in love, as she follows his experiments. And she shares his disappointment, when he tries to transport a living creature, from one futuristic-looking 'pod' to another. A baboon disappears from the 'sending' pod – but what's re-assembled, in Pod 2, is a writhing bloody unrecognizable mess. Ronnie tries to talk her lover through his dejection.

> RONNIE
> Why didn't it work?
> SETH
> I think, uh, it turned the baboon inside out.
> RONNIE
> Why?
> SETH
> Can't deal with the flesh. It only seems to work with inanimate objects, nothing that's living. Must be my fault.
> RONNIE
> *[gently]* Why?

> SETH
> Computers are dumb. They only know what you tell them. I must not know about the flesh myself. I'm going to have to learn.

Already, in Act One, we can see that what Seth wants is changing – from solving a technical problem, to comprehending a much larger mystery: "the flesh". Ronnie's said to him, in the flush of love-making, "I just want to eat you up. You know, that's why old ladies pinch babies' cheeks. It's the flesh. It just makes you crazy." Her words prompt Seth to another trial – sending a steak through the teleporter. Ronnie tries the transported steak, and says it's not good – it tastes 'synthetic'. Then Seth has a flash of insight.

> SETH
> The flesh. It should make the computer crazy, uh, crazy like the old ladies pinching babies. But it doesn't – not yet. I haven't taught the computer to be made crazy by the uh, flesh, the poetry of the steak. So I'm going to start teaching it now …

Seth 'teaches' the computer, sends another baboon from pod to pod – this time completely successfully, with Ronnie filming the breakthrough. Time for a celebration, he thinks – but Ronnie has to leave abruptly, to deal with her cranky editor (who's jealous of the time that his star reporter is spending with Brundle). The insecure inventor gets jealous, in turn, and drinks too much of what was meant to be celebratory champagne. Inhibitions down, sad and angry, Seth decides to take the ultimate step in his experiments: he'll teleport a human – himself. And he does – unaware of a stowaway, in his teleportation pod. The viewer sees what Seth does not: a lone housefly is trapped in the pod, and during the 'transportation', its DNA is fused with Brundle's.

So Act One ends with Seth believing he's just achieved his greatest goal – and the audience suspecting something terrible will be the result. Act Two plays out as Seth begins to change – in ways that he welcomes, at first: he has incredible energy, physical strength he never had before, and – reconciling with Ronnie – he's indefatigable as a lover. But other changes are happening, too; he's sprouting strange hairs in odd places, can't seem to eat enough sugar, and his intellectual focus has tipped from intense to the totally manic. Ronnie watches, bewildered by this relentless metamorphosis. After another frenzied bout of love-making, Seth wants her to share his new world with him. He insists that she has to teleport; but she's afraid and refuses. Suddenly he erupts, in an almost operatic burst of rage:

> SETH
> You're a fucking drag, you know that?
> RONNIE
> *[deeply troubled]* When you went through, something went wrong.

**48** The changed world of Act Two

> *[Turning his back on her, he starts to get dressed, ignoring her words.]*
>
> SETH
> No? If not you, if you're too chickenshit to be a member of the dynamic duo club, okay, that's great. I'll find somebody else, somebody who can keep up with me.
>
> RONNIE
> Seth, you have to listen to me –
>
> SETH
> You're afraid to dive into the plasma pool, aren't you? You're afraid to be destroyed and recreated, aren't you? I'll bet you think you woke me up about the flesh, don't you. But you only know society's straight line about the flesh. You can't penetrate beyond society's sick gray fear of the flesh. Drink deep or taste not the plasma spring! See what I'm saying? I'm not just talking about sex and penetration. I'm talking about penetration beyond the veil of the flesh, a deep penetrating dive into the plasma pool.

This bizarre confrontation happens almost exactly mid-way through the movie, and is a pivotal point in Act Two; Seth turns his back on Ronnie, and his behavior becomes more erratic. But finally even he can't deny – as his fingernails start to fall off, and tumorous growths appear on his face – that something very bad has happened. Ronnie's taken clips of the anomalous hairs he's been growing; and analysis proves they aren't human. They seem to be from some sort of ... insect? Seth doesn't believe her, and sends her away. But he turns to his computer, at last – and discovers the undeniable truth: that there were two living objects in the pod, when he teleported – "Brundle" and "Not-Brundle". A computer-animated sequence reveals what "Not-Brundle" is; in increasing detail, the image of a common housefly appears on the screen. Now Seth knows the terrible truth; and this knowledge ends Act Two.

The traditional division of a screenplay – into three 'acts' – follows the basic structure of any story: beginning – middle – end.[1] What's important to note is that this basic structure is mirrored within the act itself – that is, each act also has its own beginning, middle and end. And as the whole screenplay moves in a rising action toward a climax, the same is true for each separate act.

In *The Fly*, as we've seen, the first act develops two stories that interact with each other: the scientist Seth Brundle is on the verge of a major discovery ... and he's falling for the reporter, Ronnie, who's covering his story.

Act Two will examine the after-shocks of the scientist's rash decision, when he uses himself as a guinea pig. This act, like the first, also has three clearly delineated sections. As the act begins, Seth celebrates his success with Ronnie, even as she begins to notice changes in him that disturb her. In the middle section, Ronnie becomes an obstacle to her lover, who wants to initiate her into the wonders of teleportation. They break up, and the devastated Seth goes off on a roaring bender – fracturing the arm of a drunk who's challenged him to arm-wrestle, and taking home a prostitute, who he ends up wanting to teleport.

"I don't want to. I'm afraid," she cries as Seth starts to drag her to the device. Seth answers, "Don't be afraid!" – just as Ronnie shows up, saving the woman's life (and speaking the words that became the movie's tag-line: "No. Be afraid. Be very afraid.")

What Ronnie wants has changed, in this act – from getting a Pulitzer-Prize-winning story, to saving the life of the man she loves. But Seth, still resisting the truth, throws her out, slamming the door in her face as he tells her not to come back. He's done with her. Yet the human part of him still responds to her urgent message that something is wrong. So he starts a computer analysis of the teleportation sequence that produced the radical changes in him. And Act Two ends in a total reversal of Act One's sense of triumph; Seth now knows he's contaminated, and at a molecular level.

*The Fly* stumbles in its final act, resorting more and more to the body horror of Seth's transformation. One example: becoming more fly than human, Seth starts to eat like a fly – vomiting acid onto his food and then sucking up the dissolved remains (see Figure 5.1). It's a startling (and disgusting) effect, but that gross-out isn't the problem, here. What undercuts the film's power is that – as he loses his humanity, Seth also loses moral agency. He can no longer choose between right and wrong, becoming – in the end - just a monster, acting on animal instincts.

So *The Fly* has third-act problems – but those problems grow out of the second act, when the writers paint their protagonist into a corner he can't get out of. That dilemma is a version of what one could call the 'werewolf problem' – when the story's logic dictates an ending we can see coming too far in advance. For werewolf

**FIGURE 5.1** Jeff Goldblum eating a donut, as he evolves into *The Fly*.

movies themselves, for example, the classic Lon Chaney *Wolf Man* (1941) codified the basic traditions: the protagonist becomes monstrous not because of some fatal inner flaw, but because the story's logic demands it. Bitten by a werewolf? Then you're doomed to become a werewolf yourself. And according to standard werewolf lore, there's no escape, no cure – just death. Even worse – unlike a vampire, say – you don't stay a werewolf all of the time. You keep returning to human form, so you can suffer the guilt of knowing what havoc you wreaked as a savage beast.

The werewolf problem is one of the traps of Act Two, where too many horror movies start to fall apart. In a way, beginnings are easier – many story options are open, when one is building anticipation. But anticipation has to pay off, in Act Two, without disappointing. And then Act Two has to build again – to another, more frightening crisis: setting us up for some kind of release in Act Three, with the horror defeated, or with the horror grimly triumphant.

The trick – in Act Two – is to build an ever-increasing sense of jeopardy, without telegraphing whatever ending one's chosen – release from the terror or doom. A recent movie that does this well – keeping the audience guessing whether or not the horror's escapable – is the breathless thriller *Don't Breathe* (2016, screenplay by Fede Álvarez and Rodo Sayagues). In the movie's first act, we meet a trio of likeable, young house burglars; they don't use guns, they don't hurt anyone – and we see enough of their daily lives to know why they want to steal just enough to escape their dead-end lives, in a sadly burnt-out part of Detroit. This opening section also makes clear that our trio is a triangle: the 'quiet one', Alex, is hopelessly in love with tough-girl Rocky; but she and the trio's wannabe-'gansta', Money, are a couple. Rocky and Money are restless, and dream of moving to California. Then they get a tip, on a perfect job: an Army veteran, living alone on a block where the other houses are abandoned (so, no witnesses). The vet's daughter was hit and killed by a reckless driver, a rich young woman whose family paid up to the tune of "300 K".

"Do you think the money's in the house?" Rocky asks. And her lover Money replies, "I don't know. Let's go find out."

But Alex resists. "Guys, no. We don't do cash. Above 10 K, it's major larceny. That means ten years if we get caught." He walks away – but he's haunted by Rocky's lousy home situation: a younger sister she wants to protect from their alcoholic mother and the mother's no-good boyfriend. So he finally agrees to the classic crime story's 'one last job'. He and his partners do a surveillance, learning – when the vet walks his big attack-dog – that their target is not only living alone but is blind. This job should be easy.

Late at night, they approach the darkened house, first drugging the dog and then breaking in, assuming correctly the vet is in bed. Money sets off a sleeping-gas 'bomb', to keep the vet knocked out, and then the trio search for a safe. What they find instead is a padlocked door, apparently to a basement. Guessing the money has to be there, Money startles his friends by producing a gun – something they've never used before. Alex knows, if they're caught, the charge is now armed robbery – major jail-time. He tries to pull Rocky away.

                              ALEX
Rocky, let's go.
                              ROCKY
No, no, no, no. I think we should stay.
                              ALEX
We have to leave. This is not good.
                              MONEY
*[sneering at Alex]* You don't really think just because
you jerk off to her Instagram selfies that makes you a
Romeo? Think again, bitch.
*[Using a plastic bottle as a 'silencer', Money shoots
off the lock.]*
                              ALEX
Fuck, I'm so out.
*[He heads for the kitchen, where the trio have left
their shoes. Rocky calls after him.]*
                              ROCKY
Alex …
*[But he ignores her. Back in the hall, Money starts to
pull open the basement door. And as he does, the camera
shifts – to show the Blind Man standing in a dark
doorway.]*
                              BLIND MAN
Who's there?

(See Figure 5.2.) This scene is a solid example of truly economical writing:

- it escalates tension (when Money pulls out a gun, raising the danger for all);
- it reasserts what each character wants (and what he or she is willing to do, to get it);
- it clarifies relationships (as Money exerts his dominance, making explicit and laughing at Alex's futile longing for Rocky);
- it clues us in that the basement will be an important location – or why lock it up?;
- and finally, with the Blind Man's appearance, it pivots us out of Act One and into Act Two, as this 'simple' burglary starts to go wrong, in a very major way.

Money answers the Blind Man, claiming he wandered into the house by mistake. But the Blind Man, barefoot, steps on the shattered padlock – and knows Money's lying. Though he's blind, he's also looking buff, and dangerous as he approaches Money, closing the distance between them and then – in a lightning move he grabs the young thug. As Rocky watches in horror, the Blind Man

## 52 The changed world of Act Two

**FIGURE 5.2** Three young burglars (Daniel Zovatto, Jane Levy and Dylan Minette), about to encounter the owner of the house, in *Don't Breathe*.

wrestles the gun away, then shoots. Money hits the floor – he's dead – and Rocky backs into a walk-in closet. Cut to Alex, in the kitchen, hearing the shot and fearing the worst ... and that's the end of Act One. Now we hurtle into Act Two, as the Blind Man locks all the doors in the house and shutters the windows, trapping the two surviving burglars.

He's also checked his safe – tucked away in the closet where Rocky is hiding. When he leaves (to take care of Money's body), Alex and Rocky reconnect. He thinks they should call the cops; but Rocky's seen the safe combination. When she opens it, they find the blood-money the Blind Man got for his daughter's death. Even though she's in mortal peril, Rocky can't abandon her dream – of removing herself and her sister for good from their toxic home (and a mother who used to punish Rocky by locking her in the trunk of her car). She crams all the money into her duffle; then she and Alex descend to the basement, thinking they can find a way out by the storm-cellar doors they'd noticed before, when they were about to enter the house.

But another big scare is coming up. As Alex and Rocky make their way through a cluttered maze of basement shelves – something suddenly lunges at them: a terrified young woman in chains, handcuffed and with her mouth taped shut. She's the person who hit and killed the Blind Man's daughter with her car; and that revelation clues us in that the Blind Man's even scarier and sicker than we'd imagined.

It's also an Act Two turning-point. Alex wants to ignore the mysterious girl and get the hell out of this house. But Rocky, a child of abuse herself, is stricken by the girl's distress. She turns back, and reads a newspaper clipping the girl is frantically holding up: "Cindy Roberts found innocent of vehicular manslaughter."

                              ROCKY
    She's the one who killed his daughter. *[The girl nods.]*
    We have to get her out of here.

> ALEX
> No, no, no. Rocky, we don't have time. We'll – we'll get out of here, and we'll call the cops ... and they'll come find her, all right?
> THE GIRL
> [*muffled, through her gag*] The safe! The safe! There's the safe!
> [*In this other safe, Alex and Rocky find the keys they need to release the girl. As they do, the Blind Man opens the door to the cellar, standing – gun in hand – in the doorway.*]
> ROCKY
> [*to the girl*] I don't care what you did. I'll get you out of here.

Up until now, Rocky's had one motive: to get enough money to get herself and her sister away from their terrible home. But everything has changed – beginning with Money's sudden and shocking death. Rocky is changing, too; and Alex loves her enough to accept that. So the two of them help the Blind Man's captive, even though she's slowing them down ... with horrendous consequences that unfold in the movie's Act Three.

Fede Álvarez, the movie's director, had a success with his first horror feature: a very gory remake of the Sam Raimi classic, *The Evil Dead*. When asked what movies were on his mind when he made his second film, *Don't Breathe*, Álvarez mentioned *Psycho* and Hitchcock.

> The main thing with *Don't Breathe* was to try to do something scary in the realm of the real, not the supernatural. *Psycho* is a good example of structure and style. You start with characters with shady morals that are doing bad things in the beginning, which goes great with this kind of story. Hitchcock did that many, many times. *It makes it hard to anticipate the end of the movie with these sorts of characters because that makes it very hard to know who deserves to live and who deserves to die.* [My emphasis][2]

Because they have 'shady morals', Álvarez seems to imply, his characters (like those in *Psycho*) are unpredictable, giving their stories room enough to surprise us. But in fact, most people – 'moral' or not – are a mass of contradictions. Even 'good' people make bad choices. And bad people sometimes make good choices, only to see them backfire. Act Two of *Don't Breathe* climaxes with a shocking demonstration of that: Rocky and Alex free the captive, make it as far as the storm-cellar doors, find the right key to the lock, throw open the doors – and the Blind Man's looming there, shooting down at the intruders. Alex falls backward, grazed in the ear; the Blind Man fires again, and this time hits his luckless captive.

**54** The changed world of Act Two

The story twists and turns after this, as Rocky and Alex retreat back into the Blind Man's house, are beset by his dog (who's woken up from his pill-induced nap), scurry through crawl-spaces, fall from windows ... until Rocky is captured at last, and the Blind Man talks to her, as he sits across from his former captive's body.

> ROCKY
> Please, let me go. Please let me go! I ... I understand you. She killed your daughter. You wanted her to pay. I understand that. I won't tell anyone.
> BLIND MAN
> You understand nothing. Only a parent could know the bond between a father and his child. She should have gone to prison, but ... rich girls don't go to jail.
> ROCKY
> None of this is going to bring your daughter back.
> BLIND MAN
> That's not really true. *[He sits beside the body of the woman who killed his child.]* Cindy took my child away from me. I thought, it's only fair, that she give me a new one. She was pregnant with my baby. *[The camera moves in on the horror dawning on Rocky's face.]* You killed them both.
> ROCKY
> No ...
> BLIND MAN
> Well, they would be alive if you hadn't broken into my home.
> ROCKY
> No ...
> BLIND MAN
> You have to be held accountable.

The scene ends on Rocky, beginning to understand what the Blind Man has in mind.

In discussing the move from *The Evil Dead* to *Don't Breathe*, director Álvarez again invoked Hitchcock: "[*The Evil Dead* re-make] had a lot of blood, so for this movie I wanted a not-in-your-face shock; I wanted this to be all about *suspense*" (my emphasis).

> That's where *Psycho* comes in again. We didn't use to talk about 'scares' in a horror movie; we used to talk about how suspenseful the movie is. When we started to think about making a more classical horror movie, that's what we talked about, *the feeling of hope versus fear in every shot*. [My emphasis][3]

'Hope versus fear' is a perfect description of how Act Two should work on us, as the screenplay builds to the Act Three climax. We need to hope our protagonists can escape the menace approaching them, while growing ever more fearful that they won't. It's a delicate balancing act: to heighten the sense of danger, but keep possibility alive.

## Notes

1 There are plenty of wonderful screenplays – the thriller *Memento*, for example – that scramble chronology, playing with time to mirror the themes of the story itself. But even when the events of a screenplay happen out of order, an inescapable temporal order remains – because, while we're watching the film, time's arrow moves in only one direction, corresponding roughly to, "first part", "development", "conclusion."
2 Joe Gross, "3 Movies That Influenced Don't Breathe, and 2 That Did Not", *New Statesman*, 9/15/16, https://www.statesman.com/news/20160915/3-movies-that-influenced-dont-breathe-and-2-that-did-not (accessed 10/2/19).
3 Gross, op. cit.

# 6

# ENDING AND BEGINNING

In this chapter on endings, I'd like to look in detail at a single movie: the Spanish-language ghost story, *El Orfanato* (2007). Its screenplay (by Sergio Sanchez) is a model for how to build a gripping story – and how to pay off, in that final act, what one's carefully built before.

In an interview for "Aint It Cool News", the screenwriter Sergio Sanchez was asked if he knew the ending, before he started writing. He replied,

> Actually, we went through like maybe twenty different drafts of the script, because when we started writing it, like eight or nine years ago, there weren't many horror movies being made in Spain and suddenly it's like all of these movies came out[1] … It's like every week a new horror film would come out, Spanish or not, and all the time we had to push it a bit harder and we were thinking, "We have to do something that separates our movie from all these other films." *The one thing that stayed the same throughout all of those twenty drafts was the ending … The first act and the very ending were the same. What we had to build upon was the psychological motives of the characters to get to that, so that we could have an ending that was really moving; it's something that can be horrifying and uplifting at the same time, depending on how you read the story.* [2]

So let's take a look at that opening, first. On a beautiful summer day, a group of children – all wearing similar smocks – play a version of "Red Light, Green Light" on the lawn of a large and imposing home. Inside the building – an orphanage - the matron speaks on the phone to a couple preparing to adopt the child Laura, who's outside with her friends, not knowing her world is about to change.

It's a moment that perfectly captures a central concern of the film that follows: the transitory nature of life, the sadness that's a part of even our happiest early memories. As the prologue ends and we cut to the present, Laura – grown and married, now – has bought the old building where she once lived. With her husband and her adopted son, Laura plans to live in the orphanage, re-opening it on a smaller scale to take in children with special needs. Her own child, Simon, is on daily medication – he's HIV positive. But he's doing well, not having been told the nature of his illness (or that he's adopted).

'Normality is first threatened by the monster', in Act One. So we need to look at what would constitute 'normal', for our protagonist – which can be defined, at least in part, by *what our protagonist wants*. On the surface, what Laura wants is straightforward: to create a warm and welcoming place for children like her long-ago friends. But *she also wants something else*, that she might have trouble articulating: to protect her son at all costs (which keeps her from being totally honest with him). It's a dilemma that most parents face – children need to explore the world, and parents fear for their safety. For example, Laura shows Simon a cave at the base of a sea-side cliff – its entrance only exposed at low tide. Simon hurries in with a flashlight: Laura quickly starts to worry. When she tracks him down, he's chatting away – having found an imaginary new friend. Laura say, sharply, "Tell him to play somewhere else. It's dangerous here."

But in fact it's dangerous everywhere. Initially, the move back into the orphanage seems idyllic. But there are unsettling incidents – like a visit from an elderly woman who claims to be a social worker assigned to Simon's 'case'. Laura says that her husband's a doctor, so they won't need help with Simon. The woman leaves, reluctantly, but later that night Laura finds her skulking around a decrepit out-building. Laura scares her off, but is frightened herself by the woman's intrusions.

Meanwhile, Simon's been reading *Peter Pan* – and has questions for his mother.

SIMON
Wendy grows old and dies?

LAURA
[looking up from her sewing] Wendy grows up, but Peter Pan takes her daughter to Neverland every year.

SIMON
Why doesn't Wendy go too?

LAURA
Well.

SIMON
If Peter Pan came to get me, would you come too?

LAURA
No, I'm too old to go to Neverland, darling.

SIMON
How old are you?

LAURA
37.
[Simon thinks for a moment.]

                         SIMON
    At what age will you die?
    [Laura's startled, but tries to hide her concern.]
                         LAURA
    What sort of question is that? [Simon doesn't answer.]
    Not for a long time, when you're very old.
                         SIMON
    I won't grow old. I'm not going to grow up.
    [Laura struggles for an appropriate response.]
                         LAURA
    Will you be like Peter Pan?
                         SIMON
    Like my new friends.
                         LAURA
    There's more than one?
                         SIMON
    Six.
                         LAURA
    They won't grow up either?
                         SIMON
    They can't.

Disturbed by this conversation, Laura doesn't press Simon further. But a 'treasure hunt' set up by his 'friends' leads Simon to discover a doctor's report on his condition. The little boy melts down, claiming his mother *isn't* his mother; his friend Tomas (the imaginary one from the cave) has told Simon that he was adopted, and that he's going to die and never grow up, just like 'the others'. Laura and husband Carlos have the conversation with Simon they'd hoped to put off till he was older; they try to reassure him that, with the medication he's on, he'll be fine.

But Simon's still upset, as opening day for the orphanage arrives. When he sulks, Laura leaves him, to greet the new children who've come to live in her home. At the height of the welcoming party – with a lot of the kids and grown-ups wearing playful animal masks – Laura goes back inside to find Simon; instead she sees a child who's wearing the kind of smock *she* used to wear. The silent child also has a weird-looking sack on his head, a crude face painted on (see Figure 6.1). Thinking it's Simon, she tries to take the mask off; but the child gets violent, pushing her backwards into a bathroom. Laura trips and falls into the tub; the child locks the door and runs away.

Finally freed by her husband, Laura searches the house and grounds, in a panic – but Simon seems to have vanished. Fearing he's run away to the sea-cave, Laura races down to the beach, where a turbulent tide is coming in, fast. Husband Carlos tries to hold her back; but she glimpses a child in the mouth of the cave (as the audience does, for a second). When *Carlos* looks, the child is gone; and the surf is already strong enough to knock Laura down and injure her leg. Scuba divers search

**FIGURE 6.1** A mysterious child (Óscar Casas) appears in one of the hallways of *El Orfanato*.

the cove, police do the same for the cavern; they don't find Simon, dead or alive. Late that night, Laura's wakened from a restless sleep by a sound like something banging the walls of the old and echoing building. Hampered by her injury, she's unable to locate the source of the sound – something she'll only discover, to her horror, in Act Three.

Act One ends with Laura having tried –and failed - to protect her son. Now her action changes – as do *the stakes*, which can be defined as *what a character stands to gain, if they get what they want… and what they stand to lose, if they don't.* Initially, Laura's deepest want was 'safety' – an elusive goal. Now the stakes are higher, and Laura's goal is more specific: she *has* to find Simon, quickly, because he'll get sick without medication.

In Act One, Laura's seen evidence – but hasn't recognized - the intrusion into her world of the not-normal, the *other*worldly. Act Two begins to open Laura's eyes, as she moves from numb passivity, to actively following *any* lead, no matter how unlikely.

In a nod to the movie *Poltergeist*,[3] a team of parapsychologists and a medium come to Laura's home; their high-tech equipment seems to pick up the sound of children crying for helping. Carlos thinks this is all a trick, put on as a show for Laura. But she's begun to wonder if perhaps her house *is* haunted. Before Aurora, the medium, leaves, Laura stops her to ask for help.

> LAURA
> *[to Aurora]* What should I do?
> AURORA
> My dear – you're a good mother. Your pain will give you strength, it will guide you. But only you know how far you are willing to go … to find your son.
> LAURA
> I don't know what to do.

**60** Ending and beginning

> AURORA
> You hear, but you don't listen. Seeing is not believing.
> It's the other way around. Believe – and you will see.

What Aurora's really asking Laura to do is confront *her deepest fear*: that death is the end, that there's nothing beyond, that we lose what we love forever. It's the fear that made her overprotective; it's why she was less than truthful, when Simon would ask her difficult questions. What's at stake are all the defenses Laura's erected, to protect *herself*.

With those protections crumbling, Laura starts to accept what Carlos can't – there *are* presences in the house, and now they set up another 'treasure hunt'. Laura follows the clues to the out-building where she'd once seen Benigna, the sinister social worker, lurking about. This time, though, the discovery at the end of the hunt is horrific: the bones of Laura's childhood friends, walled up in the building's crawl-space.

The police are called in, and Laura unravels Benigna's terrible story. The woman had worked at the orphanage, briefly, when Laura was a child. And she had a son, Tomas, with birth defects – a badly disfigured face. Shortly after Laura's adoption, her friends had lured the deformed boy, Tomas, into the dangerous sea-cave (see Figure 6.2). Then they'd pulled off his 'disguise' – the sack with a face drawn on – and dared him to show himself without it. Instead, Tomas remained in the cave to hide, and drowned when the tide came in. And his mother Benigna had her revenge. Slowly she poisoned the children she held responsible, hiding their bodies.

With this grisly news, Carlos has had enough of the haunted orphanage. He wants to leave; Laura asks for two more days – 'to say goodbye'.

As Act Three starts, she now embarks on a restoration that's in fact a reversion to the past. She removes the new beds and bright bed-clothes from the orphanage

**FIGURE 6.2** Laura (Belén Rueda) discovers the fate of her former childhood friends, in *El Orfanato*.

dormitory; in their place she restores the old iron beds, cheap mattresses and plain sheets that she remembers from her childhood. She even makes a rustic meal and sets a dinner table for five. But no one shows, and finally she cries out, in fear and frustration:

> LAURA
> What do you want from me?
> [The camera moves in on her, as she has an inspiration. As if the ghostly spirits were flesh-and-blood, she tries to negotiate]
> You want to keep playing? Is that it? Let's make a deal. I'll play awhile. Then you tell me where Simon is, ok?
> [She waits, but gets no answer.] Ok? [Silence.] OK?

Though she gets no answer, Laura remembers the medium's advice: "Believe and you will see." She's offered the ghostly spirits a deal; now she has to believe they'll honor it. In one of the film's most haunting scenes, she returns to the "Red Light, Green Light" game we saw in the movie's opening.

As night falls, Laura turns her back on a room where the shadows are lengthening ... and taps on a wall, as she'd tapped on a tree that sunlit day, so long ago: "One, two, three – knock on the wall!" She turns, to catch anyone moving ... no one is there, at first. But as she keeps playing, first one child in a smock appears – then another, and another ... moving closer whenever her back is turned to 'knock on the wall'. Finally one of them touches Laura – the signal for all to scatter. As they run for hiding places, Laura follows one to a tucked-away utility closet under the stairs. The child disappears; Laura wonders if she was led here for a reason. She begins to investigate the closet, moving piles of scaffolding to reveal an inner door ...

Beyond, a dim staircase leads down into a basement she's never seen before. Apparently this was where Benigna often hid her son from the world. And Laura thinks, at first, she's found Simon too – wrapped up in a blanket. But she's only fantasizing, and reality comes creeping back in. She notices that the guard-rail to the basement steps is broken; and on the floor, below the break, is a body. It's Simon. She's found him at last.

Back upstairs in the dormitory, Laura sits by the window, holding Simon's broken body. For a second, she flashes back to the night of the little boy's disappearance. She remembers the banging she heard; now she finally understands what it was. Only dimly aware of what she's doing, she takes an overdose of pills; and we see her losing consciousness.

But then a light plays over her face; it's the beam from the neighboring lighthouse, which was always a part of her childhood. The lighthouse has been dark for years; but now it's shining out again. Laura wakes, and discovers – joyfully – that Simon is alive (see Figure 6.3).

**FIGURE 6.3** Laura (Belén Rueda), about to encounter a ghost, in *El Orfanato*.

>                         SIMON
> I wish you'd stay and look after all of us.
> [Laura follows Simon's gaze; in the dormitory beds, she
> sees the five friends of her childhood, sitting up. And
> entering the room is Tomas - free at last of his gro-
> tesque sack. He guides one of the children - Alicia,
> who's blind - to Laura's side. Alicia uses her hands to
> 'see' the grown-up's face, then tells her friends,
> amazed:]
>                         ALICIA
> It's Laura …
> [The other children run over, crying out Laura's name,
> and laughing.]
>                      ANOTHER CHILD
> She's grown old, like Wendy in the story.
> [But Alicia insists on the miracle.]
>                         ALICIA
> It's Laura.
> [Simon asks for a story - about 'the house, the beach,
> the lost children.' And Laura begins:]
>                         LAURA
> Once upon a time … there was a house near the beach …
> where the lost children lived …

The camera slowly pulls back from Laura, surrounded by the children, as she starts to spin her *own* "Peter Pan" tale. The film's conclusion movingly connects with its beginning.

In Act One, as we've seen, *the threat appears*: Laura tries to protect her child from an understanding of his mortality. But he finds out he's been lied to – and then he disappears.

In Act Two, *Laura learns the meaning of the threat, and begins to fight back*. At first Laura can't accept even the possibility that Simon might die. But months pass; her quest to find her son expands, as she turns to parapsychologists and even psychics for help. Without quite acknowledging it to herself, she's begun to accept possibilities she would never have entertained before: that her son might be in 'another realm', beyond the 'normal' one that she can perceive with her limited senses. This act ends with a gruesome discovery - the skeletal remains of Laura's childhood friends. Those remains – which have been there all along – are a potent metaphor for the secrets Laura is uncovering. Now she's more convinced than ever that she can solve her child's disappearance.

In Act Three, there's a final shift in Laura's perception of reality. The ghosts her husband can't believe in start to manifest themselves; Laura lets them guide her to the heartbreaking end of her quest – when she finally finds her little boy's body. It's been in the house the whole time, but hidden away – the most terrible secret of all. Laura could *never* protect her son from the sad and horrific things of life. And Laura now *truly* understands why: because he was always mortal. Like her. As we noted in Chapter 3 (p. 36): "In Act Three, the characters face a *final confrontation with the threat* – and either survive – forever changed – or die." In effect, the end of *El Orfanato* moves us by giving us *both* alternatives: Laura *is* forever changed; and her death makes it possible for her to live, with her son and her childhood friends, in this 'life beyond' that she's discovered – a life where time has stopped, and there is no end.

## Notes

1 Quint, "Aint It Cool News", 10/12/07, http://legacy.aintitcool.com/node/34414 (accessed 10/7/19) Sanchez is referring to movies like *The Others* (2001) and "all the films from the Fantastic Factory", which made low-budget horror movies like *Arachnid* (2001) and *Beyond Re-Animator* (2003.)
2 Quint, op. cit.
3 Quint, op. cit. The director, Juan Bayona, says, re: *Poltergeist*: "Yeah!…It was quite an obvious homage to *Poltergeist*, but the thing is that we were looking for a more realistic atmosphere, so that's why we were avoiding digital effects and things like that. The thing is that we were trying to keep, the whole time, an ambiguous reading on the story. The idea of telling a ghost story and at the same time you could read the story as something real, like the story of a woman losing her mind, so we couldn't use [things like digital special effects], because we couldn't use something that we couldn't finally justify."

# 7

# DIALOGUE

In the history of the Academy Awards (beginning in 1929), only two horror movies have ever won an Oscar for best screenplay: *The Silence of the Lambs* (1991), and *Get Out* (2017). In part this is just a reflection of common attitudes toward the genre. Horror movies have often been seen as more than slightly disreputable; only six have received nominations for best picture.[1] The Oscars are also primarily awards for American movies; and many of the greatest horror films are from other countries.

Even so, it's a fact that good *writing* isn't something that leaps to mind, when people think about horror movies. If they're fans, they remember the scares, which are most often visual;[2] how the screenwriters *build* to those scares isn't so readily apparent. This is where the craft of writing good dialogue comes in.

Dialogue in film is tricky because – in a time-based art form – it has to do so much at once, in the limited time available: establish character, sneak exposition in, paint a mood (from the comic to the ominous), and advance the plot while creating suspense.

For a simple example, let's look at an early scene from *I Walked with a Zombie* (1943) - one of ten films that producer Val Lewton made for RKO Studios. Each of these film had rules to follow: a limited budget ($150,000), a short running time (seventy-five minutes or less – *Zombie* clocks in at 69), and a title test-marked by the studio ("Yes, I *would* like to see a movie called *The Leopard Man!*") – and often bearing minimal relationship to the film that was made). Yet with all these restrictions (maybe because of them?), the films that resulted are wonders of imaginative story-telling.

*Zombie* opens in snowy Ottawa, as Betsy Connell is hired to nurse the wife of a sugar planter. The job will take her far from home, to the island of St. Sebastian; looking out at the snow, Betsy thinks a job in the tropics could be wonderful.

Cut to the small sailing vessel taking Betsy to the island. On deck but standing apart from her is her new employer, Paul Holland. Betsy looks out at the night, narrating her thoughts to us, in voice-over:

> BETSY
> 
> *[voice-over]* It seemed only a few days before I met Mr. Holland in Antigua. We boarded the boat for St. Sebastian. It was all just as I'd imagined it. I look at those great glowing stars. I felt the warm wind on my cheek. I breathed deep, and every bit of me inside myself said "How beautiful."
> *[Her reverie's interrupted, when Paul Holland speaks to her.]*
>
> PAUL
>
> It's *not* beautiful.
>
> BETSY
>
> You read my thoughts, Mr. Holland.
>
> PAUL
>
> It's easy enough to read the thoughts of a newcomer. Everything seems beautiful because you don't understand. Those flying fish – they're not leaping for joy. They're jumping in terror. Bigger fish want to eat them. That luminous water – it takes its gleam from millions of tiny dead bodies – the glitter of putrescence. There's no beauty here. Only death and decay.
>
> BETSY
>
> You can't really believe that. *[They look up at a falling star.]*
>
> PAUL
>
> Everything good dies here. Even the stars.
> *[He moves away from her, passing the crew who are quietly singing a chanty.]*
>
> BETSY
>
> *[voice-over]* How strange to have him break in on my thoughts that way. There was cruelty and hardness in his voice. And yet something about him I liked, something clean and honest. But hurt, badly hurt.

Betsy and Paul must've already met, off-screen, when they came on board the boat. But this is our first glimpse of them together, and the economical screenplay – by Curt Siodmak and Ardel Wray – gives us a lot, in this brief encounter (see Figure 7.1):

- Betsy's narration has the literary rhythm of a journal – 'And yet something about him I like'; it's clear that, as the story begins, Betsy fancies herself as the

**FIGURE 7.1** Sugar planter Paul Holland (Tom Conway) disillusions the nurse (Frances Dee) he's hired to care for his ailing wife, in *I Walked with a Zombie*.

heroine of the novels she's probably fond of. In fact, producer Lewton suggested the Caribbean 'backstory' of the classic Victorian Gothic *Jane Eyre* as a jumping-off point for the story.[3]

- It's equally clear that Paul Holland enjoys disillusioning dreamers like Betsy. He's smart enough to guess her thoughts; and initiates the conversation, just to tell her how wrong she is, to imagine beauty where what *he* sees – with the pride of a cold-eyed realist – is only death and decay.
- "You read my thoughts, Mr. Holland" – despite their opposing views, there *is* an instant connection between them. And at first we might guess that the writers are setting up a romance of opposites. But in fact, there's something else besides attraction that unites them. They both tend to think in binaries: beauty vs. death for him, for example … and cruelty vs. honesty for her. What gives the movie its power is the way that – as the story progresses – it breaks down *all* the binaries that the characters try to cling to: science vs. religion, Christianity vs. voodoo, 'primitive' vs. 'civilized', the living vs. the dead. By the end of the movie, it isn't clear *who* the 'zombie' of the title is.

We see that breakdown of boundaries in another great horror movie – Alfred Hitchcock's classic *Psycho*. As the film begins, we meet the protagonist – Marion Crane – who's dressing after a rendezvous with her lover in a cheap hotel. Sam

Loomis lives in another town; he connects with Marion when he can, but he's having money problems. So marriage will have to wait – something neither of them is happy with.

> SAM
> I'm tired of sweating for people who aren't there! I sweat to pay off my father's debts, and he's in his grave! I sweat to pay my ex-wife alimony, and she's – living on the other side of the world somewhere!
> MARION
> I pay too. They also pay who meet in hotel rooms.
> SAM
> A couple of years, and – the debts will be paid off and – if she ever remarries, the alimony will stop and –
> MARION
> I haven't even been married once!
> SAM
> Yeah – but when you do, you'll swing!
> *[Frustrated but very deeply in love, they embrace.]*
> MARION
> Sam, let's get married!
> SAM
> *[bitterly]* Yeah! And live with me in a storeroom behind a hardware store in Fairvale? We'll have lots of laughs! *[Marion has no answer.]* I'll tell you what. When I send my ex-wife alimony, you can lick the stamps!
> MARION
> *[quietly]* I'll lick the stamps.

Marion's line – "I'll lick the stamps" – is pathetic, and odd enough to be slightly comic; and it's honest, too. She *wants to marry Sam* – and to reach that goal, she'll do whatever it takes. Up to and including theft, when she's back at her job in a real-estate office. A wealthy and obnoxious customer waves around the cash he's using, to buy a house as a wedding present for his daughter. Afraid of having that much money – $40,000 – lying around the office overnight, Marion's boss sends her off to the bank, to deposit it.

But Marion doesn't go to the bank; instead, on a sudden impulse, she heads for home, packs a bag, stuffs the cash in her purse, and hits the road. She's broken a major boundary – between 'law-abiding' and 'criminal'; but she wants so badly to be with the man she loves, she's not thinking clearly. And so, as she flees, she keeps making mistakes, from arousing the suspicions of a motorcycle cop, to covering her tracks by buying a new used car – in full view of the cop who's been wondering what she's up to. Finally, late at night in a driving rain, she misses a turn-off, ending up on an old side-road that leads her to her final destination – the Bates Motel.

There she meets the owner, an attractive but awkward young man named Norman, who offers – if she's hungry – to make her a sandwich, before she retires. She accepts, and Norman heads off to get food in the old Victorian mansion that looms above the motel. Marion hears him arguing with an old woman – his mother, apparently - who accuses him of intending to seduce his latest customer. When Norman returns, with a tray of food, Marion expresses regret: "I've caused you some trouble." Norman makes excuses – "Mother' … what is the phrase … 'she isn't quite herself today'." But seeing that he *has* gone to some trouble, Marion says, "We might as well eat" – and she follows Norman into a little parlor behind the front office.

Screenwriter Joseph Stefano describes the 'strange, extraordinary nature' of the room:

> It is a room of birds. Stuffed birds, all over the room, on every available surface, one even clinging to the old fashioned fringed shade of the lamp. The birds are of many varieties, beautiful, grand, horrible, preying. [Marion] stares in awe and a certain fascinated horror.

As Marion eats, Norman talks about his hobby – taxidermy.

MARION
A man should have a hobby.

NORMAN
Well, it's – it's – it's more than a hobby. A hobby's supposed to pass the time – not fill it.

MARION
Is your time so empty?

NORMAN
No. Uh – Well, I – I run the office, and uh – tend the cabins and grounds, and – do little uh – errands for my mother - the ones she allows I might be capable of doing.

MARION
Uh, do you go out with friends?

NORMAN
Well, uh – a boy's best friend is his mother. *[Marion doesn't know how to respond to that. He smiles sadly at her.]* You've never had an empty moment in your life, have you?

MARION
Only my share.

NORMAN
Where are you going? *[Again, Marion is silent.]* I didn't mean to pry.

MARION
Hm. I'm looking for a private island.

> NORMAN
> What are you running away from?
> MARION
> Well, why do you ask that?
> NORMAN
> No. People never run away from anything. The rain didn't last long, did it? You know what I think? I think that – we're all in our private traps – clamped in them. And none of us can ever get out. We – we scratch and claw, but – only at the air – only at each other. And for all that, we never budge an inch.
> MARION
> Sometimes we deliberately step into those traps.
> NORMAN
> I was born in mine. I don't mind it any more.
> MARION
> Oh, but you should. You should mind it!
> NORMAN
> *[trying to joke]* Oh, I do – but I say I don't.

Marion's tried to escape *her* trap by fleeing, with stolen money; Norman's accepted his, at a cost we'll learn as the movie continues. Both have struggled with loneliness; yet their random meeting suggests that connection with others *can* be possible. Responding to Marion's sympathy, Norman admits how hard it is, to deal with his elderly invalid mother:

> NORMAN
> Sometimes – when she talks to me like that – I feel I'd like to go up there – and curse her – and – and – and leave her forever! Or at least defy her! ... But I know I can't. She's ill.
> MARION
> She sounded strong.
> NORMAN
> No, I mean – ill. She – she had to raise me – all by herself, after my father died. I was only five and it – it must've been quite a strain for her.

He goes on to explain that his mother remarried – but then the *second* husband died.

> NORMAN
> And – when he died, too, it was – just too great a shock for her. And – and the way he died – I guess it's nothing

>                    MARION
>
> to talk about while you're eating. Anyway, it was just too great a loss for her. She had nothing left.
>
>                    MARION
>
> Except you.
>
>                    NORMAN
>
> Well, a son is a poor substitute for a lover.
>
>                    MARION
>
> Why don't you go away?
>
>                    NORMAN
>
> To a private island like you?
>
>                    MARION
>
> *[realizing, ruefully]* No – not like me.
>
>                    NORMAN
>
> I couldn't do that. Who'd look after her? She'd be alone up there. The fire would go out.

Marion makes a suggestion – "Wouldn't it better – if you put her – someplace?" – and the conversation takes a dark turn, as Norman bitterly speaks about the horrors of a madhouse:

>                    NORMAN
>
> Have you ever seen the inside of one of those places? The laughing and the tears – and the cruel eyes studying you? My mother there? But she's harmless. Why – she's as harmless as one of those stuffed birds.
>
>                    MARION
>
> I am sorry. Uh – I only felt – it seemed she's hurting you. I meant well.
>
>                    NORMAN
>
> People always mean well. They cluck their thick tongues and shake their heads and suggest – oh so very delicately … Of course, I – I've suggested it myself. But I hate to even think about it. She needs me. It – it – it's not as if she were a – a maniac, a raving thing – She just goes a little mad sometimes. We all go a little mad sometimes. Haven't you?
>
>                    MARION
>
> Yes. And sometimes just one time can be enough. And thank you.
>
>                    NORMAN
>
> Thank you, 'Norman'.
>
>                    MARION
>
> Norman.

                    NORMAN
    Oh, y-you're not uh - You're not going back to your room
    already?
                    MARION
    I'm very tired. And I'll have a long drive tomorrow. All
    the way back to Phoenix.
                    NORMAN
    Really.
                    MARION
    I stepped into a private trap back there - I'd like to go
    back and try to pull myself out of it - before it's too
    late for me, too.

Not only has Marion found common ground with the lonely taxidermist; but in talking with him, she's realized what a very bad mistake she's made. Like the script as a whole, and like each act, *this scene has a clear development, building steadily to a climax* – as Norman reveals a hitherto-unsuspected and dangerous anger. Marion's disturbed by this; but oddly enough, not frightened: she recognizes in Norman a desperation that's made *her* 'go a little mad'. Now it's time to pull herself back from the edge; in this dark film's cruelest irony, her encounter with Norman has changed her. And she knows what she has to do, now: go back to Phoenix (not "L.A.", which is what she put down in the motel register – a deception Norman's aware of), return the stolen money, and accept the consequences. Marion goes back to her room; Norman removes a painting from the wall, revealing a peep-hole. And he spies on her as she undresses, ready to take what will be the most infamous shower in movie history.

(See Figure 7.2.) In a film script, characters never just idly chat; there isn't time for that. Whenever characters speak, they do so for *a reason*, whether it's conscious or not. *Characters have goals they pursue; and dialogue is one of the tools they use, in that pursuit.*

As we've seen, a character's goals can shift; in the 'dinner' scene from *Psycho*, for instance, Norman's met an attractive young woman, someone he might – in a different movie – think of taking out on a date. His improvised late-night snack is as close as he gets, but at least he's trying; he even starts to open up, when he's talking about his strange hobby. And Marion responds to him, not romantically, but as someone with problems that seem to echo her own. Yet this moment of connection poses a threat to Norman's fragile self; he has too much to hide, and the conversation's turning dangerous. So his goal in talking shifts, mid-stream – from connecting to repulsing, going on the attack to defend himself. Marion doesn't know why the mood has changed, but clearly she's gone too far, in suggesting that Norman place his mother in institutional care: "I am sorry. Uh – I only felt – it seemed she's hurting you. I meant well." And Norman, defending himself *and* his mother, mocks her in his reply: "People always mean well. They cluck their tongues and shake their heads and suggest – Oh, so very delicately … " At that moment, with the damage done, he catches himself, and back-steps: "Of course – I – I've suggested it myself. But I hate to even think about it. She

**72** Dialogue

**FIGURE 7.2** Motel owner Norman Bates (Anthony Perkins) talks to a sympathetic guest (Janet Leigh, off camera), in *Psycho*.

needs me. It – it – it's not as if she were a – a maniac, a raving thing – She just goes a little mad sometimes. We all go a little mad sometimes. Haven't you?" Those last two words are a final attempt to reconnect with Marion, to go back to his *original* goal. But he's too late, because his words snap Marion out of the trance she's been in, ever since *she* went 'a little mad' and stole $40,000. She's grateful for Norman's inadvertent help, but now it's time for bed. He'll bring her breakfast, he tells her; she says "good night" – and those are the final words we'll hear (beyond, "Mother! Oh God! Mother, mother! Blood, blood!") for the next hair-raising sixteen minutes.

In addition to *forwarding action, building character and establishing mood*, dialogue also contributes to a film's story-telling *rhythm*. As we've seen, there's a *rising action* – a *movement toward climax/completion* – in the story as a whole, and in the parts that make up the story (acts, scenes, even individual moments). But there's *another* rhythm that's common to horror films as a genre: that of repeating *tension/release*, escalating the tension with each repetition of the pattern.

(This is the problem with jump-scares – those moments when a movie goes "Boo!", then reveals that the 'scare' was a false alarm. Jump-scares *don't* escalate tension, they simply repeat it, to ever-decreasing effect.)

The long wordless section in *Psycho* follows Norman's final attempt to make human contact with another. Though he's inadvertently helped a young woman realize the mistakes she's made, he's still alone; words have failed. Now comes horrific violence, an *explosive* release of tension that ends with Marion's terrible death – and a death of certainty for the viewer. All along we've been rooting for Marion, who we *thought* was the protagonist; suddenly, with the movie less than half over, Marion's dead – and we're both afraid and unmoored, bewildered. Who do we care about now?

The movie gives no answer, as Norman – in horror – discovers the body, clearly thinking his mother's the murderer. He spends the next fifteen minutes in silence, using the shower curtain to wrap up the body, cleaning the bathroom and straightening up the bedroom. These wordless actions start to build up a tension of their own. We know, the whole time, that Norman is in danger of being discovered. And though we can't approve of his actions – he *is* an accomplice to murder – we feel concern for this haunted man, whose loneliness has become a black hole. The sequence ends as Norman pushes Marion's car (her body now in the trunk) into a nearby swamp. The car begins to submerge; but then, without any warning, it stops. The evidence of a terrible crime is just sitting there, for all to see. Norman looks around, for witnesses; he stares at the car, which doesn't move. In that moment, most viewers – consciously or not – *want* the car to keep sinking. It's a pay-off to the long wordless sequence of Norman 'erasing' his mother's crime.

We aren't privy to his inner thoughts – as we were to those of Marion, when she was on the road with the stolen money, trying to reach her lover. For example, we heard – in voice-over – her sardonic fantasizing about the tycoon whose money she stole: "I ain't about to kiss off forty thousand dollars! I'll get it back, and if any of it's missin', I'll replace it with her fine, soft flesh! I'll track her, never you doubt it!" Marion reveals a lot of herself with these words, which match the hint of a smile on her face, as she drives through the night. She almost *enjoys* the thought of tormenting the braggart who flaunted his cash in the office, and openly, grossly flirted with her.

In contrast, we can only imagine Norman's thoughts, as he goes about the gruesome task of cleaning up a murder. He's afraid, and his actions have urgency. But he's also efficient, and thorough – as if he'd done something like this before. Maybe even – disturbing thought – *more* than once. Above all, he's alone – not even a voice in his head for company. The silence in this sequence is chilling – its power coming, in part, from the change in rhythm it creates: the back-and-forth of dialogue in the parlor, then Marion's murder, and then … no words. Furtive actions in a now-haunted motel room. A car sinking. Silence.

This kind of reversal of rhythm can also work in the other direction: from physical actions to words, often a monologue that creates some 'breathing room' to reflect and regroup, before another – maybe final – battle with the monster.

For example, as *Invasion of the Body Snatchers* progresses, the protagonists discover that almost everyone in town has been 'snatched' – replaced with an alien double. Becky and Miles have to flee their home, with much of the town in hot pursuit, and end up – late at night – in Miles's office downtown. Miles gives them both a couple of uppers.

                          MILES
We can't close our eyes all night.
                          BECKY
We may wake up changed … into something inhuman and evil.
[Miles looks out at the dark town square.]

**74**   Dialogue

>                            MILES
> In my practice, I've seen how people have allowed their
> humanity to drain away. Only it happens slowly instead
> of all at once. They didn't seem to mind.
>                            BECKY
> But just some people, Miles.
>                            MILES
> All of us – a little bit. We harden our hearts and grown
> callous. Only when we have to fight to stay human do we
> realize how precious it is to us, how dear ... as you are
> to me ...

And they finally kiss. Miles's speeches are separated by a line from Becky; but they're basically one monologue, as Miles makes the connection between the aliens' nefarious plans, and the more routine – but equally deadly - attrition of daily life. This speech also has a build, as it moves from the general – "*we* do this and that" – to the particular: what Miles feels about *one* particular human being ... the woman he finally kisses.[4]

Perhaps the most famous monologue from a horror film is the "Indianapolis" speech from *Jaws*.[5] It comes at the end of the film's second act, when the hunt for the shark has narrowed down to three men on a small fishing vessel – Sheriff Brody, the shark expert Hooper, and the ship's hard-bitten captain, Quint. As Act Two approaches its pivot into Act Three, the shark makes a major appearance, suddenly raising its head above the surface, razor-toothed maw gaping wide before it glides back into the water. The hunters finally *know*, at last, just how big this monster is.

In a fast-paced action sequence, they mobilize to chase down the shark, shooting it with a harpoon attached to a large flotation-barrel; if the shark dives, then the buoyant barrel will drag it back to the surface. Or it would, for an *ordinary* shark; but hours pass, night starts to fall, and there's still no sign of the creature.

In the cabin, the men – to relieve the day's tensions – start to get a little drunk, comparing scars and telling 'war-stories'. Finally Sheriff Brody points at a place on Quint's arm: "What's that?"

Quint says he had a tattoo, but had it removed: the U.S.S. Indianapolis. Hooper suddenly sobers.

>                            HOOPER
> You were on the Indianapolis?
>                            BRODY
> What happened?
>                            QUINT
> Japanese submarine slammed two torpedoes into her side,
> Chief. We was coming back from the island of Tinian to
> Leyte. We'd just delivered the bomb. The Hiroshima bomb.
> Eleven hundred men went into the water. Vessel went down in

12 minutes. Didn't see the first shark for about a half-hour. Tiger. 13-footer. You know how you know that in the water, Chief? You can tell by lookin' from the dorsal to the tail. What we didn't know, was that our bomb mission was so secret, no distress signal had been sent. They didn't even list us overdue for a week. Very first light, Chief, sharks come cruisin' by, so we formed ourselves into tight groups. It was sorta like you see in calendars, you know the infantry squares in the old calendars like the Battle of Waterloo and the idea was the shark come to the nearest man, that man he starts poundin' and hollerin' and sometimes that shark he go away ... but sometimes he wouldn't go away. Sometimes that shark looks right at ya. Right into your eyes. And the thing about a shark is he's got lifeless eyes. Black eyes. Like a doll's eyes. When he comes at ya, he doesn't even seem to be livin' ... 'til he bites ya, and those black eyes roll over white and then ... ah then you hear that terrible high-pitched screamin'. The ocean turns red, and despite all your poundin' and your hollerin' those sharks come in and ... they rip you to pieces. You know by the end of that first dawn, lost a hundred men. I don't know how many sharks there were, maybe a thousand. I do know how many men, they averaged six an hour. Thursday mornin', Chief, I bumped into a friend of mine, Herbie Robinson from Cleveland. Baseball player. Boson's mate. I thought he was asleep. I reached over to wake him up. He bobbed up, down in the water, he was like a kinda top. Upended. Well, he'd been bitten in half below the waist. At noon on the fifth day, a Lockheed Ventura swung in low and he spotted us, a young pilot, lot younger than Mr. Hooper here, anyway he spotted us and a few hours later a big ol' fat PBY come down and started to pick us up. You know that was the time I was the most frightened. Waitin' for my turn. I'll never put on a lifejacket again. So eleven hundred men went into the water. 316 men come out, the sharks took the rest. June the 29th, 1945. Anyway, we delivered the bomb.

In a movie filled with physical action and scream-inducing visual scares, the storytelling here quiets down to a kind of horrific campfire tale – as frightening (if not more so) than the action that's preceded it. Like the speech from *Body Snatchers*, the Indianapolis monologue moves from the general (the historical background) to the specific and personal – in this case, the gruesome moment when Quint 'bumps' into his friend Herbie Robinson. Kept afloat by his life-jacket, Herbie up-ends ... and

**76** Dialogue

Quint sees that his body is missing, below the waist. He's been bitten in two. (Quint pays off this image, a few lines later: "I'll never put on a life-jacket again.")

For a moment, at the end of Quint's story, Hooper and Brody are silent; what can they possibly say? Far off, somewhere in the dark, they hear an eerie wail.

                          BRODY
What's that?
                          HOOPER
It's a whale.
[Quint – the only one who can – starts to bring them out of the somber mood he created, quietly singing a sailor-song:]
                          QUINT
[singing] "Farewell and adieu, to you fine Spanish ladies, Farewell and adieu, you ladies of Spain ... "
[As he sings, we cut to a long shot of the ship; in the foreground, the floatation-barrel surfaces; the shark is back, though the men don't know it yet. In the cabin, Hooper picks up on Quint's invitation to change the mood.]
                          HOOPER
[singing] "Show me the way to go home, I'm tired and I wanta go to bed ... "

Quickly, Quint and Brody join in; and because they're all singing – loudly, now – they miss the first THUD against the ship. Then it happens again; a plank bulges inward, water starts running in – and we've made the turn into Act Three, the final show-down with the shark.

For a quick overview of dialogue, let's look at its many purposes, as shown in the 'Indianapolis' speech.

- **Establishing character**. We've already gotten a good sense of Quint from his actions in the movie. But the monologue reveals *a secret* we hadn't known before: that Quint has very personal reasons for hunting the movie's monster, reasons that arise out of terrifying personal trauma.
- **Painting a mood**. Quint's speech comes out of a comic moment that seems – at first – just a welcome change of pace from the action before it. The men are comparing 'battle scars' – from the bite of a moray eel, to the scrape of a shark's rough hide. Then Quint reveals that he's had a tattoo removed – "the U.S.S. Indianpolis" – and the mood starts to change. Robert Shaw, as Quint, gives a great performance, telling the story quietly – which underscores the horror of the events that he's describing.
- **Working in exposition organically** (a.k.a. "sneaking in exposition") and *advancing the plot*. Up till now, we've thought Quint's motives were primarily financial; he's demanded a lot of money, to help in tracking down the shark.

But now we learn that he has a much more personal (even obsessive) goal: revenge. Though he doesn't spell it out, he's not going home until he or the shark is dead. This *raises the stakes* for his 'passengers', who will end up threatened not just by the shark but by Quint's long-building obsession – something they finally get when Brody tries to call back to the mainland for help; Quint takes a bat to the radio. And now they're *completely* alone, to destroy the monster or to die.

## Notes

1 The six are *The Exorcist, Jaws, The Silence of the Lambs, The Sixth Sense, Black Swan* and *Get Out*.
2 Primarily visual – but horror films also do amazing things with sound. I remember the audience gasping at the unexpected sound of a tongue going 'tlock' – just the small simple cluck of a child, in 2018's nerve-shredder, *Hereditary*.
3 Roger Luckhurst, Zombies (London: Reaktion Books Ltd., 2015), p. 91.
4 Screenwriter Daniel Mainwaring added this speech, which doesn't appear in the Jack Finney novel on which the film is based. See Al La Valley (ed.), *Invasion of the Body Snatchers* (New Brunswick, NJ and London: Rutgers University Press, 1989), p. 8.
5 The credited screenwriters of *Jaws* are Peter Benchley (author of the novel on which the film is based), and Carl Gottlieb. Director Steven Spielberg has attributed the 'Indianapolis' speech to Howard Sackler, who wrote an uncredited early draft of the script. C.f. Joshua Stecker, "Spielberg Reveals the Definitive Word on the Jaws 'Indianapolis' Speech", scriptmag.com, 6/6/11, https://www.scriptmag.com/features/spielberg-reveals-the-definitive-word-on-the-jaws-uss-indianapolis-speech (accessed 10/7/19).

# 8

# FEARFUL LANDSCAPES

'The Sunken Place' – just the name alone is ominous, and the terrible place itself appears at the end of Act One of Jordan Peele's *Get Out* (see Chapter 4, pp. 000 ff.). Our protagonist Chris, unable to sleep, has just come in from a smoke outside, when he encounters his girl-friend's mother Missy, who's a night-owl too. Inviting Chris to sit with her, she expresses concern about his smoking endangering her daughter's health. We've learned, from an earlier conversation, that Missy is a therapist. Now, talking about how hypnosis works, she keeps on stirring her teacup, as she 'innocently' interrogates Chris about a bad time from his childhood – it was raining, he was home alone watching TV, awaiting his mom's return from work ... but she never came ...

On the soundtrack, we hear the occasional clink of the teaspoon, in the present; and also the gentle sound of rain, from that terrible afternoon long ago. Much later, we learn what happened: Chris's mother was hit by a car, and could've been saved, if someone was looking for her. Instead, as Chris tells his girlfriend, Rose, "Nobody was looking ... there was time, there was time ... there was time, but nobody, nobody was looking." So his mother died by the side of the road, "cold and alone."

This is the harrowing memory that Missy is 'helping' Chris to remember, as he slips – without being aware of it – into a deep hypnotic trance.

        MISSY
 You didn't call anyone?
        CHRIS
 No.
        MISSY
 Why not?

*[Awkwardly grinning, embarrassed, he struggles to find an answer.]*

CHRIS

I don't know. I just thought that if I did, it would make it real.

MISSY

Hmm. You're so scared. You think it was your fault. *[Tears are streaming down Chris's face.]* How do you feel now?

CHRIS

I can't move.

MISSY

*[agreeing]* You can't move.

CHRIS

Why can't I move?

MISSY

You're paralyzed. Just like that day when you did nothing. You did *nothing*. *[She almost smiles.]* Now, sink into the floor.

CHRIS

Wait, wait, wait –

MISSY

*[calm but firm]* Sink.

Cut to Chris as a boy, in the rainy blue TV light of his memory – sinking into the floor. Then we're into a void, a vast black space, where grown-up Chris is falling backward, slowly, down and down and down … Missy appears up above, way off, like an image on a TV screen, but getting smaller and smaller, as Chris falls farther and farther away. Finally, his feet come to rest – in the middle of this fathomless dark. Missy leans forward, to fill him in: "Now you're in the sunken place."

Suddenly the film has moved to a whole new level of danger – from the microaggressions of awkward white liberals trying hard to be 'woke', to a calculated malevolence that has stranded Chris in limbo. A very scary place that's completely unexpected, for starters – and worse, a place that's totally empty, pitch dark and seemingly endless.[1] Chris shouts to the far-away Missy, but his words are swallowed up by the infinite nothingness around him.

A few moments later, Chris wakes, with a jolt; he's in bed, and thinks he just had a bad dream. But during the 'sunken place' sequence, the movie has cut – more than once – to show us what's happening in the *real* world, where Chris is sitting across from Missy, hypnotized, unable to move. He's *physically* safe – but now we know his hosts have power over him. And when they choose, they can 'banish' him to a place that seems like a nightmare (see Figure 8.1).

**80** Fearful landscapes

**FIGURE 8.1** Chris (Daniel Kaluuya) falls into the Sunken Place, in *Get Out*.

Which, of course, is the power the *film-maker* has – to put us into a dream-like space (in our heads), like the one we used to be warned about, on ancient maps: "Beyond this point are monsters ... "[2]

Andrew Tudor uses a wonderful phrase, in discussing how we construct 'our everyday sense of fearfulness and anxiety' – the *'landscapes of fear'* [3] (my emphasis). The successful horror screenplay carefully builds its fearful landscapes, to embody the plot *and* to mirror the interior lives of the characters. *Like dialogue, a film's 'sense of place' (including location, season, time of day, and weather) has several things to accomplish.*

- It heightens mood (in particular, the steady build-up of tension).
- For characters on a quest (to solve a mystery, for example), it provides a specific (often frightening) end-of-the-road destination.
- It creates obstacles, both exterior and interior. An example of the latter: late in Roman Polanski's *Repulsion*, the schizophrenic protagonist – holed up in her apartment with the body of a man she's killed – stumbles down a hallway that suddenly starts to sprout arms that grab at her. It's a terrifying moment – as we realize we're now seeing the world from the point-of-view of a woman who's having a *serious* break with reality. It means we can't prepare ourselves for *anything* – making us helpless.
- It can paint in 'real life' details of a specific historical moment – like the "War of the Cities" during the Iran–Iraq War (c. 1985), which serves as the backdrop to the Persian-language movie *Under the Shadow* (which we'll be looking at in Chapter 11, pp. 122 ff.).

Some of the earliest horror films – from *Nosferatu* (1922) to *Frankenstein* (1931) – took their visual cues from literature, in particular the 'Gothic' vein that began with Horace Walpole's creaky (literally and figuratively) *The Castle of Otranto* (1764). Crumbling abbeys, ruined castles, cobwebbed crypts – these were standard décor for a cultural movement engaged in re-imagining (and re-purposing) the distant past. Rejecting the Age of Enlightenment and its embrace of rationality,

> the Gothic was chaotic ... ornate and convoluted; where the classics offered a world of clear rules and limits, *Gothic represented excess and exaggeration, the product of the wild and the uncivilized, a world that constantly tended to overflow cultural boundaries.*[4] [My emphasis]

What links the Gothic 'mission' to the early days of the cinema is that both are engaged in a kind of de-stabilizing of the 'real'. Modern audiences take for granted the cinema's basic grammar: shots, cutting, camera movement, zooms and other optical effects. But this wasn't the case with people who were exposed to a new – and startling – form of visual story-telling. There's a famous (and, many scholars assume, apocryphal) anecdote about the Lumière Brothers' fifty-second film, *Arrival of a Train at La Ciotat* (first shown in December 1895 in Paris.) It's just a single, unedited take – a train appears in the distance, approaches a station (getting ever larger as it does so) – slows does as it reaches the station platform and finally stops, with passengers getting on and off. A straightforward slice-of-life. But according to legend, audiences were so alarmed by the sight of the train bearing down on them, that they fled, or ducked under their seats. What's much more likely is that these movie-goers were simply *astonished* – no one had ever seen 'real life' represented this way before. *Photographs*, yes – but photographed life *in motion* was utterly new.

This astonishment – this *seeing anew* – should be a horror-film writer's goal.[5] And a strong 'sense of place' is one of the most effective tools for that purpose. This doesn't mean one has to abandon the legacy of past visions. The fearful locations of Gothic stories – for instance, the insane asylum (featured in *Caligari* and 1931's *Dracula*) – recur in modern horror films, from *Gothika* (2003) to *Shutter Island* (2010), and even in recent experiments like Steven Soderbergh's *Unsane* (2018), shot entirely on an iPhone 7 Plus. The technology is modern, but the stories are haunted by the presence of still-effective Gothic tropes.[6]

Early horror films also used the techniques of expressionism – an artistic movement which focused on representations of inner experience, in media as different as painting, theater and fiction.[7] The most extreme cinematic example is Robert Wiene's *The Cabinet of Dr. Caligari* (1921); in that film the world is depicted as a series of weirdly angled sets, deliberately artificial-looking, complete with lighting effects like shadows *painted* on the floor. Ultimately, we learn that the film's protagonist is a madman; and his off-kilter way of seeing the world is reflected in the film's design.

Another influential expressionist classic is *Nosferatu* (1922) – a totally unauthorized version of *Dracula*, Bram Stoker's late-Victorian Gothic novel.[8] Though director F.W. Murnau loved the natural world – and some of the film is shot in the actual mountains of Transylvania (one of the novel's primary locations) – *Nosferatu*'s most powerful scenes are interiors, building 'landscapes of fear', from heavily contrasting shadow and light, in eerie locales like the title vampire's moldering pile of a castle.[9] As the film progresses, the horror migrates – following "Count Orlock" (a.k.a Dracula) as he travels from the wilds of Transylvania, to a quaint little German village, where he's bought a new house to serve as a base, intending to prey on the populace. At the story's climax, he enters the home of a victim he's selected; but we don't see *him* – we see his *shadow*, looming large against a wall and creeping up the stairs. It's a frightening moment – this shadow seems to have a malevolent life of its own. In fact, this ominous shadow has *substance* – again, very much like the filmic image itself.

In western horror films – from the 1920s through the 1930s, the "Bad Place" stays in some version of Europe, and also tends to be set in the past; *Nosferatu*, for instance, moves the Stoker novel from the 1890s (when the book was set), back to a mythical nineteenth century ravaged by what the locals think – at first – is a frightful return of the plague. *Frankenstein* is equally fluid about where exactly it's set, and when. The novel is set in 1818; the 1931 movie, in contrast, wavers between the present (complete with the latest marvels, like telephones), and an *ersatz*-rural 'long ago' (home of your standard torch-wielding villagers). Bottom line: horror's still localized in the past, and far from Hollywood.

This changes, in the 1940s; and Jacques Tourneur's *Cat People* (1942) is the first horror movie clearly set in the present, in America. It's the film that begins a strategy which continues on into the present, of finding horror in everyday life: an architect's office in New York City, the swimming pool of a woman's hotel, and – in the film's most famous sequence – one of the pedestrian traverses in Central Park.

Tourneur and his producer Val Lewton (the team behind *I Walked with a Zombie*) firmly believed in the power of *suggestion: what we imagine is there in the dark can be a lot more alarming than whatever the film might show us*. In the Central Park scene a woman is walking alone, at night, on the sidewalk of one of the sunken roads that crosses the park from east to west. The woman, Jane, hears footsteps behind her – but far enough back in the shadows that her pursuer isn't visible. We've seen who it is: the jealous Irina, wife of Jane's colleague Oliver. Irina's a Serbian émigré, who suffers from the neurotic belief (at least we *think* it's neurotic, at first) that she's a direct descendant of the 'cat people' of her village: women who – in the grip of strong emotions, like passion or jealousy – can turn into savage panthers. Jane knows that Oliver's wife is suffering from this strange 'delusion'; and though she's not superstitious herself, she grows uneasy, crossing the park, as she keeps on hearing footsteps. The movie sets up a hypnotic pattern of aural and visual doubling: Jane crosses the screen from left to right, from relative darkness into the glow of a streetlight and back into shadow again; behind her, Irina does the same, left to right, dark/light/dark. The sound of the women's shoes on the sidewalk also repeats in a pattern, the click of Jane's heels, and then Irina's following. And then suddenly the pattern breaks down; Irina's footsteps cease, as Jane moves into a darker area. Sensing something wrong, she hurries ahead, to another streetlight, looks back – and sees only the lonely traverse sidewalk, curving into the distance. Frightened now, she starts to run – reaching another pool of light, still certain that something's after her. As she fearfully looks around, there's a jarring animal *screech* on the soundtrack. Jane jumps (as did I, the first time I saw the movie); and the screech is revealed as the brakes of a bus, pulling up to the grateful pedestrian.[10] She hops on, asking the driver, "Did you see it?" He gives her a jaded look and drives on, and we cut to the park's Sheep Meadow, where a keeper has found the bodies of four slaughtered lambs … and a big cat's paw-prints leading away. Strangely, the paw-prints end, turning into the prints of a woman's shoes … (see Figure 8.2).

As horror moves into the present day, there's another shift – from the supernatural threats of the 1930s and 1940s. Anxieties of the post-war era find their way into movies like *Them!* (giant ants resulting from nuclear testing), *Invasion of the Body Snatchers* (discussed in Chapter 4, pp. 38 ff.), *Invaders from Mars*, *The Day the Earth Stood Still* (superior aliens threatening Earth with destruction, unless it stops building nuclear weapons), *The Incredible Shrinking Man* (who's shrinking because of nuclear testing), *I Married a Monster from Outer Space* (because the aliens' females are extinct, and the aliens need to mate with earth women, to continue their species), and perhaps the most haunting giant-irradiated-creature film of all time, *Gojira* (1954), a Japanese movie released only nine years after the destruction of Nagasaki and Hiroshima. Americans saw a bastardized version, badly cut and with new scenes featuring English-speaking actor Raymond Burr added in. But the Japanese

**FIGURE 8.2** Alice (Jane Randolph) wonders if she's being stalked through Central Park, in *Cat People*.

original – with a furious beast laying waste to the city of Tokyo – is a somber visual echo of the chaos that followed the dropping of the atomic bomb.

And then, in 1960, comes *Psycho* – a movie that changes the nature of the horror film forever. Norman Bates is a new kind of monster – a serial killer who doesn't *look* like a killer,[11] an 'organized' psychopath who's able to cover his bloody tracks.[12] And the film's main locations – a run-down motel and an old Victorian mansion – perfectly capture the nature of Norman's lethally divided self.

Almost sixty years after *Psycho*'s debut, the murder-in-the-shower sequence is still incredibly shocking. Not only does it kill off the woman we *thought* was the protagonist, but the stabbing takes places in the most ordinary of settings – a motel bathroom: about as far as possible from the sweeping cobwebbed staircase of Dracula's castle in Transylvania. This process – finding the ominous in the familiar – had already begun in the 1940s, with films like *Cat People*;[13] but it reaches a definite climax with *Psycho*. If one isn't safe in the privacy of an anonymous hotel bathroom, then *no* place is safe. (By the time we get to the French 'extreme horror' film *Inside* [2007], not even the womb is a refuge; in that home-invasion story, a woman's besieged – the night before she's due to give birth – by a maniac who's determined to perform an impromptu cesarean.)

In *Psycho*, screenwriter Joseph Stefano use location to generate horror in two very different ways – roughly corresponding to the famous distinction director Alfred Hitchcock made, between 'surprise' and 'suspense'. His classic example involves a couple having a chat in a restaurant; suddenly a bomb goes off. "The public is *surprised*, but prior to this surprise, it has seen an absolutely ordinary scene, of no special consequence." But what if the public *knows* there's a bomb beneath the table, set to go off?

> In these conditions, the same innocuous conversation becomes fascinating because the public is participating in the scene. The audience is longing to warn the characters on the screen: "You shouldn't be talking about such trivial matters. There's a bomb beneath you and it's about to explode!" In the first case we have given the public fifteen seconds of *surprise* at the moment of the explosion. In the second we have provided them with … minutes of suspense.[14]

Hitchcock concluded that, in general, suspense trumped surprise – "except when the surprise is a twist, that is, when the unexpected ending is, in itself, the highlight of the story."[15]

The death of Marion Crane in the shower is one of the most effective 'twists' that horror movies have given us. It ends completely one strand of the plot (the one we'd *thought* was central); we have to re-orient ourselves, as the movie's second story begins – picking up Marion's sister Lila, Marion's lover Sam, and a private detective named Arbogast, as they try to solve the mystery of Marion's disappearance.

In this second half of the movie, the screenplay carefully ratchets up the suspense – using the movie's other primary location, the old Victorian home on the hill above the Bates Motel. Looking much like a classic haunted house, it's – at first – just an ominous presence, like the dead weight of the past made tangible, looming over the action below. But after Marion's murder, we know that the house is a murderer's lair; and the film begins to play with our fear, in sequences that take us – one floor at a time – into the "Bad Place".

After his talk with Marion, Norman goes back home – and we see the entry, the stairs and a hall that leads to the kitchen. Nothing *visibly* scary here – but we're only shown a small part of the house. The *second* time we go in, we're with the private detective Arbogast. He hasn't found Norman at the motel, so he climbs the path to the house, lets himself in and looks around. On a hunch, he starts up the stairs to the second floor – not knowing what *we* know: that Mrs. Bates is up there, and she's waiting … (see Figure 8.3).

Arbogast only gets to the top of the stairs, before he's attacked and killed. So the second floor remains an Unknown – until the climax of the movie, when Marion's sister Lila sneaks in, hoping Norman's mother might know *something* that could be helpful.

Now the movie starts to intercut – as Sam, in the hotel office, chats Norman up, to keep him occupied. Lila makes it up the stairs, unharmed – for now – and starts exploring: first Mrs. Bates' bedroom, filled with heavy antique furniture … and then, the floor above, where Norman apparently sleeps on a little cot, with the broken-down toys of his childhood. There's a bewildering sadness in what Lila finds: evidence of lives that seem to be trapped in a long-ago past. And the sense that Lila's in danger builds, as the intercut scenes to the office show Norman growing more and more upset.

**FIGURE 8.3** Private detective Arbogast (Martin Balsam), about to end his investigation, in *Psycho*.

**86** Fearful landscapes

Finally he explodes, knocks out Sam and hurries up to the house. Seeing him coming, Lila heads for the only place she *hasn't* explored: the basement (where, from an earlier scene, we know Mrs. Bates may be lurking.) This is the point when the audience wants to start screaming: "No! Don't go down there!" Basements and attics – places like traps with only one exit, shadowy places where the past (with its dangerous secrets) is hidden away. "Don't go in the basement!" – though of course, when we shout that out, we're hypocrites: we *want* to know what's down there, lurking, waiting to be revealed. So Lila descends to a basement, and then to a fruit cellar even further down – and finally sees an old lady, back turned, sitting alone in a rocker, lit by a bare lightbulb on a cord.

Lila approaches. "Mrs. Bates?" She gently taps the old lady on the shoulder; and the chair rocks around ...

To conclude this chapter on 'sense of place', we'll take a quick look at *Ringu* (1998) whose 'bad place' isn't a *place* at all, at first – it's an eerie videotape. This haunted tape – a strange montage of disconnected images, including a volcano erupting, a woman combing her hair, and a long-held shot of a well – has a curse upon it; anyone who watches it dies without warning, seven days later. For reporter Reiko Asakawa, this story is personal; her niece is one of the victims, having watched the tape with several friends, all of whom have died. So Reiko – with the help of ex-husband Ryugi – starts to investigate: who made the tape? What do its images mean? And why does its horrible magic work?

Inadvertently, Reiko watches the tape herself – and then so does her little boy. Now both of them are in danger, and the Hitchcockian clock is ticking. Seven days to solve the mystery – or Reiko dies, and her son will too, a day later.

The story Reiko uncovers goes back decades, involving a powerful psychic, her equally gifted daughter and the scientist who exploited them both. The daughter was killed by the scientist (who may have been her father); and the daughter – dumped into the well that features so prominently in the videotape – somehow was able to curse the tape. Reiko and her ex-husband have to find the well with the daughter's bones, thinking the curse may be ended if the daughter's remains are laid to rest.

In the movie's climactic sequence, the well is discovered, beneath a modern building. With only hours remaining before Reiko's week-to-live is up, she and Ryugi bail out the water; at last, Reiki reaches down and pulls up the skull of the murdered woman. Instinctively, she tenderly shelters the skull against her body; it's an odd and powerful image, both grotesque but also moving, as Reiko hopes that the murdered woman's spirit can finally rest in peace.[16]

In movies made decades apart, and as seemingly different as *Ringu* and *Psycho*, it's intriguing that both have scenes near the end, when the movie's protagonists have to descend to a "Bad Place" (a forgotten well in a crawlspace in *Ringu*, a basement in *Psycho*), where they come face-to-face with all that remains of a long-dead murder-victim (*Ringu's* bones, *Psycho's* mummified Mrs. Bates). It's as if horror stories had an almost literal 'architecture' – dictating where the characters *have* to go, to reach revelation.

Which brings us back to *Get Out* – and protagonist Chris falling backward and downward, into a kind of infinite darkness. It's where, without conscious awareness, he's *always* been heading. Where he *had* to go – paradoxically, to learn where he may have always been: "Now you're in the Sunken Place."

## Notes

1. Visually, 'the sunken place' is similar to the featureless black tar-pit where 'the Female' takes her victims, in the earlier horror film *Under the Skin* (2013).
2. According to an article in *The Atlantic* by Robinson Meyer, no ancient maps have been found with the actual words, "Here be Dragons" (or the equivalent) anywhere on them, though those words do appear on one globe, circa 1510. C.f. Robinson Meyer, "'No Old Maps Actually Say 'Here be Dragons'", *The Atlantic*, 12/12/13.
3. Andrew Tudor, "Why Horror? The Peculiar Pleasures of a Popular Genre", *Cultural Studies*, 11:3 (1997), 443–463.
4. David Punter and Glennis Byron, *The Gothic* (Malden, MA: Wiley-Blackwell Publishing, 2004), p. 7.
5. On this subject, I've wondered if gimmicks of recent decades – like IMAX and the return of 3-D – are Hollywood's way of bypassing the vision of writer and director, to jump-start that sense of astonishment in an audience too familiar with the basic grammar of cinema.
6. The 'found footage' genre alone is keeping alive the 'ruined building' trope – e.g., *Grave Encounters* (Canada, 2011) and *Gonjiam Haunted Asylum* (South Korea, 2018) where young urban explorers decide to record their forays into abandoned buildings – this most often being a very bad idea.
7. Edvard Munch's *The Scream* (1893) may be the most famous expressionist work of art (and also provided the model for the killer's stylized mask in *Scream* [1996] and its sequels).
8. Stoker's widow Florence sued the production company, Prana, which went out of business, having produced a single (but crucial) movie. She also tried to have all copies of *Nosferatu* destroyed, but luckily failed.
9. This kind of chiaroscuro lighting influenced the development, some years later, of *film noir*, where shadowy landscapes mirror the protagonists' moral quandaries.
10. This technique – of building up tension to a jolt that turns out to be harmless – came to be known, at the time, as "the Lewton 'bus'" (after producer Val Lewton.) The Central Park sequence itself was included in Bravo's TV special on the "100 Scariest Moments" in horror-film history.
11. In the novel that inspired the movie, author Robert Bloch describes Norman, a forty-year-old, as having a plump face and thinning hair. In the film, Norman's played by the slim and appealingly boyish Anthony Perkins, who was twenty-eight at the time.
12. Andrew Tudor, *Monsters and Mad Scientists: A Cultural History of the Horror Movie* (Cambridge, MA: Basil Blackwell, 1989), p. 103. Tudor suggests that western horror films divide roughly into two periods: pre-1960s, with films he calls 'secure', and those that follow *Psycho*, which he gives the label 'paranoid.' In the realm of 'secure' horror, "the movies presume a world which is ultimately subject to successful human intervention … There is rarely any sense that the monster will survive and prosper long enough to overwhelm the movie's principal protagonists, let alone the whole of humanity, and our anticipatory involvement in both dramatic event and character always presumes secure narrative resolution." In paranoid horror, "both the nature and course of the threat are out of human control … Threats emerge without warning from the disordered psyche or from disease, possessing us and destroying our very humanity. Lacking control of our inner selves, we have no means of resisting, and there is a certain inevitability to humanity's final defeat."

**88** Fearful landscapes

13 In addition to the Central Park sequence, *Cat People* also features an eerie scene in a hotel swimming pool, and another – late at night – in an architect's office, where one character has to brandish a T-square (in lieu of a cross) to protect himself.
14 Francois Truffaut, *Hitchcock* (New York: Simon and Schuster, 1984), p. 73.
15 Truffaut, op. cit,p. 73.
16 Ringu, like the original *Poltergeist*, has a 'false' ending, followed by a final return of the danger. In *Ringu*, it seems our protagonists have escaped the curse of the videotape, when they find the murdered woman's bones. But afterward, back in his own apartment, Ryugi's killed when his TV comes on, and the ghostly murder victim appears on the screen, crawling out of the haunted well. In a truly frightening moment, she slithers out of the television, and Ryugi dies of fright. Reiko figures out the one thing she's done, that Ryugi didn't: she made a copy of the original videotape (the copy that doomed the skeptical Ryugi, when he watched it). Realizing that's the only way to escape the curse – by passing it on, like a virus – Reiko has to protect her son (who, we recall, has seen the tape, and is only a day away from death) by making another copy. As the movie ends, she's driving off to show her father the video. Presumably he can protect himself, by making a copy and sharing it – but it's an unsettling ending, with its suggestion of a necessary and endless contagion.

# 9
# HUMOR IN HORROR

Late at night, two railway clerks deliver a shipment to a wax museum – "McDougal's House of Horrors". It's a creepy place that gets creepier when a thunderstorm causes a blackout. But the men have a job to do, and open up one of the crates they've brought – revealing a coffin and a display card: "Dracula's Legend – Count Dracula sleeps in his coffin but rises every night at sunset…" The timid Wilbur's upset, but down-to-earth Chick only scoffs.

> CHICK
> I wonder if Mr. McDougal expects people to think that
> Dracula's really in there.
> [*He starts to open the coffin, but Wilbur stops him.*]
> WILBUR
> No, don't. Please don't.
> CHICK
> Oh, now come, come, come. Dracula was just a legendary
> character. He never existed.
> WILBUR
> No?
> CHICK
> Certainly not. Fold up this canvas. I'm going out and
> get the other crate.

Chick exits and Wilbur's left alone, with the coffin and just one candle – in the light of which he reads from the "Dracula's Legend" placard again – as the coffin behind him starts to open (*from the inside!*) – revealing the laid-out Dracula in his customary black cape. Seeing the coast isn't clear, the vampire lets the lid drop back – with an eerie 'creak!' that gives Wilbur the willies. He stands, fighting down his panic, and yells.

WILBUR

Chick? CHICK!
*[Chick re-enters, lit by a flash of lightning.]*
CHICK

What's the matter now?
WILBUR

You know that person you said that there's no such person?
CHICK

Yes?
*[Wilbur points at the coffin.]*
WILBUR

I think he's in there, in person.

Chick dismisses his fears and leaves. But Wilbur, despite himself, goes back to the placard.

WILBUR

*[reading]* "Dracula can change himself at will into a vampire bat, flying about the countryside ... "
*[The coffin lid starts to rise again – and this time a hand creeps over the edge, unseen at first by Wilbur.]*
WILBUR (cont'd)

Flying ... *[Imagining what that would be like, Wilbur flaps his arms.]* Woooo ... *[He circles about – until he sees the hand coming out of the coffin – and his 'Wooo" modulates into:]* Chick! CHICK!
*[As the lid drops back down, Chick enters again, impatient.]*
CHICK

Listen, you're making enough noise to wake up the dead!
WILBUR

I don't have to wake him up. He's up. I saw a hand ...

*Abbott and Costello Meet Frankenstein* (1948), a huge hit for the two comedians, effectively signaled the end of the reign of Gothic 'monsters at the movies', which had begun with Universal's original *Dracula* (1931.) Creatures that had seemed terrifying – less than twenty years earlier – were now becoming figures of fun.[1] And those tropes that had been so unnerving – like the dreaded figure stealthily emerging from his coffin – were now such a part of the cultural landscape, that turning them upside down could provide an easily recognized comic jolt (see Figure 9.1).

Decades later, we see the same process at work in movies like *Scream* (1996) and *Scary Movie* (2002) and their sequels – 'meta' fictions that mine the humor in genre

**FIGURE 9.1** Baggage clerk Wilbur Grey (Lou Costello) doesn't notice that Dracula's about to rise, in *Abbott and Costello Meet Frankenstein*.

conventions of *their* day. What unites all these films is the recognition that *humor and horror are closely related: both involve subversions of what we expected to hear or see*. In horror, that subversion produces a shiver or a yelp of surprise; in humor, of course, the result is a laugh. But *both share a common structure – that of a set-up and a pay-off*.

In the Abbott and Costello scene, two workers deliver a shipment to a spooky wax museum. 'Dracula' is in one crate; 'Frankenstein' in the other. In a horror film where this scene was played straight, the workers would *expect* that they were delivering wax figurines; and *the pay-off to this set-up* would show us the 'statues' coming to unexpected and dangerous life.

But by 1948, this kind of reversal's no longer surprising. We *know* that has to be Dracula himself – and we're waiting to see him emerge. So the film-makers play a trick on us; Dracula *tries* to exit his coffin, but keeps getting interrupted. Now the surprise is not the reveal itself – but the monster's frustration at not being able to make the grand entrance he'd planned. And that frustration is funny, in a way that mirrors the constant set-ups and pay-offs in the dialogue:

- "You're making enough noise to wake the dead!"
- "I don't have to wake him up. He's up … "

This kind of *comic break in narrative rhythm* can work as well in dramatic films. There's a classic example in *Jaws* – right before the 'Indianapolis' speech (c.f.

Chapter 7, pp. 74 ff.) – when the three shark hunters are waiting impatiently for their prey. The ship's captain Quint has ordered Sheriff Brody to the back of the vessel – to ladle bloody fish-parts into the water, as a lure. And to the shark expert Hooper, who's acting as pilot, Quint gives the order: "Slow ahead."

>BRODY
>[dipping into the smelly bucket of chum] 'Slow ahead.' I can go slow ahead. Come on down and chum some of this shit. [As he mutters, disgruntled, his back to the water, the shark unexpectedly breaks the surface, its head rising part-way out of the water, right beyond the stern. It's enormous. Brody, turning, sees it just before it sinks back into the deep. Stunned, he slowly backs into the cabin, where Quint is checking out some gear.]
>BRODY (cont'd)
>You're going to need a bigger boat.

It's a sequence with a one-two punch: first, as we're laughing at Brody's discomfort, the shark makes a terrifying appearance. *Maybe* we laugh again, out of shock – but mostly what we're feeling is fear – when Brody changes the mood *again* with his line: "You're going to need a bigger boat." It's classic understatement – and we laugh again, this time in relief, at the comic easing of tension.[2] Then, as we've seen – while we're catching our breath, the movie shakes us again with Captain Quint's horrendous war memories.

*Because* comedy and horror are linked (in their use of the unexpected, and their reliance on extremes of behavior), the horror story is often in danger of slipping into laughter. Sometimes this 'slip' is deliberate; long before *Young Frankenstein* (1974) stage parodies of Shelley's novel cropped up – with titles like *Frank-in-Steam* and *Frankenstitch*, "in which the mad scientist, appropriately enough, is a tailor".[3]

In the famous French theater of the macabre, the Grand Guignol (1897–1962), actors were well aware of the razor-thin line between a scream and a laugh. One of their leading ladies, Paula Maxa

> described the atmosphere of a performance as being "tense, nerves all on edge, the slightest thing could spark off laughter" … She also says: "Just a word or a phrase delivered a little too quickly, a little too harshly, could cause laughter. It required millimeter precision … If the atmosphere was broken it had to be recaptured, which was at times very difficult and often impossible."[4]

One programming trick that helped was 'la douche ecossaise' – a 'hot and cold shower' of one-act plays that made up a night at the Grand Guignol, alternating gruesome horror pieces with broad sex comedies:

The horror plays were all the more successful for the comic relief provided by the comedies (and vice versa.) The contrast between the styles exaggerated both the horror and the comedy and an evening was structured so that the increase and subsequent release of suspense was repeated, climaxing in the main horror at the end of the evening … *It is a technique of tension and release that has been put to good effect by a range of horror writers and film-makers.* [My emphasis.][5]

*An American Werewolf in London* follows this pattern, and startled viewers (in 1981) with its sudden shifts from comedy into gory horror and back again. It follows two college students hitch-hiking across the Scottish highlands. Attacked, on a full-moon night, by a werewolf, Jack is killed and David – badly mauled – is taken to London, to recover.

Having breakfast one day in his hospital bed, David looks up – and sees Jack standing there, his face and throat horrifically mangled, jacket soaked in blood.

> JACK
> Can I have a piece of toast?
> [David stares at his dead friend, stunned.]
> DAVID
> Get the fuck out of here, Jack.
> JACK
> Thanks a lot.
> DAVID
> No. I can't take this … [Jack ambles over to David's bedside.] Am I asleep, awake or what?
> JACK
> I realize I don't look so hot, David, but I thought you'd be glad to see me. [Casually, he takes a piece of David's toast. David can't speak.] David, you're hurting my feelings.
> [He sits on the edge of the bed.]
> DAVID
> 'Hurting your feelings?' Has it occurred to you that it might be unsettling to see you rise from the grave to visit me?

Jack describes his own funeral – he's surprised at how many people showed up – and mentions one in particular, the girl he had a crush on, Debbie Klein.

> JACK
> So – so you know what she does? She's so grief-stricken, she runs to find solace in Mark Levine's bed.
> DAVID
> Mark? *Levine*?

*[Jack nods.]*

                        JACK
That asshole. Life mocks me even in death.
                        DAVID
I'm going completely crazy.
                        JACK
Now I'm really sorry to be upsetting you ... but I have to warn you.
                        DAVID
Warn me?
                        JACK
You were attacked by a werewolf.
                        DAVID
I'm not listening to this.
                        JACK
On the moors, we were attacked by a lycanthrope, a werewolf. I was murdered, an unnatural death, and now I wander the earth in limbo until the werewolf's curse is lifted.
                        DAVID
Shut up.
                        JACK
The wolf's bloodline must be severed. The last remaining werewolf must be destroyed. It's you, David. Please believe me. You'll kill people.
*[David jams the call-button.]*
                        DAVID
Nurse!
                        JACK
The supernatural, the power of darkness? It's all true. The undead surround me. Have you ever talked to a corpse? It's boring! I'm lonely. Take your life, David. Kill yourself – before you kill others. *[David whimpers.]* Please don't cry. *[Down the hallway, a nurse is running.]* Beware the moon, David.
*[Nurse runs into the room – and finds David alone, in tears.]*

Jack's *visual* appearance in this scene is a shock; his wounds are sickening. But his *tone* – self-deprecating, profane – and his *actions* (like helping himself to David's breakfast) – are familiar and funny. And that clash – of the dreadful and the mundane – keeps the viewer off-balance. In effect, these ghostly/ghastly visits provide both release *and* tension: we laugh, at the offhand grotesquerie – but Jack's warning (that much worse is to come) makes us fearful of what will happen next.

*One problem with rhythmic variation is that the regular shifting of moods can itself become repetitious*; it's the biggest problem with *Paranormal Activity* (2007), the very successful micro-budgeted haunted-house movie,[6] which alternates daytime scenes (where nothing much happens), with static camera night-vision scenes of the movie's protagonists sleeping (or trying to), while the Paranormal does its increasingly ominous thing around them. As you watch the movie, you realize there will be no scares in the daytime; and you're *prepared* to be startled, every time the night-vision sequences start.

*An American Werewolf* suffers this kind of diminishing return, with its shocks. Jack reappears, twice more, the rot of his body accelerating – but *what he wants* remains the same: for David to kill himself, so Jack can move on from the limbo in which he's trapped. And David himself is caught in the Werewolf Problem (that once he's a werewolf, he's doomed – c.f. Chapter 5, p. 49); so the movie's left with nowhere to go, in terms of dramatic development. There are still some funny sequences – including the morning when David wakes up, stark naked, in the London Zoo, after a full moon's brought about his first bloody night as a werewolf. And there are the make-up wonders of special-effects artist Rick Baker, who won an Oscar in 1981, for David's painful (and painstaking) transformation into a monster. Overall, though, the movie feels hollow – its comic/horror *style* can't cover a story that's thin on substance.

An example: that Jack's dead and rotting is treated as a sight gag, one that becomes a *running* gag, as Jack makes return appearances. He jokes about the problems of being dead – "Have you ever talked to a corpse? They're boring!" – and says he's lonely. But we never get a sense of what it might *feel* like, to have 'passed over' and yet remain (in some awful way) still conscious.

Oddly enough, we *do* get that sense, from a very unlikely contender: the 1985 comic-horror film, *The Return of the Living Dead*. With a plot involving what happens when you cremate a zombie body (the ashes mix with rain, and re-animate corpses in a graveyard), the film moves toward its climax as new zombies besiege a mortuary, hoping to eat the brains of the few living humans remaining inside. Coroner Ernie manages to tie down one of the fragmented zombies (she's only a rotted torso, and is referred to in the credits as "½ Lady Corpse"); he wants to know what motivates the undead, and starts to grill her.

ERNIE
*[to the half-corpse tied down on a table]* You can hear me?
CORPSE
*[hissing]* Yes …
ERNIE
Why do you eat people?
CORPSE
Not people, brains.
ERNIE
Brains only?

                    CORPSE
Yes.
                    ERNIE
Why?
                    CORPSE
[moaning] The pain...
                    ERNIE
What about the pain?
                    CORPSE
The pain of being dead.
                    ERNIE
[realizing] It hurts to be dead ...
                    CORPSE
I can feel myself rot.
                    ERNIE
Eating brains, how does that make you feel?
                    CORPSE
It makes the pain ... go away.

It's a moment of pathos that *shouldn't* work; until then, the zombies have only been the Other, the motiveless enemy. The visual itself is disturbing – an elderly woman's head, naked torso and part of her spine, which thumps like a tail on the table where she's been tied down but keeps on struggling[7] (see Figure 9.2). Given zombie-movie conventions (e.g., the undead can't talk), it's a surprise that the corpse can speak; *more* surprisingly, it's articulate. And what it has to reveal – "the pain of being dead" – is haunting. Prince Hamlet may have worried about "what dreams may come", if he kills himself; but he didn't pursue the thought to *this* horrible end: that one could stay conscious, feeling one's body rotting away.

Stuart Gordon, director and co-writer of the wildly over-the-top horror-comedy, *Re-Animator*, once said in an interview, "The thing I have found is that you'll never find an audience that wants to laugh more than a horror audience."[8] Echoing the Grand Guignol actress Paula Maxa, he talks about how horror-makers are always engaged in a balancing act:

> You don't want to be laughing at the expense of fright. It's best if you can alternate between the two, build up the tension and then release it with a laugh. It is a double degree of challenge. You're walking a tightrope, and if something becomes inadvertently funny, the whole thing is over.[9]

As we've seen, one way to side-step this trap is to play *into* horror-movie clichés – to make the genre's conventions a *deliberate* source of humor (c.f., the Gothic tropes sent up in James Whale's *The Bride of Frankenstein*). Screenwriter Kevin Williamson updated this old tradition with *Scream* (1996) – where a film-buff interrupts a house-party screening of *Halloween*, to explain 'the rules'.

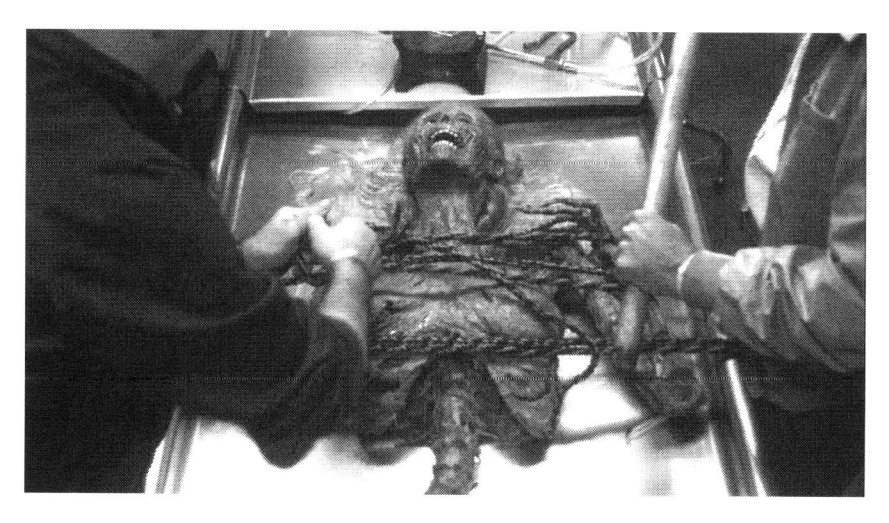

**FIGURE 9.2** The vocal half of a zombified woman (Cherry Davis) reveals the pain of being dead, in *The Return of the Living Dead*.

> RANDY
> There are certain rules that one must abide by in order to successfully survive a horror movie. For instance, Number One: You can never have sex. *[The party-goers jeer, but Randy insists.]* Big no-no! Big no-no... Sex equals death, ok? Number Two: You can never drink or do drugs. *[More cheers and jeers from the crowd, and clinking of bottles.]* No, the sin factor. It's the sin. It's an extension of Number One. And Number Three: Never, ever, ever, under any circumstances, say, "I'll be right back." 'Cause you won't be back.
> STU
> *[getting up]* I'm getting another beer. You want one?
> RANDY
> Yeah, sure.
> STU
> *[wildly exaggerating]* "I'll be right back!"
> *[The crowd roars.]*
> RANDY
> You see, you push the laws, and you end up dead, ok? I'll see you in the kitchen with a knife.

In a heavy-handed irony, the movie's characters end up breaking *all* the supposed 'rules' (or have broken them already); so the body-count swiftly rises, just as it does in the less 'meta' movies that *Scream* is ridiculing.[10]

*The Cabin in the Woods* takes this self-consciousness one step further. That film has a typical slasher plot: attractive teenagers off in the woods, being stalked one by one and 'creatively' killed (like the body-count movies mentioned earlier, Chapter 1, p. 05). Except that the slasher story is in effect a film-within-a-film: from the top of the movie, we're shown that the teens' vacation is being monitored – and even controlled – by workers in a gigantic lab. And the movie keeps cutting back and forth – from the teens exploring the rustic (but surprisingly spacious cabin), to the blasé workers betting on the outcome of the 'story', which requires certain archetypes: the Fool, the Whore, the Athlete, the Scholar and the Virgin. When the *actual* teenagers don't conform to these types, the lab-workers intervene, pumping aerosols into the cabin that make the protagonists dumber, or hornier – so they'll fulfill their 'roles' in what turns out to be a dark ritual. Four of the five *must* die; and the fifth – the "Virgin" – has to survive to the end (the film-makers' nod to the 'final girl' trope).

In an interview with *Total Film*, co-writer and producer Joss Whedon explained his intentions, in creating the film:

> It's basically a very loving hate letter. On some level it was completely a lark ... On another level it's a serious critique of what we love and what we don't about horror movies. I love being scared. I love that mixture of thrill, of horror, that objectification/identification thing of wanting definitely for the people to be alright but at the same time hoping they'll go somewhere dark and face something awful. The things that I don't like are kids acting like idiots, the devolution of the horror movie into torture porn and into a long series of sadistic comeuppances. Drew [Goddard, the director] and I both felt that the pendulum had swung a little too far in that direction.[11]

The problem is that in making his point, Whedon produces something too close to the very thing he's critiquing. He doesn't like 'kids acting like idiots' – but, in *Cabin*, the kids are *forced* to act like idiots – and are then punished. To make the blood-ritual work, a lab-worker explains to a fellow employee, it's not enough that the teenagers *die*; they have to *suffer* beforehand. And suffer they do, in the film's second half – which pretty much kills the 'meta' jokes.

In another interview, Whedon explains:

> I like to do two things, I like to entertain people and I like to have something to say. And with *Cabin*, you could talk about it like it's a lecture on horror movies but for me it's just an extraordinary amount of absurd fun. Without the absurd fun there's no point in listening to the lecture. Without the lecture the absurd fun can just become a string of events and not an actual film.[12]

In lecturing us, Whedon makes his points *at the expense of his characters*; we laugh *at* them, but not with them, and the 'feel' of the movie is cold. A good counter-example is *Shaun of the Dead* (2004), a British horror-comedy about a zombie apocalypse.[13] It's as knowing as *Cabin*, in recognizing and playing with standard genre tropes – but it cares about its characters, who constantly surprise us (and themselves) with their responses to a world that's collapsing around them.

At the start of the movie, the sad-sack Shaun is getting dumped by his girlfriend; she wants more of a 'night on the town', than hanging out at the shabby local pub. So of course the pub is the only safe place Shaun can think of, once the zombies swarm. Shaun may not be a 'go-getter' at work, but he's ready to fight for the people he loves – even his noxious step-dad. He rounds them up, in the film's second act; and in the third, Shaun's friends and family hunker down' for a bloody 'last stand' – in the midst of which the unthinkable happens: Shaun discovers his mum has been bitten, and though she hasn't changed yet, it's only a matter of time. "I didn't want to say anything...I thought you'd be upset," she explains, with classic mum self-effacement. Finally, she dies – and when she *does* change, Shaun has to shoot her.

In a film that's been comic until then, the shift in tone is wrenching. The comedy has set us up; and the pay-off is devastating. It's a perfect example of how to heighten the horror, by making us laugh at first. We drop our guard; and the moment we do, the Scary is ready to pounce again.

## Notes

1 One could make a case that this 'deconstructing' of horror began much earlier – perhaps with the 1927 silent film, *The Cat and the Canary* (based on a horror-comedy play, and set in a possibly-haunted house, where a family – under the terms of a rich uncle's will – has to spend the night.) James Whale, director of *Frankenstein* (1931), provided another candidate with his own sequel, *The Bride of Frankenstein* (1935) – from a screenplay credited to William Hurlbut (though the website IMDB lists nine other writers who worked on the script). In *The Bride*, the Creature learns how to talk and even get drunk – and in one amazing sequence smokes cigars and chats, in a crypt with the diabolical Dr. Pretorius, who ends the scene with a wonderfully disorienting toast: "To a new world of gods and monsters!" *Abbott and Costello Meet Frankenstein* was written by Robert Lees, Frederic Rinaldo and John Grant.
2 This sequence appears in a much abbreviated version – minus the set-up of Brody alone seeing the shark, and the pay-off of Brody's line about the bigger boat – in the 'Final Draft Screenplay' by Peter Benchley (author of the novel on which *Jaws* was based), available at ScriptCity.com. So I'm assuming this much-improved scene was the work of the screenplay's other writer, Carl Gottlieb (whose other credits include comedies like *The Jerk* and *Doctor Detroit*.)
3 Donald Glut, *The Frankenstein Legend* (Metuchen, NJ: Scarecrow Press, 1973), p. 33.
4 Richard J. Hand and Michael Wilson, *Grand Guignol: The French Theater of Horror* (Exeter, UK; University of Exeter, 2002), p. 37. The actress quoted here, Paula Maxa, was the subject of a 2018 bio-movie, *The Most Assassinated Woman in the World*.
5 Hand and Wilson, op. cit.
6 And its five sequels and prequels.
7 This scene is reminiscent of the moment in *Alien* (1979) – also written by Dan O'Bannon – when *part* of a hostile creature (in *Alien*'s case, the severed head of the psychotic robot Ash) is interrogated.
8 *Dark Visions*, ed. Stanley Wiater (New York; Avon, 1992), p. 84, quoted in Noel Carroll, "Humor and Horror", *The Journal of Aesthetics and Art Criticism*, 57:2 (1999), 145–160. Gordon's co-writers on *Re-Animator* were Dennis Paoli and William Norris.

9 Wiater, op. cit., p. 84.
10 The simplest definition of 'meta' is 'being self-reflexive' – the thing aware of itself (the film that signals its awareness that it's a film, for example).
11 Quoted in Steve Barton, "Joss Whedon on *The Cabin in the Woods* – 'A Loving Hate-Letter', dreadcentral.com, 2/16/12, https://www.dreadcentral.com/news/31045/joss-whedon-on-the-cabin-in-the-woods-a-loving-hate-letter (accessed 10/7/19).
12 Sam Ashburn, "Joss Whedon: Social Media Interview", https://www.gamesradar.com, 4/ 11/12 (accessed 1/14/20).
13 *Shaun of the Dead* was co-written by its director, Edgar Wright, and one of its co-stars, Simon Pegg – who also collaborated on two other genre comedies, *Hot Fuzz* (2007) and *The World's End* (2013).

# 10

## "BEYOND THIS POINT ARE MONSTERS" – DIGGING UP INSPIRATION

Long ago, standing in line to catch a screening of *Rosemary's Baby*, I saw a pregnant woman leaving the theater after the previous show; she was very unhappy and looked almost green – and I have to assume she somehow hadn't known what the movie would be about. Or maybe she did; but wasn't prepared for how effective the movie would be, in adapting a very scary best-selling novel to the screen.

Author Ira Levin wrote about his novel's genesis:

> Having observed that the most suspenseful part of a horror story is before, not after, the horror appears, I was struck one day by the thought (while not listening to a lecture) that a fetus could be an effective horror if the reader knew it was growing into something malignly different from the baby expected. Nine whole months of anticipation, with the horror inside the heroine![1]

Then he had to figure out what his fetus might be growing into. He rejected actual medical horrors, and narrowed the remaining choices down to two: "my unfortunate heroine had to be impregnated either by an extraterrestrial or the devil." John Wyndham's novel *The Midwich Cuckoos* had already tackled alien spawn, as had the excellent movie version, *Village of the Damned* (1960). So, Levin concluded, "I ... felt I was stuck with Satan. In whom I believed not at all. But I had no other intriguing ideas and a family to support. I read up on witchcraft and, late in 1965, set to work."[2]

Three things to note, in Levin's description of his working process:

- He thought of a resonant fear (and it's probably also worth noting that he was daydreaming – 'not listening to a lecture' – when this fearful thought began to take shape in his mind).

- He worked through several genre options, in deciding what kind of story to write, to best convey his Fear. He rejected the sci-fi option, here; but went for it, with two of his later books – *The Stepford Wives* (1972), and *The Boys from Brazil* (1976).
- He did his homework – he researched witchcraft (even though he himself was not a believer in the occult).

I don't know that I agree with him, that 'the most suspenseful part of a horror story is before, not after the horror appears'. I think suspense breaks down into different types: that of anticipation (starting to suspect that something's wrong), and that of knowing (there is something wrong, it's deadly and it's after you).

*Rosemary's Baby* – both novel and film – gives us both.[3]

Ira Levin suggests that his basic concept – 'a fetus could be an effective horror' – came to him out of the blue ("I was struck by the thought … "), one day while his mind was wandering. But my guess is that his mind – at least the unconscious part – was hard at work; he was writing for a living, and couldn't wait for inspiration to strike. The practical question then becomes: how do I jump-start inspiration?

The horror-movie writer has many resources to draw from, which we'll look at now.

## 'True-life' news stories

The murderer and grave-robber Ed Gein was tried, in 1957, and found "not guilty by reason of insanity." The heads of two women (and the butchered body of one of them) were found on his property – along with leggings made from human skin, four noses, bowls made from human skulls, a belt made of human nipples, a lampshade made from the skin of a human face, and a pair of lips on a window-shade drawstring.

Is it possible to imagine what could have made Gein do the things he did? Film-makers seem to think so – an internet search of 'Ed Gein movies' comes up with many titles: *In the Light of the Moon, Deranged, Ed Gein: The Butcher of Plainfield, Three on a Meathook, Ed and His Dead Mother.*

And of course, *Ed Gein: The Musical* (2010). I admit to having been curious about that one, until I saw the trailer (where Ed sings – to the tune of "All Shook Up" – to a stew-pot full of body parts). But for now, I want to look briefly at three better-known "Ed Gein movies" – *Psycho, The Texas Chainsaw Massacre* and *The Silence of the Lambs*.

*Texas Chainsaw*'s marketing claimed that the film was 'based on a true story'; and the movie begins with a narrative crawl that implies as much:

> The film which you are about to see is an account of the tragedy which befell a group of five youths… For them an idyllic summer afternoon drive became a nightmare. The events of that day were to lead to the discovery of one of the most bizarre crimes in the annals of American history, the Texas Chainsaw Massacre.

But according to actor Gunnar Hansen (the one with the human-skin mask and the chainsaw):

> [Director Tobe Hooper] had heard of Ed Gein, the man in Plainfield, Wisconsin, who was arrested in the late 1950s for killing his neighbor and on whom the movie *Psycho* was based. So when [Hooper and screenwriter Kim Henkel] set out to write this movie, they decided to have a family of killers *who had some of the characteristics of Gein*: the skin masks, the furniture made from bones, the possibility of cannibalism. But that's all. The story itself is entirely made up. So, sorry folks. There never was a massacre in Texas on which this was based. No chainsaw either.[4] [My emphasis]

What the Ed Gein story suggested was *a uniquely frightening 'sense of place'* (see Chapter 8), with hard-to-fathom cruelty lurking behind the sunny exterior of an all-American farmhouse.

In *The Silence of the Lambs*, the Ed Gein story gave novelist Thomas Harris a motive for the killer – who's sewing together a 'woman-suit', from the skin of women he's murdered. Apparently Gein attempted to make such a suit, to evoke his mother – a domineering religious fanatic whose death left Gein completely alone.[5]

*Psycho* goes one step further. The character based on Ed Gein, Norman Bates, doesn't just dress up like his mother; he becomes his mother, violently acting out her dread of (and fascination with) sex. But Norman's dual identity is a secret withheld from the audience. This enabled screenwriter Joseph Stefano to structure the film like a mystery – with the characters in the film's second half attempting to find the murderer, not knowing that he's been hiding in plain sight all along, in Norman's divided consciousness.

So – many creative reactions to one true and horrible story.

These 'Ed Gein' movies share at least the pretense of being 'realistic' – from *Texas Chainsaw*'s opening crawl to the intertitles across the skyline, in *Psycho*'s opening sequence – PHOENIX, ARIZONA; FRIDAY, DECEMBER THE ELEVENTH; and TWO FORTY-THREE P.M (as if what we're about to see is a documentary.)

*A Nightmare on Elm Street* seems far away from this surface realism. It's a story about teenagers being stalked in their dreams by a monster, his face scarred with burns, his hands encased in gloves that have knife-blades for fingers. And the scariest sequences all take place in dreamscapes where Freddy Kruger, the monster, chases down and kills his prey.

But this supernatural story was also inspired by real events. Of the origins of *Nightmare*, writer/director Wes Craven said,

> I'd read an article in the L.A. Times about a family who had escaped the Killing Fields in Cambodia and managed to get to the U.S. Things were fine, and then suddenly the young son was having very disturbing nightmares. He told his

parents he was afraid that if he slept, the thing chasing him would get him, so he tried to stay awake for days at a time. When he finally fell asleep, his parents thought this crisis was over. Then they heard screams in the middle of the night. By the time they got to him, he was dead. He died in the middle of a nightmare. Here was a youngster having a vision of a horror that everyone older was denying. That became the central line of *Nightmare on Elm Street*.[6]

Many horror films of the supernatural claim to be based on real events, including the highly successful *Conjuring* series (*The Conjuring 1* and *2*, *The Nun*, and *Annabelle* and her sequels), which began with tales of 'paranormal investigators' Ed and Lorraine Warren (who also show up in a separate movie, *A Haunting in Connecticut*). The truthfulness of these films is often questionable, at best; but it's interesting that 'based on a true story' is a selling point. It seems we want to believe these stories are true – as if, in our increasingly secular age, we welcomed – even if fearfully – the suggestion of a World Beyond.

One final example: *Verónica* (2017), a Spanish film loosely based on the 'Vallecas case' (named after the Madrid neighborhood where the incident took place). Police responded to an emergency call, involving a teenaged girl who was having seizures and hallucinations, after having played with a Ouija board. The subsequent police report described what they found as "a situation of mystery and rarity."[7]

In a Q&A at the Toronto International Film Festival, director Paco Plaza spoke of the freedom he felt, to use the true story for his own purpose:

> In Spain it's very popular, this story, because it is, as we say in the film, the only time a police officer has said he was witnessed something paranormal, and it's written in a report with an official police stamp and it's really impressive when you look at it… But I think *when we tell something, it becomes a story, even if it's in the news*. You only have to read the different newspapers to know how different reality is, depending on who's telling it. *So I knew we were going to betray the real events. I just wanted to make a whole vision.*[8] [My emphases]

'Betraying the event' is an extreme way of making what I think is a crucial point: if a true story sparks your imagination, you ought to feel completely free to change the story as much as you want – as long as your intention isn't to do a documentary.[9]

## Folk tales and urban legends

Folk tales deal with our darkest fears, often ones that go back to our childhood – like the nightmare of being abandoned by one's parents, in "Hansel and Gretel". As such, folk tales make perfect sense, as material for the horror film.

In 2013 alone, there were four movie adaptations of "Hansel & Gretel" – including a straightforward horror take ("Before Wes Craven … before John Carpenter … before Stephen King … there was … the Brothers Grimm"); a horror-comedy version in which Hansel and Gretel, now grown, have become professional witch-hunters; and *Hansel and Gretel Get Baked*, with Lara Flynn Boyle as the witch who's luring the unwary with her 'Black Forest' weed, instead of sweets.

Perhaps the most haunting version is the earlier South Korean *Hansel & Gretel* (2005). In that movie, a young executive wrecks his car on a lonely stretch of road, and wanders into a forest, ending up at a story-book-perfect house – which seems too good to be true, and is. Slowly he figures out that the children who live in the house (two girls and a boy) were terribly abused, long ago, when the house used to be an orphanage. Tormented beyond endurance, the boy found he had serious psychic powers (like *Carrie*, in the Stephen King novel and Brian De Palma movie). With those powers, he killed his abusers, and he's kept himself and his sisters young. He'd also trapped any hapless adults who wandered into his eerie domain – hoping to find parent stand-ins who will complete his 'happy family'. The movie in essence flips the basic plot of the classic fairy tale: the children, victims of trauma have become 'witches' in this story, and it's the adults – instead of the young – who suffer their wrath. Piecing together this story, the young executive has to grow up himself – to help the kids break the cycle of abused becoming abuser.

Urban legends tend to address more modern fears – like waking up in a bathtub of ice and discovering that organ thieves have removed your kidneys. Some version of this plot has appeared in both 'serious' films (like Stephen Frears' *Dirty Pretty Things*, 2002), and straight-out thrillers like *Turistas* (2006.)

An older urban legend – the chain-letter you have to copy X number of times, to avoid bad luck – has been revamped in the Japanese film *Ringu* (1998) and its American remake, *The Ring* (2002). In these movies, the item that has to be copied and passed along is a haunted videotape – and both versions feature one of the scariest moments in modern cinema: when the woman who cursed the videotape appears on the television screen, walking up to the camera ... and then starts to crawl out of the TV set and into the home of the horrified characters. It's a shock, because it challenges our belief that – no matter what happens on the screen – we're always safe, as viewers (see Chapter 8, pp. 86 ff., for more on this movie.)

One final example: 'Bloody Mary', the belief that one can summon a demon by staring into a mirror (most often in a dark bathroom, candle in hand), and saying the name 'Bloody Mary' three times. Why one would want to summon a demon is certainly a question worth asking. In previous eras, the presence evoked was more benign; 'she' would tell young girls who their husband would be. But the updated version – in films like *Urban Legends: Bloody Mary* (2005) or the Russian *Queen of Spades: The Dark Rite* (2015) – is hateful, and, when she's called up, begins a gruesome killing spree.

## Personal experience

We've already looked at how one film-maker, David Sandberg, used his own experience (with depression), to expand his prize-winning short, *Lights Out*, into a feature-length film (Chapter 2, pp. 23 ff.).

Stephen King's novel *The Shining* is another horror story with a strongly personal background. The setting came from a trip the writer made to Colorado:

> In late September of 1974, [his wife] Tabby and I spent a night at a grand old hotel in Estes Park, the Stanley. We were the only guests as it turned out; the following day they were going to close the place down for the winter. Wandering through its corridors, I thought that it seemed the perfect—maybe the archetypical—setting for a ghost story. That night I dreamed of my three-year-old son running through the corridors, looking back over his shoulder, eyes wide, screaming. He was being chased by a fire-hose. I woke up with a tremendous jerk, sweating all over, within an inch of falling out of bed. I got up, lit a cigarette, sat in the chair looking out the window at the Rockies, and by the time the cigarette was done, I had the bones of the book firmly set in my mind.[10]

The setting is part of the story; but there's another unhappier part. At the time he wrote *The Shining*, King was still a heavy drinker – very much like his protagonist in the haunted hotel, Jack Torrance. In his 'memoir of the craft' of writing, King is frank – at least in retrospect, about his problem. Maine had just passed a recycling law; so his empties, instead of being thrown into the trash, had to be collected.

> One Thursday night, I went out [to the recycling bin] to toss in a few dead soldiers and saw that this container, which had been empty on Monday night, was now almost full. And since I was the only one in the house who drank Miller Lite … Holy shit, I'm an alcoholic, I thought, and there was no dissenting opinion from inside my head – I was, after all, the guy who had written *The Shining* without even realizing (at least until that night) that I was writing about myself.[11]

King is on record as quite disliking the Kubrick film of *The Shining*; and one reason may be that the story he wrote was personal – "I was writing about myself."

Protagonist Jack's descent into madness is gradual, in the novel – whereas in the film, Jack seems to be a lost soul from the very beginning. King also gives 'his' character in the novel a moment of grace at the end – when Jack manages to warn his little boy Danny to escape. No moment of redemption like that in the movie – which reaches its climax as Jack (who's devolved into a murderous animal) chases his son through the snow that fills the hotel's topiary maze (see Figure 10.1).

Ari Aster, writer/director of the recent *Hereditary* (2018), has spoken of what inspired that film, which follows a family struggling with increasingly horrible tragedies. He's said, without going into detail, that his loved ones went through a bout of bad luck that left him wondering if there could be such a thing as a curse on a family:

**FIGURE 10.1** With murder in his heart, a haunted hotel caretaker (Jack Nicholson) pursues his young son in, *The Shining*.

The beautiful thing about the horror genre or just genre filmmaking in general is that you can take personal material and you can just sort of push it through the genre filter and out comes a work of relative invention, right? ... So I can say that the feelings that fueled the writing of the film were very personal and coming from personal experiences ... [But] none of the characters in the film are surrogates for anybody in my life. And ultimately the movie did take on a life of its own. So again, the beauty of the genre is that you can exercise demons without ultimately putting yourself on the slab. But, yeah, when I watch the film I do feel that the feelings behind it are close to home.[12]

## Literary forebears

A single novel, Bram Stoker's *Dracula* (1897), created the modern vampire, whose descendants appear in the *Twilight* movies and TV's *True Blood* series. *Frankenstein* (1818), in its story of 'the creator' and his relationship to his creation, is so resonant (much like the myth that gave the novel its subtitle: "The Modern Prometheus") that it can still power provocative films like *Ex Machina* (2014) – where the 'creation' is an artificial intelligence.

Henry James's *The Turn of the Screw* has been adapted multiple times – most notably in *The Innocents* (1961), with Deborah Kerr as the governess who fears the children in her charge have been targeted by malevolent ghosts. This story has also inspired other supernatural tales, with different plots but a similar feel – like Alejandro Amenábar's *The Others* (2001).

**FIGURE 10.2** Distraught mother Annie (Toni Collette) shows her husband and son (Gabriel Byrne and Alex Wolff) that there is a 'world beyond', in *Hereditary*.

Late Victorian and Edwardian tales of terror are a gold mine; one M.R. James story alone, "Casting the Runes" has inspired films as different as Jacque Tourneur's *Night of the Demon* (1957) and Sam Raimi's *Drag Me to Hell* (2009).

## Other movies

Whenever I teach Murnau's unauthorized *Dracula* adaptation, my students often realize they've seen Nosferatu's far-from-dashing, rat-like vampire before: as a sight-gag in an episode of *Spongebob Squarepants* (where he's off in a corner, being annoying by turning a light switch off and on).

We live in a visual culture, and can't help but be influenced by all the movies we've seen since childhood. And horror-movie creators often consciously turn to previous films, for examples from the past that can illuminate current story-telling problems.

Neil Marshall, writer/director of *The Descent*, cites four films that most influenced his movie. Number 1 was *Deliverance*: "It is the ultimate survivalist movie. People going out into nature and finding out what's good and bad about it."[13]

Another inspiration was Ridley Scott's *Alien*:

> I love "Alien" because of the creation of a totally real and atmospheric world that is totally believed. I wanted to create that kind of atmosphere in the caves in "The Descent". It obviously works, because nobody knows we shot in a studio ... It's all shot on soundstages. There [aren't] any caves in the whole film. "Alien" was just full of the creation of the world inside the space ship, this howling wind and dripping water and stuff. More organic sounds that you'd never expect to find in a technological environment [see Chapter 1, pp. 10 ff.]. That was a really interesting play on the concepts.[14]

A third influence was *The Texas Chainsaw Massacre*.

> Because of its ferocity. Although it's famous for not being as gory as everybody thinks it is, it still has a real ferocious nature to it, a primal kind of nature to it. And it's intense as well. Some scenes just kind of leave you shattered. And that's exactly what I'm trying to achieve with this. I want people to be traumatized and shell-shocked by this movie.[15]

And finally, there's *The Shining*:

> The slow build. That's something that ... *The Shining* did well. It doesn't go for the horror thing straight away. There's a long build of really, really intense suspense and fear, and then finally in the last third of the film it just goes berserk ... You've got the audience in the palm of your hand. You can sustain it for the rest of the film. And by the end you just leave them as quivering wrecks.[16]

(See Figure 10.3.) We've already mentioned director Fede Álvarez (Chapter 5, pp. 53 ff.), whose film *Don't Breathe* was influenced by *Psycho* – specifically, the 'shady morals' of Hitchcock's characters, that make it hard to predict the way the story will twist and turn. Another surprising influence is the 1960s' movie *Bande à part* ("A Band Apart"), an early film by one of the founders of the French "New Wave", Jean-Luc Godard. Álvarez says,

> The characters' dynamics for *Don't Breathe* come to a certain extent from the French film *A Band Apart*, the triangle of robbers, two guys and a girl, both of them love her. There was actually a dance scene for *Don't Breathe* at a diner, just like in *A Band Apart*, that we ended up taking out. It was pretty cute.[17]

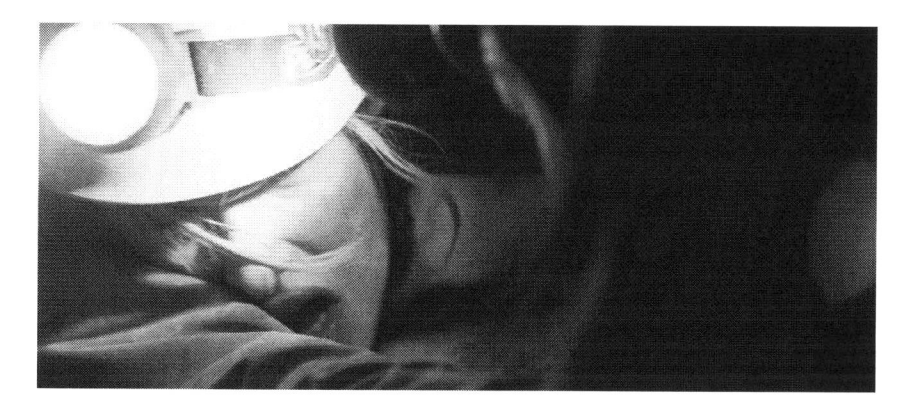

**FIGURE 10.3** Spelunker Sarah (Shauna Macdonald) in a tight spot, in *The Descent*.

In other words, it's not just horror movies that can inspire you. So a horror-movie writer should watch all kinds of films, in every genre.

John Krasinski thought often of *Jaws*, when directing his debut film, *A Quiet Place* (2018) – whose story involves an invasion of earth by aliens with super-sensitive hearing.

> I knew I wanted to give it more of a classic feel. There's something about Hitchcock and "Jaws" and "Alien" and other films that weren't so much about horror as they were suspense and psychological fear. That was really the wellspring of inspiration. I remember "Jaws" was one of the first movies Emily [Blunt – his wife and co-star] and I watched together. We'd already seen it separately but we watched it together during the first few weeks of us dating and I think by the end of those first weeks we wound up seeing it like eight times. What's weird about that is that while both of us don't like to be scared there's something cool about watching a movie you think is a scary movie but it's really something else entirely. The more you watch "Jaws" and the more you pay attention, it's one of the best-written films ever with one of the best setups ever for exploring people's plight. Really the movie's about three men dealing with their own fears and what they want to accomplish in their lives and the shark is this backdrop.[18]

What I hope is clear by now is this – that inspiration is everywhere: in the stories that make up your life, in what you read (online, or in newspapers, magazines, books), all the movies, TV shows and online content you watch, and in the stories you hear from friends (or 'friends of a friend' – FOAFs, in the lingo of urban mythology).

Keep a record of your thoughts/ideas/stories/snatches of dialogue. I'm old-fashioned, and find it helpful to carry around a small notebook. But use whatever works for you – your cellphone, tablet or any device that will let you remember that shiver you felt, when something made you think: "I wonder if … "

And I'll close with an example, from the *New York Times,* June 18, 2019:

> The horrifying news came in just as New York City was waking up on a routine Tuesday morning: a jogger in a Queens park had spotted a lifeless baby in the grass and called the police. Dozens of police officers quickly arrived to find a discolored infant on its stomach in Crocheron Park in Bayside … The authorities began releasing details – 3-month-old baby found, no heartbeat – and set up a crime scene as news crews arrived … But more than two hours after the police arrived, there was another news development: The dead baby was actually a doll.
> 
> It was not until 10:45a.m. – a full three hours after the emergency medical technicians first declared it a dead infant – that a team from the city's Medical Examiner's office made the doll determination … The doll wore a diaper and a T-shirt with the words, "Crawling Dead", suggesting that the whole thing might've been a ghoulish prank. While the city seemed to collectively exhale

in relief, another question arose: How could dozens of responders mistake a doll, one that looked like a prop out of the "Walking Dead" for a real baby.[19]

Good question: how could they? Collective hallucination? If it was that, did it just happen – or did something (or someone) cause the hallucination? If it was caused, what was the reason? Would the perpetrators try an even grander deception?

Or if it was just 'a ghoulish prank' – who was the prankster? What was their motive?

What else does this 'bizarre' story suggest to you?

## Notes

1 Ira Levin, "'Stuck with Satan': Ira Levin on the Origins of *Rosemary's Baby*", first appearing as the afterword to the 2003 New American Library edition of the novel *Rosemary's Baby*, and reprinted as 'liner notes' to the Criterion Collection DVD of the Roman Polanski film.
2 Levin, op. cit.
3 Of the film version, Levin wrote that it was "possibly the most faithful film adaptation ever made. It incorporates whole pages of the book's dialogue… It was not only director Roman Polanski's first Hollywood film but also the first one he made based on someone else's material; I'm not sure he realized he had the right to make changes. His understated directorial style perfectly complemented the style of the book, and the casting couldn't have been better." Levin, op. cit.
4 Eric Shorey, "Is 'The Texas Chainsaw Massacre' Based on a True Story?", oxygen.com, 9/6/18, https://www.oxygen.com/martinis-murder/texas-chainsaw-massacre-based-true-story-ed-gein (accessed 10/7/19).
5 In the film of the Harris novel, one disturbing scene shows the killer dressing up as a woman (complete with a woman's scalp and hair), dancing in front of a mirror with his penis tucked between his legs. The movie's been criticized for portraying transsexuals as psychopaths. And in fact, there's a scene in the book – which was deleted from the movie – in which a Johns Hopkins sex-reassignment surgeon makes the same objection to this kind of reductive labelling. (In the book, the FBI Director calms the surgeon down by explaining that the killer isn't in fact a transsexual – he only thinks he is: a 'clarification' that makes matters even murkier.)
6 Craig Marks and Rob Tannenbaum, "Freddy Lives: An Oral History of A Nightmare on Elm Street", 10/20/14, https://www.vulture.com/2014/10/nightmare-on-elm-street-oral-history.html (accessed 10/7/19).
7 Andrew Whalen, "Is 'Veronica', the New Netflix Horror Movie, a True Story?", *Newsweek*, 3/2/18.
8 Whalen, op.cit.
9 The documentary genre itself is subject to 'fictionalizing' – as in 'mockumentaries' like the pitch-black Belgian film *Man Bites Dog* (1992), which follows an increasingly desensitized film crew, as they record – and ultimately participate in – the crimes of a charismatic serial killer.
10 Stephen King, "The Shining: Inspiration", stephenking.com, https://www.stephenking.com/library/novel/shining_the_inspiration.html (accessed 10/7/19).
11 Stephen King, *On Writing* (New York City: Scribner, 2000), pp. 94–95.
12 Don Kaye, "'Hereditary': What Inspired the New Horror Classic", 6/8/18, https://www.denofgeek.com/us/movies/hereditary/274081/hereditary-what-inspired-the-new-horror-classic (accessed 10/7/19).

13 Ryan Peterson, "'The Descent' Director's Horror Homage," 8/4/06, https://www.pilotonline.com/entertainment/article_b220b485-d4ec-5622-b69b-4a84b3213814.html (accessed 10/7/19).
14 Peterson, op. cit.
15 Peterson, op. cit.
16 Peterson, op. cit.
17 Joe Gross, "3 Movies That Influenced Don't Breathe, and 2 That Did Not," *New Statesman*, 9/25/06, https://www.statesman.com/news/20160915/3-movies-that-influenced-dont-breathe-and-2-that-did-not (accessed 10/7/19).
18 Christopher Campbell, "Watch A Quiet Place, Then Watch These Movies," 4/27/18, https://filmschoolrejects.com/movies-to-watch-a-quiet-place (accessed 10/7/19). Director John Krasinski began with an original script by Bryan Woods and Scott Beck, which he revised enough to receive a co-writing credit.
19 Corey Kilgannon and Ashley Southall, "A Horrific Discovery in a Park Turns Bizarre: It Was a Doll, Not a Baby", *New York Times*, 6/18/19, https://www.nytimes.com/2019/06/18/nyregion/dead-baby-doll-park-queens.html (accessed 1/14/2020).

# 11
# POLITICS AND GLOBAL HORROR

In a basic sense, *all* horror movies are political. Normality is disrupted by the Monstrous – and that end-of-the-status-quo is either a *good* thing (the radical stance) or it's bad (the conservative view). Similarly, as a horror film ends, we either *return* to 'life as it was' – or we wind up in a 'new normal'. In *28 Days Later*, for instance, survivors of a zombie plague make their torturous way to 'safety' – a fortified mansion which has been broadcasting offers of refuge. The problem is that this new society – founded by army personnel – is as vicious, in its own way, as the zombie world it's fighting to keep at bay. The women in the survivor group are dragged off, to be raped by the soldiers (under orders of the commander, who plans to repopulate the world). And the women's male companion, protesting their treatment, is sentenced to die. But he escapes and wages a one-man 'war' on the mansion, freeing his friends and finally killing the psychopathic commander. In a coda, we learn that the three survivors have made their way to the countryside – where they signal to a passing plane that they're still alive, and need rescue.

The first two-thirds of this movie – the zombie part – are strong and effective: with zombies who no longer shamble, but run (an innovation, at the time) … and infection that happens so fast, one has no more than a second or two to dispatch a bitten comrade (or the comrade will start chowing down on *you*). The band of survivors faces adversity bravely; and we root for them. We're briefly relieved, when they get to what they think is civilization. But civilization has changed; the 'new world order' is a nightmarish one, where the horror itself has changed. So the threat is no longer a frightening Other; instead it's the very people we thought would save us. It's a wrenching shift in the movie, where the 'new normal' is worse than the chaos before it, which helped to create it. Frightening as it is, the 'rage virus' starts to fade into the background; as if it were just an echo of a more fundamental human flaw.

We see the same problem – a crisis bringing out the worst in people – in the movie that formulated the 'modern' zombie,[1] *Night of the Living Dead* (1968). The dead have started emerging from their graves to feast on the living;[2] and a group of strangers find themselves trapped in a farmhouse near a graveyard, where they try to barricade themselves against the ravenous horde outside. Tensions build among the survivors – with one white man, in particular, resenting the leadership skills of Ben, a young black man. Finally the growing zombie mass presses through the barricades; Ben retreats to the basement, the only one of the still-human group to survive.

Next morning a posse of neighboring locals moves through the fields surrounding the farmhouse, on a mission of 'search and destroy' – like American troops at that time, who'd adopted that strategy in Vietnam.[3] They're shooting anything that moves; seeing something stir in the farmhouse, one of the searchers aims and fires – killing Ben, the lone survivor, who'd just emerged from the basement. As Roger Luckhurst writes of this film, in *Zombies*: "Survival has been an epic struggle. It is cast away worthlessly."[4]

Director George Romero has said that considerations of race weren't a factor, in casting the role of Ben (played by Duane Jones); he simply chose the best actor. But racial antipathies *do* play a part, in Ben's struggles with Harry, the cranky white man. And after Ben's killed, the posse drags his body away with meat-hooks, finally throwing it on a bonfire. "This is done over the closing titles in still images, photographs explicitly used to echo the photos of murdered blacks that were often taken by lynch mobs and circulated as mementos."[5]

In *Night of the Living Dead*, there's no possibility of salvation. So it's not a surprise that in the sequel – *Dawn of the Dead* (1978) – society has collapsed, and people are running out of places to hide. *Dawn* tracks the futile efforts of a small group to re-purpose a sprawling shopping mall as a safe haven. Landing their stolen helicopter on the roof, they look down through skylights, watching a crowd of the undead wander aimlessly through their former haunts.

FRAN
What are they doing? Why did they come here?
STEPHEN
Some kind of instinct. Memory. What they used to do. This was an important place in their lives.

This is about as subtle as the film's social commentary gets. There are several 'comic' sequences – of the zombies getting tripped up by the mall's escalators, a Hare Krishna in saffron robes (a frequent sight in 1970s malls) who starts as a sight gag and bumbles his way to becoming a menace, the undead encountering mannequins (raising the question of which is scarier). And the humans – after they've sealed the mall and hunted and killed all the zombies inside – plunder the place which is now their home. Like the monsters who operate out of habit, the humans resort to conspicuous consumption with a vengeance; briefly, they enjoy "the good life" – but an oddly cobbled-together one, in the windowless interior 'back room' spaces of the mall. It's a pseudo-paradise that can't last; in the film's third act, a gang of bikers discovers the mall and blasts it open, letting the zombie horde outside come sweeping in, as the bikers go on a rampage – which Romero directs as slapstick, complete with goofy music and pies in the face (where the heck did those cream pies come from?). By this point, only Fran and Stephen are left – and they make a last-second escape, the helicopter taking them into a totally uncertain future.

*Juan of the Dead* (2011) – Cuba's first horror movie since Castro took power in 1959 – is another comic/political riff on the tropes of the undead genre. The writer/director, Alejandro Brugués, says he grew up loving American zombie films – "and it seemed natural to make one in a city [Havana] worn down by scarcity and resignation. 'I was walking through Havana one day and looked at the expressions on people's faces. Zombies. They didn't even need make-up.'"[6]

Brugués was also a fan of the British horror-comedy *Shaun of the Dead* (c.f. Chapter 9, p. 98), a movie that *Juan* makes a nod to, in its title, and often emulates – from its early scenes of people walking through life like zombies *before* they've been bitten, to Juan's relationship with Lazaro, a childish but devoted best friend.

*Juan* takes aim at the Cuban government, who first respond to the zombies by denouncing them as 'dissidents'. It also suggests that socialism (at least as practiced in Cuba) has hollowed out its people, leaving them passive and mostly hopeless. As the movie opens, Juan and Lazaro are on a home-made raft in the ocean, 'fishing' but catching nothing. This is not a problem, as Juan explains.

JUAN
This isn't about how many fish we catch, this is about having a good time.
LAZARO
Don't you just want to paddle to Miami sometimes?
JUAN
What for? There, I have to work. Here, I'm like the aborigines, waiting for fruit to fall out of the tree. This is paradise and nothing will change that. It's just a matter of sitting and waiting, something will come up. Besides – I am a survivor … Just give me a chance and I'll sort it out.[7] *[As if to demonstrate his point, he suddenly gets a pull on his line.]* Look – this is getting better …
*[But what appears, at the end of the line, is a body, floating face down.]*
LAZARO
Is he dead?

**116** Politics and global horror

> [*Juan gives Lazaro a look, then bends down to touch the corpse – which suddenly comes to life, raising its skeletal head, jaws opening wide. Startled, Lazaro reflexively shoots his harpoon gun, spearing the 'thing' in the head. It sinks back into the water.*]
>
> JUAN
>
> This stays between us, ok?

Juan *is* a survivor – so, as more zombies start to appear in Havana, he senses a golden opportunity to launch a private business. A socialist with the savvy of an entrepreneurial capitalist, he names his company "Juan of the Dead" – with the slogan, "We kill your loved ones". And he and a rag-tag band of friends begin killing zombies wholesale – in scenes of gory mayhem that are played for laughs, not scares. By movie's end, Juan's business is running out of living customers; so he helps his friends and family escape, in a car-turned-jet-propelled-boat. They beg him not to stay; but he seems to have finally found a calling, at last. And an animated closing sequence implies that his loved ones return, to re-enlist in "Juan Of The Dead Inc."

In an interview, director Brugués spoke about his intentions in making *Juan*:

> I thought I could do a film about zombies, and do a lot of social commentary, and show people how we are, how Cubans react to problems … First, they act as if it hasn't happened, and then they try to set up a business to make some money out of it, and then if things keep getting worse then they try to escape.[8]

Asked about the global appeal of *Juan*, Brugués responded,

> I'm pretty sure this will be a unique version of Cuba. But what I tried to do is make a funny zombie film, something that you can enjoy if you don't know or you don't care about Cuba. There is a Cuban social commentary in there but it doesn't get in the way of having a good time.[9]

Brugués hints at *a tension implicit in political horror movies – between 'social commentary' and 'having a good time.'* Finding a balance is tricky: too much 'message', and the film becomes preachy; bury the message too deep, and the audience misses what you're up to. I think *Juan* has the latter problem, failing to follow through on the implications of its satire. Its jokes and slapstick are funny,[10] but it's lacking in narrative energy; instead it feels like a somewhat aimless portrait of a slacker.

Guillermo del Toro faced this problem of balance – between the pleasures of genre, and the meaning of an historical event – in *The Devil's Backbone*, a ghost story set in the waning days of the Spanish Civil War (1936–1939). The film centers on a young boy, Carlos, who doesn't know that his father, an anti-fascist fighter, has died. He's brought by his tutor to stay at an orphanage/school, a remote location in the middle of a desert plain; the actual war is far away, but there's an ever-present reminder: an unexploded bomb, that fell on the courtyard, embedding itself in the ground.[11] In a prologue showing what seem to be disturbing random images – the bomb being dropped, an injured child, and a body sinking down into a well – an unidentified narrator sets the scene:

> NARRATOR
> What is a ghost? A tragedy condemned to repeat itself, over and over again? An instant of pain, perhaps. Something dead which still seems to be alive. An emotion suspended in time. Like a blurred photograph. Like an insect trapped in amber.

As the story unfolds, young Carlos discovers there *is* a ghost who's haunting the school – the spirit of one of the orphans, Santi, who disappeared the night the bomb fell. 'Santi' is pale and has spectral blood trailing off his body *upward* – as if he were moving through water, somehow. (It's a truly eerie effect.)

Carlos runs into the ghost one night, when the other boys have forced him to go fetch water from the cistern – a deep pool in the shadowy basement of the orphanage (the movie's "Bad Place"). He's frightened – but he also senses the ghost wants to tell him something. And because his curiosity is greater than his fear,[12] he makes it his mission to find out how Santi died, and why he's haunting the place.

The answer involves the adults, whose political sympathies are Republican (anti-fascist); they've been caring for the children of other Republicans called away to the war. And being human, they also find themselves caught up in a tangled triangle. Dr. Casares, benevolent head of the school, is in love with Carmen; Carmen, the widow of one of Casares' friends, is fond of the older man – but finds herself drawn to Jacinto, the brutal young handyman, who was himself once an orphan at the school.

It isn't clear what Jacinto believes in, politically – he hangs out with a couple of Nationalists, but apparently he's a deserter (from one side or the other); and Carmen and Dr. Casares have given him refuge in the school. They aren't aware that Jacinto's obsessed with something *else* they're hiding – a cache of gold bars they've agreed to safe-guard, belonging to the Republican cause.

Despite herself, Carmen gives herself to this man she knows is using her. One afternoon, after a sweaty bout of love-making, he tries to kiss her.

> CARMEN
> Don't kiss me.
> JACINTO
> Right – I forgot.
> CARMEN
> This is the last time.
> JACINTO
> "This is the last time." Same old story. *[He gets up and lights a cigarette, his back to Carmen.]* Scared the old man will hear?

**FIGURE 11.1** The ghost of a murdered child (Junio Valverde) in *The Devil's Backbone*.

CARMEN

I've never been scared. I'm ashamed.

JACINTO

Yeah. *[Unseen by her, he returns a key to her key-ring, and steals another.]* You're ashamed of me. Not him. He's a gentleman. What a pity that isn't enough. You need a hard cock as well. And your husband and the doctor? – tough luck.

*[Now he turns back to her, helping her strap back on her artificial leg.]* [13]

JACINTO (cont'd)

The old man looks at you with love. He did that even when your husband was alive. I was seventeen. By then, they took care of the poetry ... and I of the flesh.

*[They stare at each other – mutual enemies badly needing each other.]*

CARMEN

This leg – I don't like to think about this leg. It hurts. Some days I can't bear it. But I need it to stay on my feet.

*[His face is closer to hers, and the gaze between them is intense. Slowly they begin again to make love.]*

Foregrounding these relationships, del Toro keeps the Civil War – at first – a distant threat, with a single (but crucial) visual reminder: the unexploded bomb, only partly buried into the courtyard. Though experts have defused it, the orphans are sure it's still 'alive' – they think, if they press their ear against it, they can hear it ticking away.

The other shocking reminder of the war is the single scene that takes place away from the grounds of the orphanage. Dr. Casares has ridden into town for supplies; while there, he sees Carlos' tutor with several other captured Republicans. Almost casually, their fascist captors line them up by a wall and shoot them. Dr. Casares, horrified, races back to the orphanage, knowing that time is running out.

Now (in the film's third act), ghost story and love-triangle start to converge, with the hateful Jacinto central in both. Carlos has learned that Jacinto killed the boy Santi, after Santi spied him hunting for the Republicans' gold; Jacinto weighted down Santi's body and sank it in the cistern. It's Santi's spirit who's tried to warn Carlos that all of them are in danger: "Many of you will die," he moans. And this isn't a supernatural threat – it's a warning of what *does* happen.

(See Figure 11.1.) Dr. Casares and Carmen try to escape, with all the children in tow; but Jacinto, who feels abandoned by them, wrecks their truck – setting off explosions that fatally wound Casares and kill his beloved Carmen. At last Jacinto learns where the gold was hidden all along – inside Carmen's artificial leg. His 'comrades' have left him behind, afraid that his greed has made him crazy. But Jacinto thinks he's won – ignoring Carmen's final words to him: "Of all the orphans, you were always the saddest. The lost one. A prince without a kingdom. The only one who was really alone."

Meanwhile the orphans escape the room where Jacinto had locked them up, and enact their revenge. Taunting him, they trick him into chasing them into the basement; and there, with home-made javelins, they stab him and finally push him into the water of the cistern. Weighted down by the gold, Jacinto sinks into the watery deep, where the ghost of Santi's waiting to embrace him.

As the film concludes, the orphans (helping each other, no adults needed) head out onto the road that will lead them to town, and the rest of their lives. Appearing in the foreground to watch them is Dr. Casares' spirit, speaking the words that began the movie – "What is a ghost?" – and ending with the recognition: "A ghost. That's what I am."

*The Devil's Backbone* in fact is doubly haunted: obviously, by the spirit of Santi, but also by the historical fact of Spain's fratricidal conflict. Originally, del Toro – who's Mexican – set his story in the midst of the Mexican Revolution. But later he decided that the tale he was telling was wider in scope; so he moved the action to Spain, where the story became a kind of parable. "The civil war, which was never completely healed in Spain, is a ghost; anything pending is a ghost." As the truth of Santi's murder is lost, until Carlos re-discovers it, so the Spanish Civil War – to del Toro – is such a traumatic event that the country hasn't yet completed the painful task of understanding it.[14]

My one reservation with the film has to do with its villain, Jacinto. He *does* seem lost, as Carmen observes, but we never learn what damaged him. And his cruelty doesn't seem specific to this particular time or place. So the film-as-parable doesn't quite work, if it's meant to examine the *causes* of the Spanish Civil War; Jacinto's 'evil' is too generic, and even melodramatic.

Ghosts of a very different sort materialize in Kiyoshi Kurosawa's *Pulse* (2001). Set in what feels like the late 1990s – the earlier days of the internet – the movie tells two parallel stories that only connect at the very end. In one, a group of florist co-workers discovers that a colleague has killed himself; as they try to figure out *why*, they find evidence linking the death to searches the colleague was making on the internet.

In the other story, a young technophobe decides to finally go online. When he does, he ends up at a website that asks: "Would you like to meet a ghost?" Puzzled at first, and then frightened – when his computer starts turning on by itself, to show him ominous images (e.g., a figure seated alone in a chair, a bag over its head, like a kidnap victim) – he seeks the help of another student who's more computer-savvy. "Can the Internet dial you up itself?", the technophobe Kawashima asks. The student he's appealed to, Harue, doesn't have the answer to that; but when she starts to investigate, she stumbles upon something stranger than an internet with a will of its own.

Websites in both of the stories seem to be warning about a "Forbidden Room" – a place with a door outlined by red tape (these rooms multiply, as the movie goes on) where one encounters ghosts (like the seated figure whose head is hooded). And the ghosts aren't openly hostile; they're just … there, like an infection that's slowly seeping into our world. The characters who meet up with them don't die; but they seem to be robbed of will, so drained that some of them end up as nothing more than body-shaped stains on walls. The city of Tokyo literally becomes an empty ghost-town.

After Harue has seen such a ghost, she talks to Kawashima about the feelings it's stirred up in her.

> HARUE
> I always wondered what it's like to die. From when I was really little … I was always alone.
> KAWASHIMA
> Any parents or family?
> HARUE
> Sure, but they're irrelevant.
> KAWASHIMA
> Right …
> HARUE
> … that after death, you live happily with everyone over there.

KAWASHIMA
Can we stop talking about this?
HARUE
But it may be true.
KAWASHIMA
Sure, but …
HARUE
Then in high school it dawned on me you might be all alone after death, too.
KAWASHIMA
There's no way to know. How could you?
HARUE
The idea was so terrifying, I couldn't bear it. That nothing changes with death, just right now, forever. Is that what becoming a ghost is about?
KAWASHIMA
You can't mess with that. It's really bad. What have ghosts got to do with us? Besides, we're alive.
[Harue turns on a bank of computer monitors.]
HARUE
Then who are they?
[All the monitors show one single person or another, alone in a room, in front of a desktop computer.]
HARUE (cont'd)
Are they really alive? How are they different from ghosts?

Kawashima claims that those people alone in their rooms are crazy, that's all. He won't admit that ghosts exist – "even if I see one" – and hopes that, one day, someone will invent a drug "to cure death". When Harue doesn't respond, he starts to backtrack – but she corrects him.

HARUE
No … It'll turn out just like you say. I'm sure.
KAWASHIMA
What?
HARUE
Ghosts won't kill people. Because that would just make more ghosts. Isn't that right? Instead, they'll try to make people immortal …
[She drifts away from Kawashima, into another room.]
HARUE (cont'd)
… by quietly … trapping them in their own loneliness.

*Pulse* isn't exactly a warning of the dangers of technology. It's more subtle than that – suggesting that the internet is simply a portal onto a world that's *always* co-existed with ours. Yoshizaki, another student Kawashima meets, details *his* theory: that 'the afterlife' is a finite space – and once it's full, ghosts *have* to go somewhere else ... like the world of the living. If the internet opened that door, it was inevitable that *something* would: "Once that realm [of ghosts] reached critical mass, any device would have sufficed."

> YOSHIZAKI
> But if this [has] really happened, there's no turning back. No matter how simple the device, once the system's complete, it'll function on its own – and become permanent. In other words, the passage is now open ... that's how it looks.

The film ends with two survivors having made it onto a ship that's sailing away from a crumbling Tokyo. The ship's captain tells Michi (the last one left, of the group of co-workers) that they're still receiving signals from South America; so that's where they're heading. Michi goes below, to share the news with her fellow refugee, Kawashima; but even as she sits with him, he fades into a shadow/stain on the wall.

Michi says, in a closing voice-over: "Now, alone with my last friend in the world, I have found happiness." Cut to a shot high above the ship, alone in an empty ocean.

It's a vision of the end of the world much bleaker than the zombie apocalypse in *28 Days Later*. In that movie, there was clear evidence that *some* part of the world was still functioning. In *Pulse*, on the other hand, no one knows if they'll find anyone alive, when they get to their final anchorage. This vision of death seeping into the world goes beyond any local politics; it's a global phenomenon, born of 'progress' and seemingly unstoppable.

Regarding his tale of the supernatural, *Under the Shadow* (2016), Iranian-born director and writer Babak Anvari commented on a headline he'd seen, on a government-sponsored Iranian news website: "Anti-Iranian film at American film festival."

"I guess I'm already in the public eye," Anvari said,

> and it hasn't even screened yet ... I don't think I'm offending anyone but you never know, the government are quite sensitive, they might take offense. But it doesn't concern me, what can you do? The thing that annoys me is that they haven't seen it.[15]

Anvari's producer Lucan Toh adds,

> At the end of the day this isn't intended to be a political piece, and we were not intending the film to be challenging the government, [but] I think an Iranian filmmaker making a film about Iran is always going to be taken politically.[16]

Politics and global horror 123

The movie is set in Tehran in 1988 – the final year of the eight-year struggle between Iran and Iraq. Rumors abound that Iraq is about to start shelling civilian areas. And in this uncertain climate, Shideh – a former medical student – goes back to the university, hoping that she can continue her studies. A hijab covering all but her face, she patiently waits for a college official to tell her her fate.

SHIDEH
Being a doctor and serving society has always been my main goal in life. I don't want my future destroyed because of one mistake.
OFFICIAL
So, you do admit it?
SHIDEH
Admit what?
OFFICIAL
What you've done?
SHIDEH
Well, I don't know the details of my case, but I guess the reason I can't return is because I was politically active. But sir, everyone was politically active during the Revolution. I was young, naive. I mean, I didn't even understand the difference between left and right. I was just passionate like everyone else that age. I was concerned about my country. I'm sure you understand. He stares at her, not responding. [*Out the window, a missile leaves a trail as it crosses the sky.*] If I ended up in one of those radical leftist groups, it was only because I didn't know any better.
[*Through the window, they can see – far off – the smoke of an explosion.*]
OFFICIAL
Every mistake has consequences. I let you in so you could hear this directly from my lips and stop wasting your time by coming here every day. Let me tell you this frankly. You cannot continue your studies. Based on your history, there is not even the slightest possibility that you can ever return to the University. I suggest you find a new goal in life.

With stark clarity, this opening scene sets out *what Shideh wants: to resume her studies and become a doctor.* And it's equally clear about *the obstacle she has to surmount* – her past involvement in politics, which has become a liability. Going home that day, she starts to fill a garbage bag with her textbooks ... until she comes to one that has an inscription: "To my daughter – congratulations on beginning medical school. I'm proud of you. Your loving mother." That one she saves, but locks it away in a drawer, out of sight.

Tensions in her household increase as she learns, the next day, that her husband Iraj has gotten his yearly draft notice. This time, as a doctor, he's being sent to a dangerous part of the country (see Figure 11.2). Worried about his wife and their five-year-old, Dorsa, he wants them to stay with his parents in the north, where it's safer. But Shideh refuses.

> SHIDEH
> I'm not going to be a burden to your parents.
> IRAJ
> You're not a burden.
> SHIDEH
> Last time we went there, your sisters kept saying, "Tehran gets bombed and we get the shrapnel."

Shideh keeps doing household chores – putting glasses away in a cabinet, straightening up Dorsa's room – as husband Iraj *tries to get what he wants*: for Shideh to do what *he* thinks is right, so he won't be so worried about them. The conflict between them builds, as her frustration leaks out that he gets to do the work he loves, and she doesn't.

> IRAJ
> I'm not going out of choice. I'd lose my right to practice.
> SHIDEH
> If you don't have the right to practice, it's a catastrophe. But if I don't, it's for the best.

**FIGURE 11.2** As Iraqi missiles explode in the background, an Iranian pre-med student (Narges Rashidi) learns she won't be allowed to continue her studies, in *Under the Shadow*.

IRAJ
Are you mad that I'm practicing?
SHIDEH
No, I'm not mad about that ... *[She calls out:]* Dorsa, how many times have I told you to put away your toys after playing?
*[She moves from Dorsa's room to the kitchen, where she finally takes a seat.]*
IRAJ
Is it my fault you can't finish your studies? Didn't you waste your time on politics at University?
SHIDEH
You sound exactly like them.

It's one of those marital arguments that starts with what seems like a reasonable request – "Please stay with my parents, where you'll be safer" – and quickly escalates; given the treatment Shideh's received at the hand of 'the authorities', we know how harsh it is to tell her husband: "You sound exactly like them." And he responds by questioning her motives – why is it *now* that she's decided she wants to go back to school?

SHIDEH
When the universities reopened after the Cultural Revolution, who was it that told me studying could wait, stay home and raise the child?
IRAJ
Do you have a problem looking after your child?
SHIDEH
Are you calling me a bad mother?
*[Before responding, Iraj shuts the kitchen door, so Dorsa can't hear.]*
IRAJ
No, I'm saying don't blame your shortcomings on me and our child. Tell me, why do you want to go back, all of a sudden?
SHIDEH
I didn't leave out of choice, the Cultural Revolution happened.
IRAJ
That was four, five years ago. The universities reopened after a year.
SHIDEH
So?
IRAJ
You only want to go back now because your mother died.

SHIDEH
Becoming a doctor has always been my dream!
IRAJ
No, Shideh, it's your mother's dream.
SHIDEH
Dead people can't dream.

Iraj doesn't get what he wants, but neither does Shideh; it's a stalemate. He has to depart for the front, and Shideh is left behind with their five-year-old, who's started to think she hears someone walking around the apartment at night. She's also wetting the bed again, and having nightmares. At breakfast, Shideh tries to find out what's going on.

DORSA
Mummy – now that dad is not here ... can I sleep next to you at night?
SHIDEH
Aren't you a big girl? Big girls don't wet the bed either. Why do you have trouble sleeping? Well? Tell me. What are you scared of?
*[Dorsa reluctantly tells her.]*
DORSA
Djinn ...
SHIDEH
Djinn aren't real.
DORSA
They are. We just can't see them.
SHIDEH
Who told you that?
DORSA
Mehdi.
SHIDEH
Who's Mehdi?
DORSA
Sogand and Ali's cousin. He gave me a ball of magical cat fur to protect myself from them. But I lost it.
SHIDEH
Djinn are just a fairytale made up to scare little children.
DORSA
Mehdi said djinn are real. They're evil and they want to hurt us ...
SHIDEH
Mehdi is talking nonsense.

For Shideh, whose dreams have been shut down by the government, the real world is scary enough. All the windows in her apartment are taped with a giant X, in case an explosion shatters the glass. And several air-raid warnings interrupt scenes – with the building's residents racing down to the basement, hoping for safety.

Shideh wants to make sure Dorsa's head isn't filled with 'nonsense' that will haunt her dreams. So she visits her landlady, Mrs. Ebrahimi – requesting that her nephew not tell Dorsa scary stories. Mrs. Ebrahimi is puzzled; she tells Shideh that Medhi is mute (and has been, since his parents were killed in the war).

> MRS. EBRAHIMI
> Has she said what stories?
> SHIDEH
> Djinn and stuff ...
> MRS. EBRAHIMI
> Oh, God, have mercy!
> SHIDEH
> Djinn are not real, Mrs. Ebrahimi.
> MRS. EBRAHIMI
> *[emphatic]* They are very real. It's even in the Quran.

This is how the supernatural starts to creep into this well-crafted movie: a lump of cat fur Shideh throws away, unaware of its meaning ... sounds of a presence in the apartment that only a five-year-old can hear ... stories another child tells – except that he *can't*, because he's mute ...

Then there's another missile attack – this one *much* closer to Shideh's home. Shideh tries to round up Dorsa, so they can rush down to the basement. But Dorsa runs back, to fetch her doll – and is knocked out, when a missile directly hits the building. Panic-stricken, Shideh revives her daughter – just as her upstairs neighbors run in, begging her to help their ailing father, who's collapsed. Shideh's torn, but the neighbors remind her of her medical training; they *need* her. So she follows them upstairs, and is stunned by what she sees – an unexploded bomb that's ruptured the ceiling and is jutting halfway into the damaged apartment. (It's a visual echo – conscious or not – of the courtyard bomb in *The Devil's Backbone*.) Shideh gives CPR to the father, but she's too late; the shock of the bomb has killed him.

Or was it something *other* than the bomb, that scared him to death? The next morning Pargol, the upstairs neighbor, brings Shideh flowers – to thank her for her help.

> PARGOL
> I'm also here to say goodbye.
> SHIDEH
> Goodbye?
> PARGOL
> I'm going back to Kurdistan for awhile.

> SHIDEH
> But it's so dangerous over there.
> PARGOL
> My father always wanted to be buried in his home-town. *[Dorsa appears by Shideh's side, and Pargol addresses her.]* Dorsa, my dear. Remember, yesterday, after the missile hit, you said you saw something, or someone? You said they were scary. You were crying.
> *[Shideh sends Dorsa back inside, then confronts her neighbor.]*
> SHIDEH
> Dorsa is a child. She imagines things when she's scared.
> PARGOL
> You probably think I'm going crazy ... but my father was fine yesterday, after the missile hit. He was talking to me. I swear. I left the room to get him a glass of water, and then I heard him scream. I ran back and saw ... he looked so terrified... His eyes were fixed on something behind me I couldn't see. Something terrifying ... Like ... *[Shideh looks at her with a kind of skeptical tolerance.]*
> SHIDEH
> I understand how hard it is to deal with the death of someone so close. You know I lost my mother six months ago. But it was the shock of the missile that gave your father a heart attack.

This sequence – from the missile attack, to Pargol sharing her fears of a frightening 'something' – concludes Act One of the script, and begins Act Two – as Shideh's confidence erodes, in 'rational' explanations of what seems to be going on in her home. Dorsa's beloved doll Kimia disappears, Shideh finds her contraband 'Jane Fonda workout tape' tangled up in the garbage[17] – and then one night, a sleepy Shideh wakes up just enough to find her husband, his back to her, lying next to her in bed.

> SHIDEH
> I missed you.
> IRAJ/DJINN
> I'm here for Dorsa. I always knew you were useless. *[Startled, Shideh goes on the alert.]*
> SHIDEH
> This can't be real.
> IRAJ/DJINN
> Why not?

Shideh pulls back the covers to see her husband – who suddenly changes into an unseen presence under the blankets. Terrified, she struggles with the 'presence', tumbles out of the bed – and we cut to her downstairs neighbors trying to calm her down, as they search the bedroom and fail to find an intruder.

In Act Two, the other residents – weary of life in a war-torn city – move out, one by one, leaving Shideh and Dorsa alone in an empty building that's feeling haunted. In one disturbing sequence, Shideh's watching over her sleeping child, when she sees a naked stranger passing the doorway of the room. Frantic, she searches for the intruder, who seems to have disappeared; then Dorsa reports that *she's* seen someone else, a nice lady who talked to her. Completely unnerved, Shideh grabs Dorsa up and runs out of the building, to find a safe place. But no place is safe, in war-torn Tehran; and Shideh is stopped by patrolling guards who arrest her for daring to show herself in public without her head covered. Supernatural fears collide with the real-life horrors of a repressive regime; Shideh is told that she ought to be grateful she's being let off with a warning, instead of the lashes she deserves.

Now Shideh knows that she *has* to leave; *what she wants has changed* – protecting her daughter is all that matters. But Dorsa refuses to go without her doll Kimia – so Shideh turns the apartment upside down, in a search that gets ever more desperate. The djinn's manifestations – subtle, at first – are becoming increasingly brazen. In the form of a woman we only ever see as a startling swirl of cloth,[18] the djinn tells Dorsa *she'd* take better care of the child than her worn-out mother does. Shideh finds the textbook her mother gave her upstairs, in the ruined apartment. She'd locked that book away in a drawer; wondering what's in the drawer *now*, she unlocks it and discovers the doll – with its head and limbs torn off. When Shideh tries to explain to Dorsa that this is a spirit's doing, Dorsa replies that her mother had told her things like djinns weren't real. Shideh has no answer to that – she can only promise to fix the doll, which she can because she's a doctor.

That night there's another air-raid, and Shideh decides that this will be the end – when they get the 'all clear', they'll leave the building and drive to her husband's parents. But the djinn has other plans – and, in the eerie, emptied-out building, Shideh fights the djinn a final time. At last she gets Dorsa into the car – and they drive away from the ruined Tehran. The final shots are of Shideh's textbook, fluttering in the breeze from the open hole in the neighbor's ceiling – and the gaping hole itself, a wound of war that may never heal.

I've spent this much time with *Under the Shadow* because it's a great example of the 'political' horror film – demonstrating *exactly* how "the personal is the political".[19] What's more of a threat to your understanding of how the world is supposed to work – a malevolent djinn, or a bomb that comes crashing into a neighbor's apartment? The movie suggests that, in some very frightening way, they could be the same - eruptions of the irrational, over which you have no control.

## Notes

1 The first horror movie to use the word 'zombie' was 1932's *White Zombie*, with Bela Lugosi skulking about as "Murder Legendre", a sugar-cane plantation owner in Haiti. Legendre's tapped into voodoo to build his workforce, animating dead bodies who end up being his will-less slaves ('zombies'). In the script for *Night of the Living Dead* – co-written with John A. Russo – director George Romero referred to his creatures as 'ghouls', not 'zombies'.
2 There's no real explanation for the cause of the zombie outbreak. Scientists on a TV show speculate that 'radiation from a NASA probe' could be the culprit. But beyond that, we – and the characters – are left in the dark.
3 A movie that more explicitly makes the connection – Vietnam/horror – is the 1974 *Deathdream*, in which an American family learns that their son has been killed in action. The mother, overwhelmed by grief, won't believe that her son is really dead – and seems to be vindicated, when Andy suddenly shows up at their door. But because this is yet another version of the ubiquitous "Monkey's Paw", Andy is in fact dead, and is starting to rot – a process he can only halt by killing people, injecting himself with their blood. At the film's finale, pursued by police, Andy forces his mother to take him to the local cemetery. There he tumbles into an open grave, pulling dirt on top of his rotting body and finally coming to rest. His heartbroken mother holds his hand; as police approach, she says, "Andy's home … Some boys never come home." It's a very powerful moment.
4 Roger Luckhurst, *Zombies: A Cultural History* (London: Reaktion Books Ltd., 2015), p. 145.
5 Luckhurst, op. cit., p. 145.
6 Rory Carroll, "Zombie Horror-Comedy Hopes to Bring Cuban Film Industry Back to Life", *The Guardian*, 4/20/11, https://www.theguardian.com/world/2011/apr/20/cuba-zombie-juan-dead-movie (accessed 10/7/19).
7 My transcription of this passage is based on the English subtitles to the film, and a slightly different version of the passage quoted in "All That's Ideology Melts into Flesh", Alan West-Duran, https://cubacounterpoints.com/archives/3205.html (accessed 1/17/20).
8 Sarah Dobbs, "Juan of the Dead Director Alejandro Brugués on Cuba's First Horror Movie," 2/5/12, https://www.scifinow.co.uk/interviews/juan-of-the-dead-director-alejandro-brugues-on-cubas-first-horror-movie (accessed 10/7/19).
9 Dobbs, op. cit.
10 One sour note in the comedy - a glut of homophobic 'jokes' from Juan and his friends. The writers may have intended them as an indictment of Juan's machismo; if so, that indictment goes nowhere, and the 'jokes' stand out as mean-spirited.
11 The unexploded bomb gives its title to *The Bomb*, an unproduced screenplay by Antonio Trashorras and David Munoz, which del Toro bought the rights to, after he'd made the decision to move his own story from Mexico to Spain. As Trashorras writes, of his subsequent collaboration with del Toro, "Many of the elements that are present in *The Devil's Backbone* were present in the story that David and I did, albeit in a somewhat different way: school, war, bomb, ghost, murder… That having been said, I remember that the adults were less important in our story… The elements of love, sex and secrets between adults were all Guillermo." C.f. Matt Zoller Seitz and Simon Abrams, *Guillermo del Toro's 'The Devil's Backbone'* (San Rafael, CA: Insight Editions, 2017), p. 149.
12 In an interview in *Gizmodo*, del Toro talks about his own encounter with a ghost: "[My uncle] and I made a deal, because he was one of the earliest influences for me we talked about the paranormal and the supernatural and all that. He said to me that if and when he died, he would come back and let me know if there's anything else. So it was a couple years after he had died. I was not thinking about it, I was doing my homework, the TV was on. And then I started hearing a voice, a human voice breathing and sighing really close to my ear. Really sad, long sighs filled with sorrow. *I didn't panic. Strangely enough, I started trying to logically figure out where the sound was coming from, and what it was.* As I moved around the

room, I noticed that the voice basically walked next to me. This happened for about five minutes. The last few seconds that I recognized the voice as my Uncle's. And then I ran out of the room. That was the first time." Meredith Woener, "Guillermo del Toro Describes His Real-Life Encounter with a Ghost," 1/25/13 (my emphasis), https://io9.gizmodo.com/guillermo-del-toro-describes-his-real-life-encounter-wi-5978987 (accessed 10/7/19).
13 I don't think it's ever explained, in the film, how she came to lose a leg. But a book about the film asserts that, "Santa Lucia's headmistress, Carmen, lost her husband and her leg to the war." Matt Zoller Seitz and Simon Abrams, op. cit.
14 Jacob Trussell, "Healing Through Trauma: Guillermo del Toro and Trauma", 8/3/18, https://filmschoolrejects.com/guillermo-del-toro-and-trauma (accessed 10/7/19).
15 Tom Grater, "Sundance 2016: Babak Anvari talks 'Under the Shadow'", 1/21/16, https://www.screendaily.com/features/sundance-2016-babak-anvari-talks-under-the-shadow/5099093.article (accessed 10/7/19).
16 Grater, op. cit.
17 At the time, it was illegal in Iran to own a VCR player, or tapes.
18 The djinn in *Under the Shadow* – tangible but invisible – resembles the ghost in the famous short story by M.R James, "Oh, Whistle, And I'll Come To You, My Lad". In that story a man inadvertently summons something that appears in his bedroom, using the sheets to take on a form, with "an intensely horrible face of crumpled linen." M.R. James, "Oh, Whistle, And I'll Come To You, My Lad," in M.R. James, *'Casting the Runes' and Other Ghost Stories* (Oxford: Oxford University Press, 1987).
19 'The personal is political' was a rallying cry of the student left in the 1960s.

# 12

## "OUR NAME IS LEGION" – VARIETIES OF HORROR

In choosing what to write about, it's also helpful to think what *kind* of horror most appeals to you. The horror genre has a head-spinning number of variations: slasher, psychological horror, ghost story, zombie apocalypse, horror-comedy, body horror, monster movie (vampire/werewolf/clown), supernatural tale, 'natal' horror (*Rosemary's Baby, Still/Born, It's Alive*), to name a few.

These subgenres *also* break down into ever-more specific types. In the 'found footage' genre, for instance, there's a subgroup involving abandoned buildings, often institutions, which a team of either (a) TV journalist 'ghost hunters', or (b) doomed curious teens, decides to investigate (always, of course, overnight). One could break this subgenre down even further, into what *type* of 'haunted' building the characters will be wandering through – former prisons are popular (*Death Row, The Task*) as are hotels (*Hell House LLC, The Innkeepers*). But the most-frequented haunted building is probably the asylum – which has been a locus for dread and unease from the earliest days of the cinema. Examples of this sub-subgenre include *Grave Encounters* (2011) and *Gonjiam: Haunted Asylum* (2018) – the former recording a cynical TV crew, the latter a group of teens involved in an internet ghost-hunting show.[1]

It would take another book (at least) to examine all the possible permutations of the horror film. So, for the sake of brevity, we'll narrow our focus down to three: the 'slasher', 'found footage' and 'psychological horror.'

For decades, 'slasher films' have been a popular (often disturbing) subgenre. It's a long way from the killer house-party in 1920's *The Bat*, to the self-conscious murders in *Scream* (1996) and its sequels; but the basic template's proved impressively durable. A group of people – sometimes strangers, sometimes friends – is being stalked by a killer; the killer's motive could be revenge, some twisted notion of justice (in the *Saw* films, for example) or random malevolence. The killings can happen in many locations, or one – as in Agatha Christie's 1939 novel *And Then*

*There Were None* (first filmed in 1945, and several times since then). In Christie's novel, a group of strangers are summoned to an island; when they get there, they're confronted with a recording (by their unseen 'host') which accuses them all of various crimes for which they were never punished. And then – as the horrified 'guests' discover they're trapped on the island with no escape - they start to be murdered, one by one.

(In the sub-subgenre of 'isolated location' slashers, it'll be hard to top the restricted environs of 2010's *Devil*, which traps its group of strangers in a malfunctioning elevator; each time the power goes out, somebody gets it, until the surprise reveal, at the end, of the 'killer' – who isn't human.)

The term 'slasher' starts to appear in the 1980s, referring to films with a stalker whose murders are shown in explicit, R-Rated detail. *Psycho* is often cited as a precursor, as is *Peeping Tom* – released the same year as *Psycho* (1960), and directed by Michael Powell (whose ballet film, *The Red Shoes*, is a very different kind of classic). Hitchcock's film was dismissed by many critics; but Powell's was *loathed*, and effectively ended the director's career. Its portrait of the photographer-as-voyeur *is* deeply unsettling; the killer uses a knife blade in his tripod, as his weapon – and films the horror his victims (all of them women) feel, as they realize they're about to die. We're put inside the killer's head, as we watch his crimes, from his point of view – and it's a horrific place to be.

Italian *gialli* [2] definitely had an influence on the slasher film. These highly stylized movies had titles to match, like *Bay of Blood (a.k.a. Twitch of the Death Nerve)*, *Blood and Black Lace* and – my favorite – *Your Vice is a Locked Room, and Only I Have the Key* (1972). A masked killer wearing black leather gloves became the genre's archetype; and central to almost all of them are spectacular 'set pieces' – incredibly elaborate (and most often gruesome murders), like the first death in Argento's *Suspiria*,[3] where a woman is strangled, then stabbed in the heart – in close-up - and finally hung, her body smashing through a sky-light, so broken glass can skewer a helpless bystander below.[4]

Other movies which have champions as 'the original slasher' include *The Texas Chainsaw Massacre* and *Black Christmas* (both 1974), and the original *Halloween* (1978.) I'd eliminate *Chainsaw*, if only because its killers don't stalk their victims. Which probably gives *Black Christmas* the win, with its story of a killer hiding in a sorority attic. John Carpenter was a fan of the film, and allegedly asked the *Christmas* director Bob Clark if he'd ever thought of doing a sequel.

> "I didn't come into the business to do just horror," [Clark] said in an interview in 2005. OK but if you were going to make one, Carpenter asked, what would you do? "I said it would be the next year and the guy would have actually been caught, escape from a mental institution, go back to the house and they would start all over again. And I would call it *Halloween*."[5]

*Friday the 13th* ushers in the 1980s (and starts a franchise); four years later, *A Nightmare On Elm Street* arrives. Both are big money-makers. *Friday* ends up having ten sequels; *Nightmare* has nine, one of them pitching *Nightmare*'s Freddy Kruger against *Friday*'s Jason. (Spoiler alert: it's a draw. For both franchises, the next film up is a reboot of the original.)

Given the number of sequels (and imitations, from *My Bloody Valentine* to *I Know What You Did Last Summer*), the slasher starts to run out of steam in the 1990s – only to get a new lease on life with *Scream* (1996) and *its* three sequels. On the list of "13 Top Grossing R-Rated Movies", published by Forbes Magazine, *Scream 2* was #13, and *Scream* was #10.[6]

Which raises the ultimate question: why are these slasher movies so popular? Or more to the point, perhaps – why do we want to watch the same movie (killer stalks people, kills them one by one, until only one is left) in seemingly infinite versions and variations, again and again?

I've wondered if it has something to do with one of life's most haunting mysteries: that unless we've received a doctor's bad news, or we're on death row without appeal, *we don't know when we're going to die*. From the moment that we finally become aware that we are in fact mortal, that question lurks in the back of our minds, floating up to the surface at times of danger or illness, and then – when the crisis is over – being hustled back into the shadows. (Though the 'bucket list' of our day is an oddly upbeat *memento mori* – "Better climb that mountain *now*, because ... ")

There's a corollary question: if you *could* know the date and the hour of your death – would you want to? In one of the eeriest moments of the silent '*Dr. Caligari*' film, the title trickster sets up at a fair, exhibiting his prize 'specimen' – a somnambulist named Cesare who's been in a sleep-like trance his entire life. Caligari tells the gawking crowd that Cesare can see the future. Recklessly, the young lover Alan calls out, "How long will I live?" And the corpse-like sleep-walker, opening wide his eyes, pronounces his sentence: "Till tomorrow!" Alan, stunned, tries to laugh the moment off; but that night, he wakes up in his bed – and we see on the wall beside him a murderer's shadow, knife upraised ...

The *Final Destination* films also play with this knowledge that 'we must die'. In the first film and its four sequels, a group of characters barely avoids a catastrophe (not getting on a plane that explodes, for example, killing all aboard). But then – as if Death had been cheated, and was claiming what was owed to it – the 'survivors' one by one start to die, in wildly elaborate 'accidents'. The 'slasher' in these films becomes Death itself – though director James Wong would argue the film is *not* a slasher flick:

> One thing we were all in agreement on from the start is that we didn't want to do a slasher movie. We didn't want a guy in a dark cloak or some kind of monster chasing after these kids. That's been done again and again. I became very excited when we decided to make the world at large, in the service of death, our antagonist. Everyday objects and occurrences then take on ominous proportions and it becomes less about whether or not our characters are going to die and more about how they will die and how they can delay their deaths.

The entertainment value is in the "ride" not in the outcome, and by placing the premise of the film on the inevitability of death, we play a certain philosophical note.[7]

*"How [my characters] will die, and how they can delay their deaths"* – this, I think, is at the often-punctured heart of the slasher film. The givens of these films are a group of people we *know* are going to die; we can also assume that *one* of these people will probably survive, in the end. This formula is so ironclad that it offers a kind of 'comfort of the familiar', narrative certainty. We can watch the dance-of-death play out at a certain emotional distance; because we already know the answer to the Big Question, for most of the characters: "When will I die?" *"In the next ninety minutes!"*

And we settle in for 'the ride'.

Film historians often cite the Italian movie *Cannibal Holocaust* (1980) as the pioneer in the horror genre that came to be known as 'found footage'. In *Holocaust*, the footage appears as a movie-within-the movie: a film crew in the Amazon jungle is tracking down a *previous* crew, which has seemingly vanished without a trace. And the second team discovers the footage shot by their predecessors, which 'documents' a cycle of violence started by the film-makers themselves (who 'staged' a massacre of the indigenous people, and raped one of the women); in revenge, the tribespeople capture the film-makers, torturing, raping and killing them all.

I put quotes around the word 'documents' – because the 'documentary' footage is, of course, faked, though it's certainly brutal enough (including the actual killing, on screen, of several animals). Audiences weren't accustomed to this mix of the real and the 'make-believe'; the film's deaths were so convincing that the director was charged with murder. (His cast had to make appearances on TV, to prove they were still alive.)

Critics have argued for and against the merit of *Cannibal Holocaust* – which some see as an indictment of the brutality of 'civilized' men, and others consider shock for the sake of shock. It wasn't the first of the 'cannibal' horror subgenre; that 'honor' goes to Umberto Lenzi's *Man from Deep River* (1972).[8] But *Cannibal Holocaust* did pioneer the use of faked 'real' footage, to amplify the impact of the atrocities on display; the audience couldn't dismiss the horror (and possibly didn't *want* to).

Shock cinema was too extreme to have much effect on the ever-evolving nature of the horror film.[9] So it's not until twelve years later that 'found footage' makes an appearance again, this time as ferocious black comedy in the Belgian *Man Bites Dog* (1992).

In that movie, a camera crew follows a chatty serial killer as he goes about his daily routine: offing people, disposing of bodies, and spending time with his loving family, who seem not to know what he's up to. It's never explained how the film-makers got the killer's permission to film him; nor are the film-makers' motives clear. The implication is that they *intend* to make a disturbing movie, and aren't bothered by their role as passive observers of the crimes they record. Eventually, they even join in, in a hard-to-watch home invasion. Finally, the killer's crimes catch up with him and he's arrested. He escapes – but he's angered a mobster, whose henchmen kill the killer and then – one-by-one – the compromised film-makers. And the movie ends (like many in this genre) with a camera, dropped on the ground, recording a fallen body that doesn't move.

*Man Bites Dog* is another film that's divided critics, who find it either a one-joke joke (and a sick one), or a thoughtful and provocative look at the exploitative nature of art. One critic, citing the three Belgian film students who made the movie,[10] wrote that they "ruthlessly expose the mendacity of the media and its persistent tendency to obliterate, then manipulate, 'truth' in order to make it conform respectively to the ideological and economic agendas of bias and sensationalism."[11]

Whether the film succeeds or not – my feeling is that it doesn't[12] – it's using the documentary form in a very different way from its *Cannibal Holocaust* predecessor. The violence is so extreme, the film-makers' attitude so blasé, that the disconnect is comic – at first. (It becomes increasingly less so as the story goes along.) Other horror films that use this 'mockumentary' approach[13] include *Behind the Mask: The Rise of Leslie Vernon* (about a young serial-killer-in-training), and New Zealand's vampire-family comedy, *What We Do in the Shadows*.

Found-footage horror is still a relative rarity until 1999 – when *The Blair Witch Project* looms into view. Shot in eight days, from an improvised script, it was made for $60,000 – and grossed $250 million. That opened the flood-gates – and dozens of found-footage projects have followed (including the even more successful *Paranormal Activity*). What people seem to have missed is the fact that *Blair Witch* is a pretty lousy film (annoying characters, mundane dialogue, repetitious plot); what was *genius* was its marketing campaign, which convinced the public (at least for a while) that the film was *real*. This marketing began a full year before the movie's release, with the launch of a website made up of fake interviews and phony police reports. Even creepier was the movie's Internet Movie Database page, which – at the time the movie opened – listed the actors involved as 'missing, presumed dead.'[14]

One of the actors, interviewed many years later, spoke of how weird it was, to meet people who thought she'd died: "Well, it doesn't happen much any more, but when Blair Witch first came out my Mum kept getting sympathy cards," she said. "It was all part of their marketing scheme so, yeah, people thought I was dead. When people found out I was alive a lot of them were kind of annoyed with me and wanted their money back."[15]

*Blair Witch* made its eerie appearance in the earlier days of the internet, when people were more inclined to believe in the truth of what they read online. Those days are gone; and the problem *now* may be that we don't believe *anything*. So deceptive marketing isn't going to sell found-footage any more. The question becomes: what else does the genre offer, besides 'reality'? To answer that, I'd like to look at two fascinating – and very different - movies.

*Noroi: The Curse* (2005) purports to be the taped evidence for a TV show, hosted by Masafumi Kobayashi – an author of books on the paranormal, who's disappeared after a fire that killed his wife and destroyed his home. The tapes we see become flashbacks to a case that Kobayashi is just starting to investigate (assisted throughout by his unseen cameraman Miyajima). These tapes have not been edited; and the case itself is very complex, going back decades and introducing characters (a hostile woman whose neighbors complain about the strange sounds – crying babies? – coming from the woman's apartment ... a psychic schoolgirl who demonstrates her abilities on a TV show, and then disappears ... a paranoid young man who's wrapped his entire apartment in tinfoil) whose connections to each other aren't apparent, at first – though they *will* be.[16]

Because we're watching an episode of a show that wasn't completed, we're left to piece the increasingly ominous puzzle together ourselves; and that challenge makes the viewer an active participant in the experience. It's unsettling *and* exciting, as we get a new piece of information, and realize a pattern is beginning to emerge. Of course, the order in which we learn more is controlled by the film's director and co-writer, Kōji Shiraishi; but he offers the viewer a more than usual level of involvement, in piecing together what's happening, and what it finally means.

Crucial to this approach is the way the film presents its protagonist, the investigator Kobayashi. His job seems to be his entire life; and we never see him except at work, interviewing an expert or tracking down a witness. He's *defined completely by what he does*; and it's only his tenaciousness that lets us understand how much he cares about what he's doing. In the end, the footage he's captured doesn't just solve a disturbing mystery – it becomes a kind of tribute to a man who's tried to help a few people escape from the 'curse' of the title.

*[REC]* is an altogether different kind of viewing experience. Though it starts deceptively quietly – with a TV film crew recording the night-time routine of a fire station - it quickly ratchets the tension up, as the firemen respond to an emergency at an apartment building. Neighbors have reported that an elderly woman's in trouble; she may have fallen down, and is raising a ruckus with her screaming. So TV reporter Angela rides with the firemen to the building – where police assist in breaking open the door to the apartment ... only to find that the elderly woman's gone berserk (or rabid?), and attacks her rescuers, biting one in the neck ...

And from there all hell breaks loose – as the frightened people (residents, first responders and TV crew) discover that the government's suddenly sealed the building, placing them all in quarantine. No one can get help for the injured; and the illness – whatever it is – that turned the old woman into a bloodthirsty beast, is starting to spread from one infected person to another.

Throughout the ordeal, Angela keeps her cameraman Pablo shooting – both terrified and excited that they've stumbled upon a *huge* story. *They have a reason for being there, which solves the plausibility problem common in found-footage*: i.e., why the characters keep on filming, when anyone else would run for their lives. In *[REC]*, there's no place to run to; but Pablo and Angela *could've* just given up. Instead, they do their best to make a record of what's happening – interviewing people during momentary lulls ... and then staying on top of the 'action', when conditions start (increasingly fast) to deteriorate.

The movie's beautifully paced – so there *are* brief moments of calm, even humor; but the overall movement is toward increasing chaos no one can escape from. The device of 'found footage' helps to build that sense of claustrophobia – because its visual field is restricted to what a single person (whoever's holding the camera) sees (see Figure 12.1). One can cheat a bit, zoom in and out – to simulate close-ups and long shots. But one has to give up many basic ways of creating visual rhythm (like tracking shots, fluid camera movement, lighting, cutting, and editing).

*[REC]* is so good, in part, because it makes such frightening use of what would otherwise be limitations. For example, in the film's finale, Angela and Pablo have been chased to the top of the building, where they find momentary shelter in the building's empty penthouse. The power's out – and the government has draped the building, blocking all light. So Pablo resorts to the night-vision mode on his camera, to investigate. The simple effect is eerie, and the tension continues to build, as a ceiling-panel abruptly drops down, opening up to the dark of an attic. Pablo gets on a chair and holds the camera up in the space, to see what's there; and we see Pablo's hand-held pan of the attic, showing nothing at all, until ... but that's the movie's final shock, which I'm not about to give away.

On lists of top-grossing horror films of all time, there are often several entries in the found-footage category.[17] I think their success goes beyond basic economics – i.e., that they're cheap to produce. Though the best of them are carefully crafted,

**FIGURE 12.1** TV reporter Angela (Manuela Velasco) and firefighter Manu (Ferran Terraza), trapped in a quarantined building in *[REC]*.

they're satisfying a hunger for *scares that seem, at the moment we're watching them, to be real* – 'documented' proof of a world beyond the one we live in.

In psychological horror, the monsters are human, or internal – or both. In the classic *Diabolique*, for example, there's a *very* human monster: the headmaster of a boarding school, who flaunts his contempt for his timid wife by carrying on an affair with one of her colleagues, another teacher. Wife and mistress have had enough of this lecherous bully and sadist, and concoct a plan to murder him – drowning him in a tub, then dumping his body in the school's swimming pool. The plan works, though it puts a great strain on the wife, who has a heart condition. Then wife and mistress anxiously wait for the body to be discovered. But it turns out there's a problem – the body has disappeared ...

*Diabolique* creates an unbalanced world of mistrust and suspicion, where *no* one is innocent. The wife gets rid of the man who's been tormenting her, for years; but her desperate action brings no relief, because of her remorse and guilt. Once the body disappears, her fragile mind begins to disintegrate. *Is* her husband walking the grounds of the school, a ghost or even something worse – a re-animated corpse?

When human beings are threatening, one can run away, fight back or hide; but when the threat is your own unstable mind, there's no escape. This premise has provided the scares in films going back to *Caligari*, and onward to movies like *Spellbound* (1945), *Gothika* (2003) and *Shutter Island* (2010). One of the most disturbing is the small independent film *They Look Like People* (2015), from writer/director Perry Blackshear. Wyatt, a disturbed young man (who seems to be schizophrenic) drifts into New York City, after a break-up with his fiancée. His old friend Christian takes him in, worried about him but not realizing just *how* troubled Wyatt is. Christian has his own problems, at work; he isn't, by nature, confident – and overcompensates by being cocky and aggressive. At last he's fired; meanwhile, Wyatt is now hearing voices and seeing terrible things (like the faces of people melting into the grimace of a demon). At the climax of the movie, Wyatt shares one of his visions with Christian. He'd tracked down Christian's boss, hoping to change her mind about firing him. But then he realized that *she* was becoming one of the demons, too.

```
                    WYATT
   Her face started twisting, and then her smile started
   spreading out, further than a smile's supposed to be,
   all the way past her ears. And then her head split in
   two, and there was this thing there. You know what I
   thought? That we're all alone.
```

Now Wyatt wonders if *Christian* is also becoming one of Them. To demonstrate that he isn't, Christian lets Wyatt tie him up; and the seconds count down to what Wyatt thinks will be some kind of Apocalypse. Christian's put his life on the line, for his friend; and we hold our breath, not knowing whether Wyatt's madness will overwhelm him. We're afraid *of* him, and *for* him – which makes the tension almost unbearable (see Figure 12.2).

**140** "Our name is legion" – varieties of horror

**FIGURE 12.2** A troubled young man (MacLeod Andrews, in the gas-mask) has to discover if his friend (Evan Dumouchel) is still human, in *They Look Like People*.

As we've seen, horror movies de-stabilize the familiar world, bringing us face to face with some of our darkest and oldest fears. They can also put us *directly* into the point of view of the unbalanced – so anything can happen, leaving us helpless to prepare ourselves. We depend on our minds, to save ourselves; when they turn on us – in films like Polanski's *Repulsion* or *They Look Like People* – we're lost.

## Notes

1 Though it's not 'found footage', one of the creepiest 'haunted asylum' movies is *Session 9* (2001), which was shot in the slated-to-be-demolished Danvers State Mental Hospital in Massachusetts.
2 'Giallo' ("yellow") gets its name from a series of cheap paperback crime thrillers (originally Italian translations of hard-boiled novels like James M. Cain's *The Postman Always Rings Twice*), distinguished by their bright yellow-background covers.
3 Though *Suspiria* (1977) is often called a *giallo*, it differs from most – which are basically murder mysteries – in its emphasis on the occult.
4 Violence against women in horror films is so large a subject that it's a focus of many books, including Carol Clover's *Men, Women and Chainsaws* and the anthology *The Dread of Difference: Gender and the Horror Film*, edited by Barry Keith Grant.
5 Jason Concepcion, "'Black Christmas' Was the First 'Halloween'", 10/3/18, https://www.theringer.com/movies/2018/10/3/17932802/black-christmas-horror-film-halloween-scream, (accessed 10/7/19).
6 Simon Thompson, "The 13 Highest Grossing R-Rated Horror Movies of All Time," 10/2/18, https://www.theringer.com/movies/2018/10/3/17932802/black-christmas-horror-film-halloween-scream (accessed 10/7/19).
7 "Final Destination": Press Book, http://www.angelfire.com/stars/chaddonella/flight180/press/book.html (accessed 10/7/19).
8 Lenzi's film itself was influenced by the "Mondo" movies of the 1960s – exploitation shockers pretending to document the disturbing rites and customs of 'primitive' cultures.
9 Though extremes of violence seem to cycle through genre history. Preceding the "Cannibal" films were the very low-budget 'splatter' films of Herschell Gordon Lewis, like *Blood Feast* (1963), which may have drawn inspiration from the explicit gore of the Grand Guignol Theater (gore that might have been more effective on stage than in the

Lewis flicks, where the poster-paint-red blood – though certainly copious – looks ridiculous.). In the 2000s, gore came roaring back with *Saw* (2004) and *Hostel* (2005) – movies that focused on bodily harm and came to be known as "torture porn".

10  Remy Belvaux, Andre Bonzel and Benoit Poelvoorde, the three students (who also appear on screen) co-wrote and co-directed film (with a writing assist from Vincent Tavier) over the course of two-and-a-half years, for $100,000. And the film, upon its release, became the most successful Belgian film of its day.

11  Shane McNeil, "Mocu(docu)mentary", in *Cinema Papers*, 95, October 1993.

12  In a review of the remake of Michael Haneke's home-invasion movie *Funny Games*, Christopher Orr writes, "*being morally perturbed is not the same thing as gaining moral knowledge, and the lessons Haneke claims to impart in Funny Games are ones that his viewers already know, or will never learn*" (Christopher Orr, "The Movie Review: 'Funny Games'", *The New Republic*, March 14, 2008, my emphasis). That describes very well the problem I have with *Man Bites Dog*, a film that – like both versions of *Funny Games* – supposedly addresses the way in which we, as viewers, are complicit in the violence we're watching. To those movies that taunt the audience by asking, "Why are you watching this?", I've always thought the most honest answer was, "Because you made it, and I assumed you wanted it to be seen."

13  Probably the best-known mockumentary is Rob Reiner's *This is Spinal Tap* (1984) – a very funny and even touching look at a fading heavy-metal band.

14  This was a version of the trick that got Ruggero Deodato, director of *Cannibal Holocaust*, in trouble: he'd paid his cast to go into hiding, avoiding publicity, for a year from the film's opening – to suggest that the actors had really died. As noted earlier, the trick worked too well, and Deodato was indicted for murder.

15  Rebecca Hawkes, "Why Did the World Think The Blair Witch Project Really Happened?", 7/25/16, https://www.telegraph.co.uk/films/2016/07/25/why-did-the-world-think-the-blair-witch-project-really-happened (accessed 10/7/19).

16  Noroi's screenplay is by director Kōji Shiraishi and Naoyuki Yokota, both of whom are uncredited, presumably to reinforce the sense that what we're watching is unedited 'real' footage.

17  Thompson, op. cit. There are three on Thompson's list, at positions 9, 7 and 4.

# 13

# "DEAD MAN'S CHEST" – THE ECONOMICS OF HORROR

Oren Peli, a videogame programmer, had recently moved to a new tract home, where he and his then-girlfriend were unsettled by 'things that went bump in the night': odd creaks and groans that – Peli knows now – were just the normal sounds of a new house settling on its foundation. "I never thought we had a ghost or we were dealing with a supernatural phenomenon," Peli said in an interview. "But that's what got me thinking – if you really want to know what's going on, you set up a video camera. Then I started thinking if you did have a camera running and you did see something move, that would be really creepy."[1]

Peli wanted to quit his day-job.

> I was working as a videogame programmer. It wasn't so much that I hated the programming part, but I hated most of my co-workers. Up until then, I thought, to be a film-maker, you need to go to film school, you need to work your way up and maybe you'll get a chance to direct a movie. But then I saw *The Blair Witch Project* and looked at other films like *El Mariachi* and *Open Water*, where the film-makers picked up a video camera and made a movie.[2]

So Peli, who'd never made even a short, decided to shoot a film in his home – over the course of seven days, with only the special effects that he could do himself on his computer (see Figure 13.1).[3]

The film – *Paranormal Activity* (2009) – cost $15,000 to make – and has grossed, world-wide and domestically, $194 million.

Admittedly, a 13,000 percent return on investment is an anomaly; but the fact remains that horror has *always* been a money-maker. Following the success of two silents with horror-movie elements – *The Hunchback of Notre Dame* (1923) and *The Phantom of the Opera* (1925), Universal Pictures scored with a string of hits in the early 1930s: first *Dracula* and then *Frankenstein* (both in 1931), then *Murders in*

**FIGURE 13.1** A young couple (Katie Featherston and Micah Sloat) are troubled by strange occurrences in their home, in *Paranormal Activity*.

*the Rue Morgue, The Old Dark House* and *The Mummy* (1932) and *The Invisible Man* (1933.) All these movies were profitable; and after a pause in production (in 1937 and 1938), Universal had another success with the re-release of *Dracula and Frankenstein* on a double bill, in 1938.[4]

In those early days, horror hadn't yet been considered as a *genre; Dracula*, for example, was marketed as a 'mystery picture'. But by the end of the 1930s, the horror film had carved a niche for itself – going through lulls (the war years of the 1940s) and re-inventions (the alien-invader flicks of the 1950s, for example), but always providing studios with a reliable source of income.[5]

Reliable – but seldom 'respectable'. As Scott Meslow writes, in a story about our 'new golden age' of horror: "Hollywood has long had a kind of reflective snobbishness about horror movies – a self-perpetuating cycle in which studios, largely writing horror movies off as cheap and lazy, would race to the bottom with cheap, lazy horror movies."[6] As Jason Blum, producer of *Get Out*, puts it: "Most Hollywood executives make horror movies because they make money, not because they like them, and I think most of the fans can tell that."[7]

But the cultural climate is changing. Recent films like *Get Out* (2017) and *Hereditary* (2018) have won acclaim from critics, while also doing great box-office business.[8] To quote Scott Meslow again:

> What's the single trend that unifies all the horror movies being released right now? The answer: they're all *so damn good*. Horror movies, which were snobbishly dismissed for so long, are now routinely better reviewed than your average 'prestige' picture.[9]

*It*, for example, the adaptation of *half* of Stephen King's thousand-page killer-clown opus, has an 85 percent Certified Fresh rating, on Rotten Tomatoes, the film-review aggregate site. Perhaps more impressively, it has almost as high an "audience score" (84 percent). And then, of course, there are the *other* numbers: *It*'s budget was high, for a genre film – $35 million. But it grossed, worldwide, $697 million[10] – making it one of the most lucrative horror films of all time.

It's tempting – when looking at *It* or *Get Out* – to believe there's a new, more discriminating audience out there – and they're finally getting the smart and provocative movies they've always wanted. As Maslow puts it,

> The massive success of *Get Out* is proof that audiences are hungry for the kinds of stories and perspectives that larger, more risk-averse studios have ignored for so long … And *Get Out* reinforces horror's unique ability to tackle social commentary, because the natural empathy a film's audience feels for its protagonist forces every viewer to consider everything from his point of view.[11]

What this *doesn't* explain is the staggering success of a film like *The Nun* – a spin-off of a sequel (*The Conjuring 2*). It grossed more than $300 million worldwide, against a budget of $22 million – making it the most successful film of the "*Conjuring* Universe". And it's a *terrible* movie – with a muddled script and minimal scares. Unlike a 'new horror' film like *Hereditary*, which seems very much like a personal vision, *The Nun* has a by-the-numbers feel, a spin-off that's only spinning through the motions.

But the film was one of several releases from Warner Brothers that year, that acknowledged in its casting the impact of international audiences. (*Crazy Rich Asians* was another). *The Nun* starred a Mexican actor, Demián Bichir, and opened big both in Spain and Mexico. It also appeared in a summer without competition from other horror films.[12] And – perhaps the most crucial factor of all – it *was* part of the "*Conjuring* Universe", even if a peripheral one.

In 2018, the year that *The Nun* was released, *Black Panther* became the first Marvel 'origin story' to top $200 million (with an ultimate world-wide gross of over $1 billion). The "Marvel Universe" model is currently dominating Hollywood – a series of interconnected films that build a massive audience; its 2019 entry, *Avengers Endgame* is well on its way to grossing $3 billion.

*The Nun*'s 'universe' began with a single haunted-house movie, *The Conjuring* (2013) – a supposedly true story detailing the work of a ghost-hunting couple. The movie was successful enough to spawn a sequel, *The Conjuring 2*, with the tag-line: "The next true story from the case files of Ed and Lorraine Warren." This movie was also a hit; and from there, the 'universe' began to branch, with separate stories involving creatures and artifacts the Warrens have stumbled upon, on their adventures: so far three *Annabelle* movies (about a haunted doll encountered in *Conjuring 1*), *The Nun* (an evil spirit briefly seen in *Conjuring 2*), and *The Curse of la Llarona* (which isn't officially a '*Conjuring* Universe' film, though it shares one character). Currently in development are a sequel to *The Nun*, a third *Conjuring* movie, and a stand-alone, *The Crooked Man*, based on another villain briefly seen in *Conjuring 2*.

What exactly *is* the 'universe' these films are building? Annette Hill, a professor of Media and Communications at Lund University, Sweden, suggests that it's one that accepts a belief in the paranormal.

> The paranormal includes a range of alternative spiritual beliefs, in ghosts and spiritual communication, in witchcraft, in aliens, in extra sensory projection, all of which offer audiences an opportunity to engage with their personal beliefs, doubts and fears about the existence of life after death, and the existence of anomalous experiences.[13]

We're back to that 'desire to believe' that we touched on in Chapter 10 (p. 104). Matthew Rozsa, the *Salon* writer who quoted Professor Hill, finds something problematic in such a desire:

> While more discerning moviegoers can watch films like *The Conjuring* and the rest of that movie's cinematic universe and recognize that this is fiction, some will take the "based on true stories" claim and assume that this proves the existence of the paranormal. At a time when science is too often disregarded with terrible real-world consequences – whether on global warming, vaccines, evolution or the legitimacy of transgender experiences – any film that purports to cast scientific fact aside for unverified hocus pocus should not be dismissed lightly.[14]

I think these films occupy a less disturbing middle ground – somewhere between 'entertainment only' and propaganda for the occult. One doesn't have to believe in the factual basis of *The Conjuring* films, to enjoy their exploration of *possibilities* – the 'what if?' at the heart of many horror movies.

If modestly budgeted horror films keep making gigantic profits, one logical question would be: why isn't Hollywood making more of them? As media analyst Paul Dergarabedian says,

> Horror movies always seem to find an audience. They are extraordinarily cost efficient. You don't need a ton of money to make one. All you have to have is a darkened room and some people chasing other people and you've got a horror movie.[15]

Many great horror movies can't be reduced to 'dark room/frightened people being chased'. But the basic point is sound: horror movies *are*, in general, cheaper to make than 'prestige' pictures; for that reason, they have a better chance of breaking even (at least) and – with talent and luck – making a profit. But as Brent Lang writes, in *Variety*, "Hollywood has an addiction to sequels and reboots – and *Don't Breathe* won't be the cure."[16]

Of that movie, Lang writes,

> [*Don't Breathe*] will be one of the rare major studio releases this summer [2016] to make back its budget in a matter of days. It also extends a string of economical horror hits, building on the success of *The Purge: Election Year*, *The Shallows*, *The Conjuring 2* and *Lights Out*, four recent winners that carry an average budget of $17.9 million, a fraction of what it cost to reassemble the Avengers every summer.[17]

Lang also mentioned the costly flops of the summer of 2016, including *Teenage Mutant Ninja Turtles: Out of the Shadows*, *Ghostbusters* and *Independence Day: Resurgence*. Why risk so much, when horror films can promise a safer investment? For Lang, the culprit's the wave of 'conglomeratization' of the movie business, turning studios into ever-shrinking subsidiaries of the parent media-giants: "Time Warner, Viacom, 21st Century Fox, Walt Disney and other parent companies don't care about earning $20 million on a movie. That won't move the needle on their stock price… For all its success, 'Don't Breathe' and its gang of teenage delinquents aren't likely to inspire a Saturday morning cartoon or land on many lunch boxes. Even three or four of these movies won't cover the enormous overhead it takes to maintain global distribution networks, massive studio lots and to keep thousands of employees from Culver City to Tokyo humming."[18]

Jason Blum, the producer of *Get Out and Paranormal Activity*, told *L.A. Weekly*, "'In Hollywood, the herd mentality is massive. The reason people don't make low-budget movies is that it's completely not sexy – we're not the cool guys on the block.'"[19]

Which brings us to Jason Blum himself – the man some media analysts have declared "The New Master of Horror". As Jason Guerrasio puts it, in a *BusinessInsider* story,

> Unless you own the rights to Marvel characters or you're a streaming giant with endless capital, the best way to make a buck in Hollywood these days is finding a passionate audience for a particular audience for a particular subject, and make the content on the cheap. Jason Blum and his company, Blumhouse Productions, have done just that, and now they're reaping the rewards.[20]

Blum had worked in acquisitions for giant Miramax, in the 1990s; then he tried his hand as an independent producer, and didn't like it. But he learned a lot – and, in the end, was inspired to start his own company. Blumhouse Productions struggled, at first; but then, one day, Jason Blum saw Oren Peli's modest 'home movie'. Blum shopped it around, and only Dream Works was interested – *in remaking it*. Blum agreed (never intending to do a re-make), with the proviso:

> What I said was I will sell you the remake rights to the movie, but, and I put this in the contract: you guys set up and attend a test screening [of Peli's

> original version] ... And I said to Oren, "I promise you you'll never remake the movie – you don't want to do it, I don't want to do it, it's never going to happen. But this is the only way I can get people who make a decision into a movie theater with people."[21]

The gamble worked; when Dream Works execs watched a terrified audience watching Peli's movie, they agreed to release it unchanged (except for the ending, which was tinkered with). And Blumhouse had a hit on its hands – one of the biggest money-makers in cinema history.

In the business model Blumhouse Productions has followed, since *Paranormal*, Blum says that one of his tenets is, "Never work with first-time directors."[22] But Blum is a man of contradictions – because when he read *Get Out*, a script by first-time director Jordan Peele, he gave the project the go-ahead.

> He wrote the script and I think it was kind of making its way around town. We've had the most success with movies that are not the new bright and shiny object. *The Gift* [another Blumhouse hit] was shopped all over the place. *The Purge* [ditto] was shopped all over the place. *Paranormal Activity* was shopped all over the place. So [*Get Out*] had kind of been making the rounds. I didn't hear the pitch. I read the script and then I met Jordan afterward, but I loved it. It was so original. It is about race and it is about Donald Trump, and it's about all these other things. I loved a lot of things about it, but the politics is certainly one of the many aspects I loved about it.[23]

Audiences clearly loved it too; *Get Out* (on a $4.5 million budget) went on to gross $255 million world-wide. And Jordan Peele collected three top Oscar nominations: best director, best picture, and best original screenplay (winning for the latter).

Blum's attracted to risky projects that other studios may have avoided. But he's also immensely practical; writers and directors working for Blum have certain rules to follow (much like the constraints imposed on Val Lewton, back in the 1940s – when he produced a string of horror hits for struggling RKO Pictures). Keeping within a $4–5-million-dollar budget is one of those rules. That way, a picture's almost assured of breaking even, at least – since "digital distribution through channels like iTunes can guarantee about $2 million in sales in the U.S. and another $2 million overseas."[24]

Another of the key Blumhouse directives is that

> story and character matter – even in horror movies. "*The scares don't work if the story and characters don't work* ... If you take away the toys [multiple locations, expensive special effects, etc.], the director has nothing to focus on but those things. I think it makes the movie stronger".[25]

Another current producer, Andrew Form of Platinum Dunes, would agree. Form was given a spec script, written by two unknown writers, Bryan Woods and Scott

Beck. Called *A Quiet Place*, the script was only sixty-seven pages long, with almost no dialogue; its story followed a family trying to survive in a world that's been overrun by hostile aliens with super-sensitive hearing. Form gave the script to actor John Krasinski, who was looking for a project to direct, and Krasinski pounced on it – because, says Form, "it wasn't your typical fright fest. [Krasinski] always wanted it to be a scary movie, but it's a family drama. So he approached it that way, and then of course, the tension and the scares come along with it"[26] (see Figure 13.2).

It's not a new phenomenon, that important talents are being discovered via the horror genre. Steven Spielberg's early work includes two made-for-TV horror films. On James Cameron's resumé is *Piranha Part Two: The Spawning*. And Peter Jackson started the road to *Lord of the Rings* with low-budget 'splatter comedies', *Bad Taste* and *Dead Alive*.

But producers like Jason Blum and Andrew Form are keeping this developmental arena alive. When asked if there were risks he wished more people would take, Blum replied,

> I'm not frustrated, because the movies that are done for low budgets are actually very edgy. 'Risk' is probably the wrong word, but they're different, and they try new things … [Conversely], the higher the budget gets, the fewer storytelling risks you're able to take.[27]

And story-telling – the screenwriter's job – is key. To give Jason Blum the final word,

> One of the things I always tell the filmmakers is, if you pull out the genre parts, does the movie stand on its own as a great dramatic story? Most horror movies don't, but I like to think our movies do.[28]

**FIGURE 13.2** As he carries his son (Noah Jupe), a father (John Krasinski) fears an attack by unearthly aliens, in *A Quiet Place*.

## Notes

1. Ethan Sacks, "Box Office Champ 'Paranormal Activity' Had Scary Personal Inspiration for Film-Maker Oren Peli", *New York Daily News*, 10/26/09, https://www.nydailynews.com/entertainment/tv-movies/box-office-champ-paranormal-activity-scary-personal-inspiration-filmmaker-oren-peli-article-1.382664 (accessed 10/7/19).
2. Mekado Murphy, "Filmmaker Oren Peli on the End of 'Paranormal Activity'", *New York Times*, 10/21/15, https://www.nytimes.com/2015/10/22/movies/filmmaker-oren-peli-on-the-end-of-paranormal-activity.html (accessed 10/7/19).
3. Sacks, op. cit.
4. Murray Leeder, *Horror Film* (New York: Bloomsbury Academic, 2018), pp. 28–29.
5. In a piece for *NPR* in 2015, writer Quoctrung Bui used data from a company (Studio System) that crunches entertainment-industry numbers, to look at "what kind of films have had the best return on investment over the last years". The company looked at ROI – return on investment – which measures the amount of profit on an investment, relative to its cost. According to Studio System's study, horror films "are at the top of the list, with 13 of the top 30 films by ROI since 2010." C.f. Quoctrung Bui, "Horror is the Best Deal in Hollywood", 08/21/15, https://www.npr.org/sections/money/2015/08/21/433505958/horror-is-the-best-deal-in-hollywood (accessed 10/7/19).
6. Scott Maslow, "How We Ended Up in The Golden Age of Horror Movies", *Gentlemen's Quarterly*, 10/27/17.
7. Jordan Crucchiola, "The New Master of Horror", 2017, https://www.vulture.com/2017/03/get-outs-jason-blum-is-the-new-master-of-horror.html (accessed 10/7/19).
8. *Get Out* grossed $255 million on a budget of $5 million. *Hereditary* had a more modest but still rewarding take of $70 million, on a budget of $10 million (figures from the industry website "The Numbers").
9. Maslow, op. cit.
10. Source: http://www.the-numbers.com,https://www.the-numbers.com/movie/It-(2017)#tab=summary (accessed 10/7/19).
11. Maslow, op. cit.
12. Travis Clark, "How 'The Nun' Overcame Bad Reviews to be a Box-Office Hit," 09/12/18, https://www.newstimes.com/technology/businessinsider/article/How-The-Nun-overcame-bad-reviews-to-be-a-13224162.php (accessed 10/7/19).
13. Matthew Rozsa, "Why is a Mediocre Movie Like 'The Nun' Such a Hit?", 9/22/18, https://www.salon.com/2018/09/22/why-is-a-mediocre-movie-like-the-nun-such-a-hit (accessed 10/7/19).
14. Rozsa, op. cit.
15. Brent Lang, "Don't Breathe Won't Cure Hollywood's Blockbuster Addiction", 8/28/16, https://variety.com/2016/film/box-office/dont-breathe-box-office-1201846137 (accessed 10/7/19).
16. Lang, op. cit.
17. Lang, op. cit.
18. Lang, op. cit.
19. Amy Nicholson, "Can Budget-Slasher Jason Blum Prove the Way Hollywood Makes Movies is Horrifyingly Wrong?", 10/19/15, https://www.laweekly.com/can-budget-slasher-jason-blum-prove-the-way-hollywood-makes-movies-is-horrifyingly-wrong (accessed 10/7/19).
20. Jason Guerrasio, "How the Company Behind 2 of the Year's Biggest Movies is Blowing Up the Hollywood Playbook," 3/1/17, https://www.businessinsider.com/blumhouse-productions-get-out-split-2017-2 (accessed 10/7/19).
21. Guerrasio, op. cit.
22. Paula Bernstein, "SXSW: Low-Budget Producer Jason Blum on the Secret of His Success", 3/9/14 (my emphasis), https://www.indiewire.com/2014/03/sxsw-low-budget-producer-jason-blum-on-the-secret-of-his-success-29202 (accessed 10/7/19).
23. Crucchiola, op. cit.

24 Jason Del Rey, "The Secret Formula Behind Low-Budget Hits Like Paranormal Activity and Whiplash", 2/13/17, https://www.vox.com/2017/2/13/14603058/blum-productions-low-budget-formula-purge-whiplash-paranormal-activity (accessed 10/7/19).
25 Bernstein, op. cit.
26 Nicole LaPorte, "Why Horror Movies are Now More Important than Ever in Hollywood," 7/11/18, https://www.fastcompany.com/90199673/why-horror-movies-are-now-more-important-than-ever-in-hollywood (accessed 10/7/19).
27 Crucchiola, op. cit.
28 Scotty Macaulay, "Working through Fear: An Interview with Blumhouse's Jason Blum", 1/25/17, https://filmmakermagazine.com/104113-working-through-fear/#.XZuwZ2YpA2w (accessed 10/7/19).

# 14
# THE FUTURE OF HORROR

2017 was a banner year for the horror movie; both *It* and *Get Out* cleaned up at the box office *and* received glowing reviews from critics. Culture watchers began to proclaim a new era for the scary film. As Jason Zinoman writes, in the *New York Times*,

> Moving into territory once the preserve of prestige dramas, horror has never been more bankable and celebrated than it is right now. And while evil clowns and serial killers at sorority houses still haunt young viewers (and make tons of money), *we're in the midst of a golden age of grown-up horror.* [1]

Zinoman implies that 'evil clowns' are more standard horror fare (unlike the indie films he takes up later, in his article). And *It* – though well-made – is at heart a very traditional movie, with pre-teens as its protagonists: outsiders who come together to defeat a shape-shifting monster clown. Its antecedents go back to the kids-vs.-unhelpful-adults template of Spielberg's *E.T.*, and – more recently – the Netflix rip-off-of-Spielberg series *Stranger Things*. [2] When asked why he thought his movie had been such a hit, director Andy Muschietti replied,

> This is a story that resonates a lot with the situation that society is living in right now … It talks to us about what it is to live in a culture of fear, you know? Where fear is used as a tool to divide and control and subdue. For people who didn't know this story – and who went to the movie to see a horror movie – they went and found something else.[3]

Actually, that 'something else' – elevating the story beyond the jump scares of a routine scary picture – has been a part of horror for decades. The 'culture of fear', for example, is at the heart of the 1950s classic, *Invasion of the Body Snatchers* (c.f.

Chapter 1). What *It* does do is bring a larger scope to its story of 'fear itself'. At 135 minutes, it's much longer than average horror pics; it has a larger cast (more than ten major characters); and because a decision was made to film only *half* of its source material (a Stephen King doorstopper novel weighing in at over 1,000 pages), the movie had more freedom to build its characters and their relationships. (The sequel, *It Chapter Two* – released in September 2019 – fared less well with critics, but did even better at the box office.)

*It* is solid entertainment, but nothing about it is *truly* surprising. Good triumphs over evil (at least temporarily) – end of story. It doesn't set out to re-imagine horror's possibilities. And that's where the independents come in, re-visioning the kinds of stories and themes that the genre can tackle. As Jason Zinoman writes, "Hushed and character-driven, this [new horror] works ferociously on adult anxieties in an age of dislocation."[4] From *The Babadook* and *It Follows* (both appearing in 2014), to *Get Out* and *Hereditary* (2017 and 2018), horror's taking us now to strange new places, where evil isn't as clearly defined, and reality's harder to grasp.

In *The Babadook*, for example, a woman's still grieving for her husband, who died in a car crash the day the woman gave birth to their only child. Six years have passed, Amelia's life is stuck, and Samuel, her troubled son, is acting out in ways that are getting more and more aggressive. Into this troubled household comes a figure from an odd story-book – a sinister creature, the Babadook, who threatens to get 'inside your skin.' Convinced that the creature is real, Samuel wants to protect his mother. But his 'protection' takes violent forms– a home-made dart-gun, for instance – and Amelia's nerves begin to shred, as Samuel's suspended from school. From there, the boy's obsession with the Babadook continues to grow; he has nightmares, keeping his mother awake, till she's moving like one of the walking dead. And *she's* beginning to think she's catching glimpses of the boogeyman; when she tells the police she's being stalked, they dismiss her story and offer no help. She's alone, with a more and more traumatized child, whose melt-downs are terrifying.

But the mother's are even scarier. One morning, after a sleepless night, Samuel appears in her doorway; he's on medication he has to take with food, and needs her help. But she doesn't move, just lies there, eyes wide open, in the foreground – while Samuel is an out-of-focus blur at the edge of the frame.

SAMUEL
Mom? I took the pills, but I feel sick again. I need to eat something. *[She sighs, not stirring.]* I couldn't find any food in the fridge. You said to have them with food. I'm really hungry, mom.
*[Now she speaks, with quiet fury, back still turned to him.]*

AMELIA
Why do you have to keep talk-talk-talking? Don't you ever stop?

                              SAMUEL
I was just –
                              AMELIA
I need to sleep!
                              SAMUEL
I'm sorry, mommy, I was just really hungry.
*[Now she rolls over to face him.]*
                              AMELIA
If you're that hungry, why don't you go and EAT SHIT!
*[We see him clearly now – he looks stunned, then runs from the room. Amelia rolls back onto her side, staring at the wall.]*

It's a truly hair-raising moment, one that plays on an ancient fear going back, to Saturn devouring his children; or Hansel and Gretel, or – in the modern world, Jack Torrance chasing his son with an axe through a maze, at the end of *The Shining*. What if the 'monster under the bed' turns out to be your mom or dad – the person who you'd always believed would love you and protect you? That's Samuel's fear, in *The Babadook*; and his mother's fear is the flipside of that: what if your child began to seem like a visceral threat to your sanity? What if you *knew* you should love and care for this child you secretly wanted to die? (see Figure 14.1).

This fear of harming a loved one is at the very dark heart of *Hereditary*, another recent indie film that garnered stellar reviews. The film begins with a funeral, of the grandmother of a family; about thirty minutes in, there's another death – and it's horrific. Big brother Peter is rushing his sister Charlie to the hospital (she's having a bad allergic reaction to eating nuts, at a party); struggling to breathe, the young girl sticks her head out the window – and, as Peter swerves the car to avoid an animal in the road, a telephone pole lops Charlie's head off. Peter, in shock,

**FIGURE 14.1** The sinister children's book (with its pop-up title creature) in *The Babadook*.

drives home, not even telling his parents what happened. Next morning his mother Annie gets ready to take the car out – and we hear her screams, off-camera, as she discovers the body.

Director Ari Aster has spoken about the death of Charlie:

> I mean, *Psycho* was *the* reference for that … there's this traumatic baton-passing from a main character to what felt like a secondary character. And the movie suddenly becomes unsafe, right? We're not quite sure what we're watching any more. That is the Janet Leigh shower scene [of the film] …

He goes on to talk about a kind of complacency viewers feel, when they think they're settling into a genre film with its standard conventions: " … and that provides the storyteller suddenly with an opportunity to jolt that viewer out of that complacency and bring forth a more active engagement with the story."[5]

The jolts keep coming. The family's mother, Annie – an artist who creates miniature rooms and landscapes – is overwhelmed by her grief, and can't even speak to her son, who she blames for Charlie's death. One night Annie's husband Steve comes to tell her that dinner's ready – and finds her at work on a miniature of the roadside where her daughter died, complete with tiny head on the ground, near the fatal telephone pole.

STEVE
Jesus Christ, Annie.
[She keeps working.]
            STEVE (cont'd)
You're not planning on letting him see that, are you?
            ANNIE
Who?
            STEVE
Peter. How do you think he's gonna feel when he sees that?
            ANNIE
What? It's not about him.
            STEVE
Oh, no?
            ANNIE
No, it's a neutral view of the accident.
[Steve shakes his head, as Annie returns to her work.]
            STEVE
Are you, uh, are you coming down to dinner?
            ANNIE
I'm making dinner.
            STEVE
[with barely controlled anger] No, I made the dinner. I came to get you.

> *[Annie doesn't respond.]*
>                         STEVE (cont'd)
> Come, stay, whatever you want. I really don't give a shit.
> *[He leaves Annie to her work.]*

Of course there *is* no "neutral view" of the accident. People try to hide their feelings; but those terrible feelings fester. In the following dinner scene – the first time Annie and Peter have been together on screen in twenty minutes – no one's talking. The film's music score is silent; there's just the clatter of cutlery. Finally Peter decides to ignite an explosion.

>                         PETER
> You ok, Mom?
>                         ANNIE
> What?
>                         PETER
> Is there something on your mind?
>                         ANNIE
> Is there something on *your* mind?
>                         PETER
> It just seems like there might be something you wanna say.
>                         STEVE
> Peter –
>                         ANNIE
> Like what? I mean why would I wanna say something, so I can watch you sneer at me?
>                         PETER
> Sneer at you? I don't ever sneer at you.
>                         ANNIE
> Oh sweetie. You don't have to. You get your point across.
>                         PETER
> Ok, so fine. Then say what you wanna say, then.
>                         STEVE
> *Peter.*
>                         ANNIE
> I don't wanna say anything. I've tried saying things.
>                         PETER
> Ok, so try again. Release yourself.
>                         ANNIE
> Oh, release you, you mean.
>                         PETER
> Yeah, fine. Release me. Just say it. Just fucking say it!
> *[Annie rises from the table.]*

ANNIE
Don't you swear at me, you little shit! Don't you ever raise your voice at me. I am your mother! Do you understand? All I do is worry and slave and defend you. And all I get back is that fucking face on your face! So full of disdain and resentment and always so annoyed. Well, now your sister is dead. And I know you miss her, and I know it was an accident, and I know you're in pain. And I wish I could take that away for you. I wish I could shield you from the knowledge that you did what you did, but your sister is dead. She's gone forever! And what a waste.
[She starts crying.]
ANNIE (cont'd)
If it could have maybe brought us together or something. If you could have just said, "I'm sorry." Or faced up to what happened. Maybe then we could do something with this. But you can't take responsibility for anything! So now I can't accept … And I can't forgive, because … Because nobody admits anything they've done!

This scene is devastating – in part because *nobody* gets *what they want*. Peter wants his mother's love – or specifically, her forgiveness. Annie would like to give up her anger, but can't. And Steve wants peace – which, given what's happened, he will never have. The tragedy of Charlie's death *could* have brought these people together; instead, it's isolating them. As director Aster said in an interview,

> [The film] preys on the fears that don't really have a remedy. What do you do with a fear of death? What do you do with the suspicion that you don't really know the people you're closest to? What do you do with fear of abandonment? The fear of somebody close to you changing? The film is really feeding on those fears.[6]

We've come a long way from the vampires and werewolves, doppelgangers and aliens of earlier horror movies. Reviewer A.A. Dowd describes his initial reaction to seeing the film:

> This isn't a scary movie. It's pure emotional terrorism, gripping you with real horror, the unspeakable kind, and then imbuing the supernatural stuff with those feelings. It didn't play me like a fiddle. It slammed on my insides like a grand piano.[7]

He also compares the film's impact to that of *The Babadook*, though he adds, "Hereditary isn't as thematically cut-and-dried as that acclaimed horror hit; its emotions are somehow uglier, messier, tougher to diagnose."

I wonder if the 'messiness' comes from the writer-director's attempt to fuse a pitch-dark psychological drama to more traditional horror. *Hereditary*'s pace is slow and deliberate – and it takes a *long* time to get to the big revelation of the final act: that the family at the movie's center is *cursed*. In a very literal way. As Annie tries to order life with her miniature dioramas, the characters in *Hereditary* are being moved around by forces they can't begin to comprehend, like figures in a dollhouse. *Nobody* has free will; everything that happens – from decapitation to self-combustion – is part of a diabolical plan, with teenager Peter as the ultimate pawn. By the end of the movie, he's suffered a crushing soul-murder, he's now possessed by his dead sister's spirit, and he's become "King Paimon", one of the more obscure rulers of the Hell. To which my reaction has always been a bewildered "Huh?" I've seen the movie three times, now – and every time I get to the end, I *always* feel a disconnect. "Wait – this was about *devil worship?*" The psychic violence loved ones inflict on each other is *so* disturbing – that the more conventional threats of black magic feel like an anti-climax of sorts. (Especially when the naked old demon worshippers start to wander in; they seem to have been teleported from the world of *Rosemary's Baby*.)

Steve Rose, a *Guardian* journalist, has come up with a term to describe the new movies that try to "push beyond [the] cast-iron conventions" of the genre: "post-horror."[8] It's a term that hasn't caught on – and there was online pushback against it, when his article first appeared.[9] But I think Rose is on to *something*. In recent years, there are more and more films coming out that aren't 'governed by rules and codes' of the 'classic' horror genre. Those classic rules "are our flashlight as we venture into the unknown ... But what happens when you stray beyond those cast-iron conventions and wander off into the darkness? You might find something even scarier."[10]

Because these films are changing the rules, they can be perplexing to viewers. The indie movie *It Comes at Night*, for example, sets us up to expect some monstrous "it" to come lumbering onto the screen. But that's not what the movie's about, at all. Set in a post-apocalyptic world that's been ravaged by a deadly new plague, it centers on a family that's isolated itself in the woods – and what happens to them when *another* family shows up, looking for shelter (see Figure 14.2).

Writer-director Trey Edward Shults talks about where the movie came from:

> I had a weird relationship with my dad and he battled addiction and I hadn't seen him in ten years and then I was with him on his deathbed. He was so full of regret and he didn't want to let go and I was just trying to help him find some kind of peace. What I said to him was what Sarah [a character in the movie] says to her dad at the beginning of the film. Two months later, I just started writing. I don't know why. And this whole story spun out of that. It's obviously fictional, but it was that emotion and headspace and processing and dealing with my fears, basically. All of my fears are in this movie. The biggest one of all is mortality.[11]

**158** The future of horror

**FIGURE 14.2** Two families (Riley Keogh, Christopher Abbott, Joel Edgerton, Kelvin Harrison, Carmen Ejogo and Christopher Robert Faulkner) hide from the plague-infected outside world, in *It Comes at Night*.

What he made of his fears is a tense and disturbing film about survival – both physical and psychological – in the face of constant uncertainty and an ever-mounting tension.

We're back to that basic idea I discussed in Chapter 2: *to frighten your audience, write about what frightens you*. Shults did that, and came up with a movie that some critics picked as the best of the year. It also did well at the box-office, off of strong word-of-mouth. Yet its "CinemaScore" – a poll of viewers on a film's opening weekend – is a D minus. How to explain the discrepancy?

As noted above, the title's misleading; apparently many people *were* waiting for "It" to show up – and felt gypped when it didn't. The film's trailer also suggested that this was a standard horror movie: its editing accelerates, with increasingly violent images, building to the tagline: "FEAR TURNS MEN INTO MONSTERS." That is, in fact, what happens – but the monsters are human, not 'creatures'.

Critic Jason Zinoman notes, of these newer films, that

> now that horror attracts better actors, bigger budgets and meatier scripts, there is a sense of fun missing in some of the tasteful scary movies. Has horror lost some of its disreputable pleasures, not to mention its single-minded determination to terrify?[12]

In movies like *Hereditary*, or the ponderous 2018 remake of *Suspiria*, I'd say the answer's a qualified 'yes'. These movies are smart, and *extremely* well-made – but it would be hard to call them 'fun'. A critic for the entertainment website 'Den of Geek' suggests that *Hereditary* is "a sublime horror comedy": "It's like a wretched sinner confessing to a crime so heinous that even the priest can't stop himself from rushing out of the church and screaming for the police."[13] This critic mentions Alfred Hitchcock's often-quoted remark that he intended *Psycho* to be 'a big joke' – and wonders if writer-director Ari Aster allowed himself "a sly grin at the grim fates he metes out on his characters."[14] For my part, I think Hitchcock was pulling the leg of the BBC interviewers; *Psycho* has lines that may be painfully humorous in retrospect, e.g., "A boy's best friend is his mother," but overall, it's meant to terrify us, and it does. *Hereditary* has moments so over-the-top that one *might* be tempted to laugh (in dismay?) – like Annie suspended mid-air in the attic, sawing off her own head with a wire. That *ought* to be hard to top – yet Annie's 'emotional terrorism', the hatred with which she confronts her son, is the part of the film I find most disturbing. Somehow I connect this film, in my mind, with the French 'new extreme' horror movies (including *High Tension, Inside* and *Martyrs*), that *are* extreme in depicting ways of harming the human body. The connection is a kind of ferocious intensity that I find more exhausting at last – because what does it *mean*? – than entertaining.

Of the recent crop of scary films, *Get Out* may be the most successful, at finding a balance between its horror-movie pleasures (which are considerable) and its concerns (which are deadly serious). Writer-director Jordan Peele has said, of his movie's origins, "It began as the fun of a horror story. It's my favorite genre. I wanted to have fun while writing."[15]

As he worked on it, though, he began to discover what he *really* wanted to do. "Halfway through writing the project is when I realized what it was actually about."[16]

The horror he wanted to get at wasn't a psycho in a hockey mask, or a killer clown in a haunted house; it was racism so pervasive that it blends into the everyday, becoming *almost* invisible, but remaining a continual threat.

*"Every great horror movie comes from a true fear, and ideally it's a universal fear,"* Peele said in an *NPR* interview.[17]

> The tricky nature of this project is that the fear I'm pulling from is very human but it's not necessarily a universal experience, so that's why the first third of the movie is showing, and not in an over-the-top way, in a sort of real, grounded way, just getting everybody to be able to see the world through my protagonist's eyes and his fears.[18]

Peele does this in subtle ways that show us how his protagonist, Chris, reacts to the world around him. For example, there's an eerie scene as Chris and his white girlfriend Rose are driving through woods on their way to meet Rose's parents (who haven't been told yet that Chris is black). Chris has earlier expressed his apprehension about the meeting; but Rose has reassured him that her family's super-liberal.

ROSE
My dad would've voted for Obama for a third time if he could've. Like, the love is so real. I'm only telling you this 'cause he's definitely gonna wanna talk to you about that. And it will definitely fucking suck.

*[They both laugh.]*
                    ROSE (cont'd)
But that's because he's a lame dad more than anything
else. They are not racist.
                    CHRIS
All right.
                    ROSE
I would've told you.

They end up kissing; and we cut to the scene in the car, as Chris – in the passenger seat – starts to light up a cigarette. Rose grabs it, breaks it and throws it out the window; they bicker about whether or not Chris should smoke (setting up the excuse Rose's mother will use, when she offers to hypnotize Chris, to 'cure' his habit – c.f. Chapter 8, p. 78). Changing the subject, Chris calls his pal Rod – a TSA officer at the airport – to thank him for looking after Chris's dog while he's gone.

                    ROSE
Can I talk to him?
                    CHRIS
No.
                    ROSE
I'd like to talk to him, please.
*[Chris sighs.]*
                    CHRIS
Hold on, hold on …
*[He holds up the phone to Rose, and we INTERCUT with Rod, on speaker-phone.]*
                    ROSE
Hi, Rod.
                    ROD
Now, look here, you know you picked the wrong guy,
right?
                    ROSE
Yeah, of course I know that. This is just a ploy to get
to you. It's not too late for us.
*[Chris takes the phone back.]*
                    CHRIS
Ok, get your own girl. Goddam …
                    ROD
She's all mad at you 'cause you never take my advice.
                    CHRIS
Like what?

                            ROD
Like don't go to a white girl's parents' house. What's
she doin'? Lickin' your balls or somethin'?
                           CHRIS
Yeah, bye.
                            ROD
You know what I'm saying, Chris?
[But Chris has hung up. We stay with Rod.]
                       ROD (cont'd)
Chris ... Chri-. This motherfucker hung up on me.
[Back to the car, where Rose is smiling.]
                           ROSE
You're jealous.
                           CHRIS
I'm not jealous.
                           ROSE
I made you jealous!
                           CHRIS
I'm not jealous of Rod.
                           ROSE
It's Rod!
[In the midst of their banter, there's suddenly a loud
THUMP, as the car hits a deer, whose body is flung off into
the woods. The car comes to a halt.]

It's a perfect use of a comic scene that lulls us into relaxing, before a sudden shock. Chris and Rose get out of the car – and Chris hears a terrible moan from the woods. He starts to walk to the verge of the road, hearing the sickening moan again. Very quiet, ominous music increases our sense of unease as Chris enters the woods, seeing the wounded deer, lying still, on its side. Alone and helpless. In the background, on this bright sunny day, we hear the soft, disconcerting sound of rain – a part of a crucial memory, we'll discover, in the 'hypnosis' scene. Chris stares at the deer, we cut back and forth from the animal, to a last close-up of Chris ... and we can see that this accident has shaken him up, but we don't know why. So, with simple means, the writer's suggested a mystery we'd like an answer to. (On top of the film's *first* mystery – the kidnapping of the young black man, in the pre-title sequence – c.f. Chapter 4, pp. 43 ff.)

The answer, when it *does* come, is heart-breaking. As therapist Missy takes Chris back, he remembers the day he lost his mother. We see young Chris in a blue TV glow, the shadows of raindrops streaking the walls – waiting for his mom to come home, not knowing that she's been hit by a car, and has finally died by the side of the road. Chris ends up reliving, all over again, the helplessness he felt back then. And what makes the scene *terrifying* is that Missy – his girlfriend's mother, a woman he wanted to think he could trust – is using Chris's grief *against* him, to send him to 'the sunken place.'

At that moment we realize that Chris's original fears were justified – these white 'liberals' *aren't* liberal, and Chris is in terrible danger.

While writing *Get Out*, Peele worried that the movie would be divisive. "I thought I'd lose black people because we're victims in the movie, and that's hard to watch, that's not fun," he explained.

> Maybe I'd lose white people because white people are the villains in the movie, that would be an assault. But I stuck with it and one of the most fulfilling and validating things to see was how an audience would sort of go in with their preconceived notions on what the film [was] but by the middle, they were all Chris. They were all the main character.[19]

Peele created a protagonist who was so sympathetic – and also so beautifully played by Daniel Kaluuya – that the movie, instead of being divisive, brought audiences together.

Beyond the success of provocative works like *Get Out* and *Hereditary*, there are other promising portents, for the future of the horror film. As Nicole LaPorte writes,

> In a world where major studios are making fewer movies [so they can] focus increasingly on IP-driven franchises that are more about brand names and established characters ... than the actors who play them, horror has become a new artistic haven for talent. Meanwhile, for studios, [horror] films are filling out the void being left by mid-budget dramas, where directors and stars have historically made their mark and picked up awards.[20]

Another significant factor is the way horror films perform overseas. "Studios are keen to bet on films that have a track-record of performing well abroad – horror is chief among them, particularly in markets like Japan and South Korea."[21]

Horror also has new ways of reaching its fans – in particular, streaming services. One of the scariest films I've seen in recent years is *The Invitation*, which had only a brief theatrical run, before it showed up on Netflix. Netflix doesn't release its streaming numbers,

> but anecdotally *The Invitation* has been a sizable hit with Netflix subscribers, driven almost entirely by Netflix algorithms and word-of-mouth. "I'm sort of surprised [*The Invitation*] worked on Netflix, because I'm always puzzled by the lack of direction I feel when *I'm* trying to find a movie on Netflix," says [director Karyn] Kusuma. "I'm always surprised when I hear the number of people who saw *The Invitation* just because it was available to stream. Streaming can open a *lot* of doors for the genre."[22]

Quartz, a 'news outlet for business people in the new global economy', had this to stay about the enduring market for horror movies:

While Hollywood loses its grip on young people (18–24-year-olds are abandoning the movie theater faster than any other age group), there's no indication that the horror genre has suffered a similar fate. Younger audiences are more likely to seek out intense, thrilling experiences – an impulse that fades with age.[23]

Or maybe it doesn't. The farthest-out explanation I've read, for horror's new popularity, involves the way that smartphones could be rewiring our brains. If every notification we get releases a shot of dopamine, we may need increasing stimuli, to feed this new addiction; and horror movies are potent enough – the theory goes – to give us that dopamine kick.[24]

We live in an age of increasing uncertainty – it seems, about *everything*: from the fate of democracies under the threat of nativist demagogues, to the very survival of the planet (or the human portion of it, at least), as global warming accelerates. Horror thrives, in times like these – and it does so not by trivializing our fears, but by confronting them. As frightening as this moment can be, it's also an exciting one for a genre that can provide a way of thinking about what scares us most.

When Chris, *Get Out*'s protagonist, finds himself falling into "the Sunken Place", we – as an audience – fear for him. But there's also a sense of wonder at *seeing* what racism really *feels* like: a purposeful reduction of human worth to utter nothingness. In that awful, awe-filled place, Chris is able to *learn* from his experience. And what he learns protects him, when he finally has to save himself.[25]

Salvation is hard-earned; many horror movies don't provide it. But the best offer visions of what it means to be human in a frightening world that also contains – beyond the horror – wondrous possibilities: for change, for growth, for connection to others who share these visions with us, in the dark.

## Notes

1 Jason Zinoman, "Home is Where the Horror is", *New York Times*, 6/7/18; my emphasis.
2 Speaking of the 'nostalgia horror' trend, typified by *It* and *Stranger Things*, Adam Wingard (director of the home-invasion indie, *You're Next*) said he thought this trend might be close to running its course. "The fact that I saw, the other day, that some other movie was being called part of the 'kids on a bicycle' genre … That's when you know you're in trouble. You can't do this forever. That's not a genre. That's just a thing that happens in movies that you've seen so many times before. Everyone's gonna get sick of it." C.f. "How We Ended Up in the Golden Age of Horror Movies," Scott Meslow, *Gentlemen's Quarterly*, 10/27/17.
3 Scott Meslow, "How the Director of *It* Filmed Its Most Nightmare-Inducing Scene," Scott Meslow, *Gentlemen's Quarterly*, 9/12/17.
4 Zinoman, op. cit.
5 Katie Rife, "Director Ari Aster Tells You Everything We Can't about Hereditary", 6/11/18, https://film.avclub.com/director-ari-aster-tells-you-everything-we-cant-about-h-1826651443 (accessed 10/7/19)
6 Jenelle Riley "Hereditary Filmmaker Ari Aster Answers Burning Questions (Spoilers)", www.variety.com, June 11, 2018, https://variety.com/2018/film/awards/hereditary-ari-aster-answers-burning-questions-1202841448, (accessed 10/7/19)

7. A.A. Dowd, "Hereditary is the Most Traumatically Terrifying Horror Movie in Ages," 1/23/18, https://www.avclub.com/hereditary-is-the-most-traumatically-terrifying-horror-1822352430 (accessed 10/7/19).
8. Steve Rose, "How Post-Horror Movies are Taking over Cinema", 7/6/17, https://www.theguardian.com/film/2017/jul/06/post-horror-films-scary-movies-ghost-story-it-comes-at-night (accessed 10/17/19).
9. Scott Myers, "Reflections on *It Comes at Night, Get Out, A Ghost Story*, More", 7/9/17, https://gointothestory.blcklst.com/how-post-horror-movies-are-taking-over-cinema-99dec5036ecb (accessed 10/7/19).
10. Rose, op. cit.
11. "*It Comes At Night* Director Trey Edward Shults on How *The Shining* Inspired His New Cinematic Nightmare" (interview), 6/7/17, https://www.slashfilm.com/it-comes-at-night-trey-edward-shults-interview (accessed 10/7/19).
12. Zinoman, op. cit.
13. Ryan Lambie, "Why Hereditary is a Sublime Horror Comedy", 6/19/18, https://www.denofgeek.com/us/movies/hereditary/274318/why-hereditary-is-a-sublime-horror-comedy (accessed 10/7/19).
14. Lambie, op. cit.
15. April Salud, "Jordan Peel Says *Get Out* Was 'Meant to be a More Direct, Brutal Wake-Up Call'", 11/21/17, https://www.hollywoodreporter.com/news/jordan-peele-says-get-was-meant-be-a-more-direct-brutal-wake-up-call-1060345 (accessed 10/7/19).
16. Ricardo Lopez, "Jordan Peele on How He Tackled Systemic Racism as Horror in *Get Out*," 11/1/17, https://variety.com/2017/film/news/jordan-peele-get-out-systemic-racism-1202604824 (accessed 10/7/19).
17. Terry Gross, "*Get Out* Sprang from an Effort to Master Fear, Says Director Jordan Peele," 1/5/18, my emphasis, https://www.npr.org/2018/01/05/575843147/get-out-sprang-from-an-effort-to-master-fear-says-director-jordan-peele (accessed 10/7/19).
18. Gross, op. cit.
19. Salud, op. cit.
20. Nicole LaPorte, "Why Horror Movies are Now More Important than Ever in Hollywood," 7/11/18, https://www.fastcompany.com/90199673/why-horror-movies-are-now-more-important-than-ever-in-hollywood (accessed 10/7/19).
21. LaPorte, op. cit.
22. Meslow, op. cit., 10/27/17. In this article, Meslow also writes about the experience of director Mike Flanagan, whose home-invasion movie *Hush* became a Netflix hit. "By the time our first weekend was over, we looked at it and said, 'Wow, I think more people sat down and watched this movie than ever would have seen it if we'd released it theatrically.'"
23. Adam Epstein, "One Movie Genre is Quietly Thriving Outside the Mainstream Hollywood System," 8/20/16, https://qz.com/770020/one-movie-genre-is-quietly-thriving-outside-the-mainstream-hollywood-system (accessed 10/7/19).
24. Michael Tauberg, "Why are Horror Movies so Popular Now?", 3/27/19, https://www.google.com/url?sa=t&rct=j&q=&esrc=s&source=web&cd=1&cad=rja&uact=8&ved=2ahUKEwj0gvXxk4vlAhUSd98KHUkqAy4QFjAAegQIARAB&url=https%3A%2F%2Fmedium.com%2Fswlh%2Fdopamine-and-the-horror-renaissance-351d4c0b38ef&usg=AOvVaw0fosAR8ZphZYycIhdE8NB9 (accessed 10/7/19).
25. Whether what he learns could save him in the long run's a trickier question. In the film's original ending, Chris kills all of his white tormentors, only to face a cop car pulling up; he's immediately arrested and jailed. As producer Sean McKittrick describes it, "We tested the movie with the original 'sad truth' ending where, when the cop shows up, it's an actual cop and Chris goes to jail. The audience was absolutely loving it, and then it was like we punched everybody in the gut. You could feel the air being sucked out of the room." So writer-director Jordan Peele shot another, upbeat ending. In this one – the one the producers went with – it isn't cops but Chris's buddy Rod who rides up, to the rescue. As Bradley Whitford (playing the father of Chris's white

girlfriend), explains, "The original ending was making a statement that I think Jordan felt a white audience might be able to dismiss about mass incarceration. The ending he ended up with does a brilliant thing, because ... you see the red police lights, and then you see the door open and it says "Airport" and it's a huge laugh, and everybody has that same laugh and release. You understand from Chris's POV that if the cops come, he's a dead man. That is absolutely brilliant, non-lecturing storytelling." C.f. Adam Chitwood, "'Get Out' Filmmakers Explain Why They Changed the Ending," 2/22/18, https://collider.com/get-out-alternate-ending-explained (accessed 10/7/19).

# INDEX

Note: Page references in italics refer to images.

*28 Days Later* 37, 113, 122
*2001* 2

Abbott, Christopher *158*
*Abbott and Costello Meet Frankenstein* 89–90, *91*
Academy Awards 64, 95, 147
Act One 33, 37–45, 46–7, 51–2, 57, 59, 63, 128
Act Two 35, 36, 40, 43–5, 46–55, 59, 63, 74, 128–9
Act Three 35, 36, 49, 50, 53, 54, 56–63, 74, 76
*Alien* 9, 10–1, *11*, 37, 108, 110
aliens 2, 4–5, 9–11, 13, 37, 73–4, 83, 101, 108, 110, 145, 148, 156
Álvarez, Fede 50, 53–4, 109
Amenábar, Alejandro 107
*American Werewolf in London, An* 93–5
*Anaconda* 13
*And Then There Were None* 132–3
Andrews, MacLeod *140*
*Annabelle* 104, 144
Anvari, Babak 122
*Apocalypse Now* 8
*Arachnophobia* 13
*Arrival of a Train at La Ciotat* 81
Aster, Ari 106–7, 154, 156, 159
*Audition* 40–3, *42*
*Avengers Endgame* 144

*Babadook, The* 6, 26, 152–3, *153*, 156
*Backcountry* 37
*Bad Taste* 148
Baker, Rick 95
Balsam, Martin *85*
*Bande à part* 109
*Bat, The* 132
*Bay of Blood* 133
Beal, Timothy 14
Beck, Scott 147–8
*Behind the Mask: The Rise of Leslie Vernon* 136
Bichir, Demián 144
*Black Christmas* 133
Blackshear, Perry 139
*Blair Witch Project, The* 136, 142
*Blood and Black Lace* 133
Bloody Mary 105
Blum, Jason 143, 146–7, 148
Blunt, Emily 110
body-count movies *see* slasher movies
Boyle, Lara Flynn 105
*Boys from Brazil* 102
*Bride of Frankenstein, The* 96
Brugués, Alejandro 115–6
budget 142–8
Burke, Billy *25*
*Burnt Offerings* 9
Burr, Raymond 83
Byrne, Gabriel *108*

# Index

*Cabin in the Woods, The* 98–9
*Cabinet of Dr. Caligari, The* 1, 33, *34*, 81, 134, 139
*Caligari* 37, 81
Cameron, James 148
*Candyman* 9
*Cannibal Holocaust* 135, 136
Carpenter, John 4, 133
*Carrie* (book) 105
*Carrie* (movie) 31, 105
Casas, Óscar 59
"Casting the Runes" 108
*Castle of Otranto, The* 80
*Cat People* 82–4, *83*
Chaney, Lon 50
*Changeling, The* 9
Christie, Agatha 132–3
Clark, Bob 133
Clasen, Mathias 18
*Cloverfield* 45
clowns 3, 13, 35, 132, 144, 151, 159
Collette, Toni *108*
*Conjuring, The* 9, 104, 144–5
*Conjuring 2, The* 104, 144, 146
*Conjuring* movies 9, 104, 144–6
Connolly, Ella *31*
Conway, Tom *66*
Costello, Lou *91*
costs 142–8
Craven, Wes 103–4
*Crazy Rich Asians* 144
Cronenberg, David 46
*Crooked Man, The* 145
*Curse of la Llorona, The* 144–5

Dante 33
*Dark Waters* 9
Davis, Cherry *97*
*Dawn of the Dead* 114–5
*Day the Earth Stood Still, The* 83
De Palma, Brian 31, 105
*Dead Alive* 148
*Death Row* 132
Dee, Frances *66*
del Toro, Guillermo 115, 119
*Deliverance* 108
Dergarabedian, Paul 145
*Descent, The* 4, 8, 27–8, 108–9, *109*
*Devil* 133
*Devil's Backbone, The* 116–20, *118*
*Diabolique* 139
dialogue 64–77, 110
*Dirty Pretty Things* 105
Donahue, Jocelin *41*
*Don't Breathe* 50–4, *52*, 109, 145–6

Douglas, Pamela 37
Dowd, A.A. 25–6, 156
*Dracula* (book) 81–2
Dracula (character) 1, 5, 84, 89–90, 91
*Dracula* (movie) 81, 90
*Dracula* (movie) 107, 142–3
*Drag Me to Hell* 108
Dumouchel, Evan *140*

economics 142–8
*Ed Gein: The Musical* 102
Edgerton, Joel *158*
Ejogo, Carmen *158*
*El Mariachi* 142
*El Orfanato* 56–63, *59*, *60*, *62*
*E.T.* 4, 151
*Evil Dead, The* 53–4
*Ex Machina* 2, 107

"Fall of the House of Usher" 3
Farrow, Mia *18*
Faulkner, Christopher Robert *158*
fear 13–26, 151–2, 158, 163; 'what if' list 2
Featherston, Katie *143*
*Final Destination* 5
*Final Destination* movies 5, 134–5
'final girl' trope 98
Finney, Jack 38
*Fly, The* 46–9, *49*
folk tales 104–5
Form, Andrew 147–8
'found footage' genre 45, 87, 132, 135–9
*Frankenstein* (book) 82, 92, 107
Frankenstein (character) 91
*Frankenstein* (movie) 2, 6, 35, 37, 80, 82, 142–3
Frears, Stephen 105
*Friday the 13th* 38, 133–5
future of horror 151–63

Gein, Ed 102–3
Gerwig, Greta 40
*Get Out* 5, 43–4, 64, 78–80, *80*, 87, 143, 144, 146, 147, 151, 152, 159–63
*Ghostbusters* 146
gialli 133
*Gift, The* 147
*Girl Walks Home Alone at Night, A* 37
*God Told Me To* 37
Godard, Jean-Luc 109
Goddard, Drew 45, 98
*Gojira* 83–4
Goldblum, Jeff *49*
*Golem: How He Came Into The World, The* 1, 2

*Gonjiam: Haunted Asylum* 132
Gordon, Stuart 96
Gothic imagery 80–1
*Gothika* 81, 139
Grand Guignol 92–3, 96
*Grave Encounters* 132
Grey, Lawrence 24
gross-out 9–10, 49
Guerrasio, Jason 146

*Halloween* 4, 8, 38, 96, 133
*Hansel & Gretel* 105
Hansel and Gretel 104–5, 153
*Hansel and Gretel Get Baked* 105
Hansen, Gunnar 103
*Happening, The* 37
Harris, Thomas 103
Harrison, Kelvin *158*
haunted house 9, 85, 95, 99, 144, 159
*Haunting in Connecticut, A* 104
Hedebrant, Kåre 22
Heisserer, Eric 24
*Hell House LLC* 132
Henkel, Kim 103
*Hereditary* 36, 106–7, *108*, 143, 144, 152, 153–7, 158–9, 162
*High Tension* 159
Hill, Annette 145
Hitchcock, Alfred 53–4, 66, 84, 109, 110, 158–9
Hooper, Tobe 103
*House of the Devil, The* 40, *41*, 46
humor 5, 7, 89–99, 114–6, 135–6, 148, 158–9
*Hunchback of Notre Dame, The* 142

*I Know What You Did Last Summer* 134
*I Married a Monster from Outer Space* 83
*I Walked with a Zombie* 64–6, *66*, 82
*Ils* 13, 27
*Incredible Shrinking Man, The* 83
*Independence Day: Resurgence* 146
*Innkeepers, The* 132
*Innocents, The* 107
*Inside* 84, 159
inspiration 7, 101–11
*Invaders from Mars* 83
*Invasion of the Body Snatchers* 2, 5, 37, 38–9, *39*, 73–5, 83, 151
*Invisible Man, The* 143
*Invitation, The* 162
*It* (book) 144, 152
*It* (movie) 144, 151–2
*It Chapter Two* 152

*It Comes at Night* 157–8, *158*
*It Follows* 2, 13, 152

Jackson, Peter 148
Jacobs, W.W. 32
James, Henry 107
James, M.R. 108
*Jane Eyre* 66
Janowitz, Hans 34
*Jaws* 23, 37, 74–7, 91–2, 110
Jones, Carolyn *39*
Jones, Duane 114
*Juan of the Dead* 115–6
Jupe, Noah *148*

Kaluuya, Daniel *80*, 162
Keogh, Riley *158*
Kerr, Deborah 107
Kim Su-an 7
King, Stephen 9, 32, 105, 106, 144, 152
Krasinski, John 110, 148, *148*
Kurosawa, Kiyoshi 120
Kusuma, Karyn 162

Lang, Brent 145–6
LaPorte, Nicole 162
Leandersson, Lina *22*
Leigh, Janet 154
Lenzi, Umberto 135
*Let the Right One In* 6, 19–23, *22*, 37
Levin, Ira 101–2
Levy, Jane *52*
Lewton, Val 64, 66, 82, 147
*Lights Out* 23–6, *25*, 105, 146
Lindqvist, John Ajvide 19
locations 7, 78–87
*Lord of the Rings* 148
Losten, Lotta 24
Lovecraft, H.P. 13
Luckhurst, Roger 114
Lumière Brothers 81

Macdonald, Shauna *109*
Mainwaring, Daniel 38
*Man Bites Dog* 135–6
*Man from Deep River* 135
Marshall, Neil 27, 108–9
*Martyrs* 4, 159
Maxa, Paula 92, 96
Mayer, Carl 34
Meslow, Scott 143–4
*Midwich Cuckoos, The* 101
Minette, Dylan *52*
"Monkey's Paw" 32
*Monsters* 9

*Mummy, The* 143
*Murders in the Rue Morgue, The* 143
Murnau, F.W. 81, 108
Muschietti, Andy 151
*My Bloody Valentine* 134

news stories 102–4
Nicholson, Jack *107*
*Night of the Demon* 108
*Night of the Lepus* 37
*Night of the Living Dead* 114
*Nightmare on Elm Street, A* 103–4, 133–5
*Noroi: The Curse* 137
*Nosferatu* 80, 81–2, 108
*Nun, The* 144, 145

O'Bannon, Dan 10
*Old Dark House, The* 143
*Omen, The* 37
*Open Water* 13, 142
*Others, The* 107

*Paranormal Activity* 95, 136, 142, *143*, 146–7
Park, Joo-Suk 6
Peele, Jordan 43, 78, 147, 159
*Peeping Tom* 133
Peli, Oren 142, 146–7
Perkins, Anthony 72
personal experience 105–7
*Pet Sematary* (book) 32
*Pet Sematary* (movie) 32
*Phantom of the Opera, The* 142
*Piranha Part Two* 148
Plaza, Paco 104
Poe, Edgar Allan 3–4, 6
Polanski, Roman 13, 80, 140
politics 113–29, 147
*Poltergeist* 2–3, 8, 9, 35–6, *36*, 59
Powell, Michael 133
*Psycho* 4, 6, 10, 13, 37, 53, 54, 66–73, *72*, 84–6, *85*, 102–3, 109, 133, 154, 158–9
psychological horror 132, 139–40
*Pulse* 120–2
*Purge, The* 146–7

*Quiet Place, A* 110, 148, *148*

race 114, 147, 159–60, 162–3
Raimi, Sam 53, 108
Randolph, Jane *83*
Rashidi, Narges *124*
*Re-Animator* 96
*[REC]* 137–8, *138*
*Red Shoes, The* 133
*Repulsion* 80, 140

*Return of the Living Dead, The* 95–6, 97
*Rift* 9
*Ring, The* 105
*Ringu* 86, 105
Romero, George 114–5
Rose, Steve 157
*Rosemary's Baby* 2, 13–8, *18*, 46, 101–2, 157
Rozsa, Matthew 145
Rueda, Belén *60*, *62*
*Russian Queen of Spades* 105

Sanchez, Sergio 56
Sandberg, David 24–6, 105
*Saw III* 9–10
*Saw* movies 9–10, 132
Sayagues, Rodo 50
*Scary Movie* 90
Scheider, Roy 23
Scott, Ridley 108
*Scream* 90, 96–7, 132, 134
setting *see* locations
*Seven* 37
*Shallows, The* 146
*Shaun of the Dead* 5, 98–9, 115
Sheen, Martin 8
Shelley, Mary 92
Shiina, Eihi *42*
*Shining, The* (book) 106
*Shining, The* (movie) 106, *107*, 109, 153
Shiraishi, Kōji 137
Shults, Trey Edward 157–8
Shusett, Ronald 10
*Shutter Island* 81, 139
*Sigaw* 9
*Silence of the Lambs, The* 6, 37, 64, 102–3
*Sinister* 9
Siodmak, Curt 65
slasher movies 5, 37–8, 98, 132–5
Sloat, Micah *143*
*Snakes on a Plane* 13
Soderbergh, Steven 81
*Spellbound* 139
Spielberg, Steven 148, 151
*Spongebob Squarepants* 108
Stanton, Harry Dean 10–1, *11*
Stefano, Joseph 68, 84, 103
*Stepfather, The* 37
*Stepford Wives* 102
Stoker, Bram 81–2
*Stranger Things* 151
*Strangers, The* 13
structure 27–36; Act One 33, 37–45, 46–7, 51–2, 57, 59, 63, 128; Act Two 35, 36, 40, 43–5, 46–55, 59, 63, 74,

128–9; Act Three 35, 36, 49, 50, 53, 54, 56–63, 74, 76
*Suspiria* 133, 158

*Tale of Two Sisters, A* 9
*Task, The* 132
*Teenage Mutant Ninja Turtles: Out of the Shadows* 146
Tengan, Daisuke 40
Terraza, Ferran *138*
*Texas Chainsaw Massacre, The* 27, 102–3, 109, 133
*Them!* 37, 83
*They Look Like People* 139–40, *140*
*Thing, The* 4–5
Toh, Lucan 122
Tourneur, Jacques 82, 108
*Train to Busan* 6–7, *7*, 9
*True Blood* 107
Trump, Donald 147
Tudor, Andrew 80
*Turistas* 105
*Turn of the Screw, The* 107
*Twilight* movies 107

*Under the Shadow* 37, 80, 122–9, *124*
*Unsane* 81
urban legends 104–5
*Urban Legends: Bloody Mary* 105

Valverde, Junio *118*
vampires 20, 22, 37, 50, 81, 89–90, 107–8, 132, 136, 156
Velasco, Manuela *138*
*Verónica* 104
*Village of the Damned* 101

*Visit, The* 37
von Twardowski, Hans Heinrich *34*

*Wake Wood* 27–32, *31*
Walpole, Horace 80
Wan, James 24
werewolf problem 49–50, 95
werewolves 49–50, 93–5, 132, 156
West, Ti 40
Whale, James 6, 35, 96
'what if' list 2
*What We Do in the Shadows* 136
Whedon, Joss 98
Wiene, Robert 81
Williams, Jobeth *36*
Williamson, Keith 96
*Wizard of Oz, The* 1, 2, 3, 8
*Wolf Man* 50
Wolff, Alex *108*
Wong, James 134–5
Wood, Robin 33
Woods, Bryan 147–8
Wray, Ardel 65
Wyndham, John 101

Yeon, Sang-ho 6
Yoo, Gong 7
Yorke, John 44
*Young Frankenstein* 91
*Your Vice is a Locked Room, and Only I Have the Key* 133

Zinoman, Jason 151–2, 158
zombies 6–7, 9, 13, 66, 95–6, 98–9, 113–6, 122, 130, 132
Zovatto, Daniel *52*

Printed in Great Britain
by Amazon